NORTHEAST INDIA
Readings in Cultural Life

NORTHEAST INDIA

Readings in Cultural Life

Lanukumla Ao

RESEARCH INDIA PRESS
New Delhi (INDIA)

Northeast India: Readings in Cultural Life

ISBN : 978-93-5171-034-9

Price : 1295/-

First Edition: 2021

Published by :
RESEARCH INDIA PRESS
E-6/34, Sangam Vihar
New Delhi-110062
Phone: 011-26047013, (M) 9818085794
E-mail: researchindiapress@gmail.com

Type Setting & Design by
G. R. Sharma

Contents

Preface & Acknowledgements

Over the decades several researches have been conducted to reconstruct the cultural life of the people of northeast India. Hence, a national seminar, we thought, would allow us to take stock of existing scholarship on the region. The Seminar was organized by the Research Cell and Internal Quality Assurance Cell, Don Bosco College, Kohima, Nagaland between 1st and 2nd November 2019, on the theme *Culture Paradigm-The pluralistic Northeast India: Appreciating the Diverse Culture of Northeast India*. Held in the academic pursuit, to understand the emerging cultural studies in northeast India, the seminar included discussions on a wide variety of topics from humanities, literature and social sciences. Not all the papers from the seminar could be included in the final publication. As always there were too many seminar papers. What we have here is a selection on the basis of the recommendation from the reviewers. We have also included a couple of essays that were not presented at the seminar but seemed thematically appropriate for this collection.

Sincere gratitude goes to the following towards holding the seminar and the publication of the proceedings of the same:

The North Eastern Council (NEC), Shillong, Meghalaya for the financial contribution made for organizing the National Seminar. The grant proved significant for successful holding of the Seminar. Our special invitee *Shri. Thepfulhouvi Solo*, IFS Retd. Principal Secretary, Government of Nagaland, for gracing our inaugural function and for enlightening us with his address. *Shri. Kiremwati*, former Pro Vice Chancellor, North-Eastern Hill University for kindly accepting our invitation to be our keynote speaker. His address set the high academic quality of the seminar.

Prof. Xavier P. Mao, North-Eastern Hill University, Shillong; *Prof. Y. Ben Lotha*, *Prof. N. Das* and *Prof. Tiatoshi Jamir*, Nagaland University for chairing the academic sessions of the seminar and stirring the purpose of the seminar. The discussions during the sessions were not only helpful to the paper presenters but also to the audience.

Prof. Xavier P. Mao and *Prof. Amrendra Kumar Thakur*, North-Eastern Hill University, Shillong; *Prof. N. Das*, *Dr. Ditamulu Vasa* and *Dr. Chubala Sanglir* Nagaland University; *Dr. Toshimenla*, Don Bosco College Kohima for their contribution in peer reviewing the articles. All the reviewers helped to maintain the high quality of manuscripts through their suggestions.

Fr. Dr. P. Suresh, Principal DBCK, for all the tireless support and assistance. My co-convenors –*Mrs. Jarani Mao*, Co-ordinator, IQAC, DBCK and *Dr. Imtinaro Longkumer*, Asst. Co-ordinator, NAAC, DBCK. The organizing committee members: *Dr. Velhou Koza*, Head, Department of Sociology, DBCK; *Dr. Pinky Sagolsem*, Head, Department of English, DBCK and *Mr. Zupenthung Shitiri*, Head, Department of Political Science, DBCK. They stood firmly with me from the stage of planning of the seminar to the publication of this book.

The meticulous planning and execution require for a project like this must be considered and I want to thank my esteemed colleagues, office staff members, and the students of DBCK for doing everything possible to make the national seminar in the College a success. Bosco Music Society, DBCK, for rendition of a warm welcoming song and to the volunteers for their tireless service; without them the holding of the seminar would have been very difficult.

There are many people who contributed to the success of the seminar in the background. Particularly, I would like to express my gratitude to my family for their constant support in this project as they have done in all my academic pursuits. Finally, and above all, I thank the Almighty God for His bounty and blessings that He has bestowed.

Kohima **Dr. Lanukumla Ao**

Introduction

Culture is the very foundation of any society. It is essential to understand that culture is all inclusive, all embracing and participatory by nature. It presupposes an engaged outlook, and plays a fundamentally strategic role in territorial development by seeking to integrate knowledge. The dynamics of cultural change is directly linked to concurrent social, religious and institutional transformations that evolve over time. The implications of such changes have inexplicable complexities in every fiber of society. The fast paced change that is taking place since the latter half of the millennia till present times due to exposure to the world at our fingertips is making culture change a moot point.

There is a palpable change in the cultural sphere of northeast India today. The change is due to a number of factors such as rapid globalization, urbanization, modern education, demographic shifts, and impact of mass media. Combined stress of these factors in the contemporary world has made us forget our roots and face server identity crisis, as people are no longer bound by boundaries. Westernization, particularly, along with modernity has invaded the northeast Indian tribal oriented outlook.

Northeast India consists of diverse mosaic cultures which have to be enriched. This paradigm shift in culture can be seen to be endangering some traditional values that are deeply entrenched in our society. These are the most invaluable parts of the cultural life of the people of northeast India that need to be researched as we simply cannot afford to lose them. Even though culture change, and in some cases is inevitable, the need of the hour is to minimize their negative fallouts. In its primary objectives the seminar explored and affirmed the cultures of northeast India. It also highlighted the uniqueness of these cultures and advocated for their preservation and enhancement of all that is good and noble in them.

Prof. Xavier P. Mao paper entitled, "Language Thought and Culture with Special Reference to the Tribes of Northeast", talks about the importance of language, thought and culture which are inextricably related to each other. Language is the soul of culture. Therefore, in order to appreciate and preserve good aspects of tribal culture, tribal language should be seriously researched as they are fast disappearing in modern times. Dr. Aparna Mathur, in her paper, "Tantra and Buddhism: An Inquiry into Early Assam", explores the development of tantric practices among the Buddhist followers of Assam. The paper is divided into two parts. The first part is a general overview of the tantric tradition, including discussing the meaning of the term tantra and the critical discussions related to its antiquity and origin. The second part discusses the development of tantric practices among the Buddhists of early Assam up to the thirteenth century CE. "The Dragon, Sun, Lotus and the Cross: Religious Pluralism in Arunachal Pradesh" by Dr. Tajen Dabi gives a preview of the religious systems practiced in Arunachal Pradesh. It also raises the issue of how established religions have exerted their influence on the animistic communities. It also tries to reaffirm the effort of the indigenous religious reform movement in generating a powerful network of activities, intellectuals, temples and organizations to such influences. Dr. Pradeep Kumar Deepak in his paper, "The Cultural History of Tripura: An Overview", discussed on a number of culture that has followed in which tribal elements and elements of non-tribal cultural formation has been analysed comprehensively. The paper also successfully presents the cultural life of the people of Tripura as an assimilation of cultured society and establishing the process of change.

Tsering Yangjom, in her paper, "The Cultural Life of the Thembang Monpas of Arunachal Pradesh: Exploring through Hoi-si-na", explores the ritual, origin and addresses the interaction between Buddhism and the Bonpoistic ritual Hoi-si-na. The paper also draws a conclusion that pre Buddhist elements are still continuing even in the society which has adopted its socio-cultural life. The paper by Krishna Kumar Sharma, "Non-Buddhist Elements in Buddhism of Sikkim", investigates Buddhist and non-Buddhist culture and ritual practices that are influenced by each other. It also discusses on the accommodated of non-Buddhist elements in Buddhist solemnity and community too. Vunglunmawi, paper on, "Clothing of the Kukis of Manipur: A Study in Cultural Progress", tries to analyse objectively the technology and cultural progress of the Kukis which can be examined through manufacturing process, designs and various use of clothes. This paper opens a new vista which is not very popular in the historical reconstruction of the cultural life of the people of northeast India.

Hepuni Liba in his paper, "Rites and Rituals with Special Reference to Death and Disposal of Death Bodies of Poumai Naga Tribe before the 20th Century", analyzes the nature of rites and rituals and its importance on death and its disposal with special reference to Poumai Naga tribe. The Poumai Nagas have a unique belief system in the existence of life and soul after death. The paper by Shürhonuo Tsürho, "Oral Tradition as an Itinerary to the Past: A Reflection of the Socio-Cultural Values of the Naga" focuses on several external forces such as the coming of the British Company, the American Missionaries and the popularity of the global village to its peak that have altered the oral tradition in Nagaland. These intrusions may have taken as positive utility as they assist the community by lending their Mother Tongue to the Nagas which in turn helped the Nagas write their own stories.

Dr. Sentinaro in her paper, "An Overview of Cultural Values of the Aos in Temsula's Selected Writings" has traced to delineate the areas of cultural elements as is found in *Temsula's* writings. Her works highlight the various aspects of Ao culture, practices, beliefs, myths etc. Dr. Vizovono Elizabeth, "Cultural Context in Literature: A Study of Easterine Kire's a Naga Village Remembered", studies the cultural context of the novel with the contention that such an approach will help us better understand the ideas and events that shaped people's attitudes in that particular time and place. These details are significant in the context of the culture clash that takes place after the coming of the British colonialists and the repercussions thereafter. K. S. Mariam in her paper, "Revisiting Culture and Tradition through the Lens of Mamang Dai's Legends of Pensam and Easterine Kire's a Respectable Woman", presents how the writings of Mamang Dai and Easterine Kire undoubtedly, makes the reader to rethink the overall concept within the readings of literature as preserver of culture, in which some cultural belief systems is institutionalized and structured, that can crippled society if one fails to keep a reality check.

Kedivonu Kharutso, on her paper "Festivals as Cultural Heritage: Sekrenyi Festival of the Angamis", analyses the role of festivals in the preservation of Angami culture and tradition with special reference to Sekrenyi festival. It also highlights on the traditional festivals playing a leading role in preserving traditional culture and promote cultural continuity. Dr. Temjenwabang, paper on "Colonial and Postcolonial Imagery of the Early Nagas: Text, Context and the Discourse of Difference" is a discursive deliberation seeking to critically problematize a project of otherness and othering in the context of representing the early Nagas. Taking cues from colonial and post-colonial writings on Nagas, the paper seeks to advocate and vouch for critical agencies that operated behind this psyche of otherness. The paper "Customs and Traditional Practices of Khezhakeno Village: A Socio-Historical Perspective" by Dr. Velhou Koza and Tsutshowe-ü Sekhamo, analyzes the practices of traditions and customs in Khezhakeno village from the socio-historical perspective. The paper also highlights the influences of traditions and customs from transitional period to contemporary.

Dr. Lallianzuali Chhangte's paper entitled, "From Traditional to Modern: A Discourse on Educational and Culture Change in Mizo Society", talks about the interface between introduction of modern education and consequent change in the cultural life of the Mizos. Broadly, the paper also describes the traditional cultural life of the Mizos and the modernity which was introduced by the British mainly through education. Roja Ahmed, on her paper, "Hydropower

Development in Northeast India and its Impact", looks into the impact of large dams in Assam with special reference to the Ranganadi Dam, located in Yazali, Arunachal Pradesh. It also focuses on how the dam has contributed to climate change apart from its downstream impact on Assam.

Northeast India as an anthropological museum is a home of diverse cultures. Its unique identity must be preserved as it is fast eroding due to invading modernization and rapid radical change of taste and habits of the denizens of northeast India. On the basis of the papers presented and the discussion followed after the presentation of papers during the various academic sessions of the seminar the following major outcomes emerged:

The Culture Paradigm abounds in all sorts of activities like modes of living: (i) festivals (ii) cooking and food processing (iii) singing, dancing and playing musical instrument (iv) weaving (v) carving and engraving (vi) handicrafts of all sorts (vii) all agricultural, horticultural, piscicultural, floricultural, animal husbandry, activities (viii) drawing, painting, dyeing, tattooing, etc. (ix) gymnastics, and all sorts of games (x) religious practices, rituals and propagational activities and animist practices (xi) observing austerities/penance for self-control and discipline (xii) mystical beliefs and explorations (xiii) building monuments and loving monuments (xiv) establishing relationships and friendships (xv) Educational pursuits and institutional activities (xvi) common chores observed by household for day-to-day living (xvii) birth, upbringing and death (xviii) custom, tradition, folklore and honouring the heritage (xix) inheritance and customary laws (xx) power structure and hegemony (xxi) Linguistic and oral tradition etc.

1. The Cultural diversities in Northeast India are encountering severe challenges due to rapid changes in demographic pattern.
2. The new generation is affected by fast encroaching modernity and hence is losing the glorious tradition and culture of the past. Preserving the cultural diversities is prime necessity of our time.

   It should be permanent preservation by digitalization.
3. Identifying the individual items of cultural diversity and work on their aspects need to be the radical practice.
4. The Diversity we talk about is immense. Hence exploring into their aspects must be pursued in diverse ways by diverse agents.
5. The exploration should be accentuated by different communities and tribes tenaciously through utilitarian principle aiming at sustainable development of all concerned.
6. Extreme anthropocentric bias need to be balanced by eco centric practices to bring amelioration to the ailing Earth for furthering the wholesomeness of humanity.
7. The distortions in the history of northeast India due to the British colonial interest and/or the interest of China which have come up during the British period and even after were exposed.
8. The importance of the use of indigenous literary and archaeological sources in the contemporary researches was highlighted to correct the distortions in the history of Northeast India.

9. The elements of cultural continuity between the plains and hills of northeast India were located through some of the papers and need was felt during the discussions on the papers and during the valedictory session to have similar researches on the line.

Keynote Address

SHRI. KIREMWATI
Former Pro-Vice Chancellor
North Eastern Hill University

Introduction

At old age (90 years), I am delighted to write and address the seminar. It gives me joy and refreshing memories. Thank you for creating the opportunity. My brain due to dementia, fails to bring out a satisfactory paper, even appropriate words may be missing. Please overlook inconsistency, if any.

Development of concept and operation of culture, I leave to the specialist speakers. I have focused more on "My living culture in the world-wide cultural spectrum." God has granted privilege to me to be in this from time to time.

Culture is inclusive of all aspects of living of individuals and collectively as a community: habitats and surroundings, character and behaviour, ethics and attitudes, honest and hospitality, food and its preparation, clothing and style, singing and dancing, and so on. They are expressions of inner self. Culture is a changing dimension; and the agents of change maybe active (such as war, migration), passive (such as fashion, acculturation through software) and even dormant (such as customs and costumes). Political geography changes but the physical geography does not, except though natural forces such as atmospheric warming, isocracy, etc. Such changes though silent and unnoticed affect culture of human race globally. Political changes lead to immigration and demographic shift at regional and local levels. Northeast region of India bordering Bangladesh, Myanmar and China is being affected today by migration of Rohingya people.

Own Culture is the identity of a person/people in a fast changing world. Man has the inherent desire to see the unseen, and to know the unknown. About three weeks ago, I was talking to an American couple at Kohima visiting Nagaland to see her beauty. I told them that God has created all places in the world beautiful. Only man thinks that the unseen is more beautiful than the seen. Even in small Nagaland, every different place has its own unique beauty. In the world, differently cultured groups have to learn from each other.

Britishers advise the new entrant foreigners: Do not visit British homes without pre-appointment. When you enter the reception room, do not touch the decorative pieces, and do not ask their prices. Britishers are not talkative. They feel hurt to talk about money. If there is no issue to talk about, you start talking appreciating the flowers, furniture and so on.

Cleanliness is like a mirror reflecting the culture of a people. The image of India is not well reflected. Some people keep inside the house and furniture very clean, but they throw rubbish through window making the surroundings dirty. Once, a foreign observer described India as a Big Latrine. Posters in Nagaland say, KEEP DUNCAN CLEAN, KOHIMA CLEAN...In Great Britain, posters say, KEEP BRITAIN TIDY. In 1964, while travelling from Hull to

London with my friend Mr. Keith in his bike, we stopped in a forest for food. I threw the food wrapper away in the forest. My friend picked it up to be disposed off only in parents home. He told me, "In England, We do not throw rubbish anywhere including forest to keep it tidy". A good lesson I have learnt that day. Citizens know their culture and live by them.

India has awakened to the present need of cleanliness. Prime Minister Modi, very wisely and boldly has launched several realistic and practical programmes:

(a) To keep cities and human habitats clean;

(b) To construct public toilets to eliminate open defecation;

(c) To clean Ganges; and so on.

Such conscious efforts will surely guide the people to their future culture.

Customs/Traditions/Practices of the people of Northeast India are so pluralistic, and yet co-existing beautifully like beads of a garland joined together by a strong thread which must have been developed not only by geographical closeness, but more by the each-other love and respect in the paradigm of pluralistic culture.

During the Time, when North-Eastern Hill University was processing to take over Pachunga College in Mizoram and Kohima Science College in Nagaland to make them University Campuses, a meeting of the Executive Council was held at Aizwal. There were misunderstandings (I won't call it opposition). Students lined up both sides of the road, all wearing their dark traditional shawls as a mark of displeasure. They allowed the Councillors to walk along the middle of the road. Silently and peacefully, the students came to the meeting and submitted their Memorandum of demands. I appreciated the students for their attitude and unity. Such is the culture of Mizo community.

Pluralistic Religion in the Northeast India and their co-existence is a lesson the rest of India can learn. There is no anti feeling. If Christians, Hindus, Muslims and other faith become better believers, what a pluralistic better society that would be! No religion teaches hatred, but love. While returning from Aizawl to Shillong, the long convoy of vehicles stopped to fill in gas in a rural area petrol station in Jantia Hills. One staff member suddenly got sick, and he could not stand. Nearby, there was neither hospital nor doctor. What should we do? Shall we not pray to our respective Gods for healing, I said; and all agreed. I asked the sick whether he believes in God to heal him. Oh yes, he replied. We prayed and the sickness was gone; and we continued the journey. What a wonder!

In a Global Society, culture identifies who and where from is a person. In 1952, I attended the world student Christian Federation at Tambaram representing the student Christian movement, Assam as its president. In those days, Naga Hills was a district of Assam. I took a Naga spear, a dao and a set of customary dress for a war dance. When I danced, all in the big hall were surprised, some were even afraid! Dr. Devanesan, the first vice chancellor of NEHU was present there. After many years, we met at Shillong. He recognised me as a Naga dancer. It is surprising how culture works to identify a person.

My Experiences in global society is not all white. Even few black spots need to be mentioned to make my address balanced and realistic. I journeyed in 1965 in a ship with 600 first class international passengers for 20 days from Liverpool (England) to Bombay (India). I observed that, in a confined closed society, it is very fast to intermix, and to familiarise one with another. All sorts of activities for games, swimming, library, etc were provided free in the ship. Every night was cultural night of entertainment: singing, dancing, film show and so on. One cultural night, I was made to organize and conduct the function. I yelled in a very loud voice and sang an Ao Naga folk love song. It was well received by the audience; and they wanted me to sing more. Since that time, the passengers started asking questions regarding Nagaland, the people and their culture. In another cultural night, one lady from Bombay sang a good song with very sweet voice. Expecting positive response, I asked my German friend sitting next to me how he felt. He replied, "Good, very good, but after all, that is not her song!" She sang in English tune and language.

After crossing the Mediterranean Sea, before entering the Red Sea, the ship halted for a few hours at Aden. We, the passengers were glad to be on land. I with two Indian friends went to a shop. I enquired for a pocket size radio, and bought one for 6 pounds. My friend also wanted to buy one. The shop keeper told him that, "He (I) Japan, I give him; but you Indian, I no give. My friend did not buy the radio."

IN 1975, God has given me the privilege of touring for 40 days as a member of the first Naga choir to Northern Europe. The 14 members were fully ready wearing Naga traditional dress and to sing folk songs and gospel based English songs. As the journey progressed, demand to sing indigenous folk songs increased. We sang in churches, markets and streets. We sang folk songs in two sessions of the Baptist world Congress at Stockholm (Sweden) attended by 10,000 participants from 85 countries on July 13. One German singer told me: Do not let your music go out of the world of music. After the congress, few choirs were selected from among the participants for a special programme to be televised to the whole world. Naga choir was also among them. We were allotted 3 and half minutes. The choir also sang in the Billy Graham crusade in Skansonia. All those programmes were televised live.

The impact of culture is clearly confirmed when I received a letter from a university student of Hull. She wanted to visit Nagaland, the letter stated. She was a small girl, daughter of Rev. Hulme, pastor of Hull Baptist church. I used to push her in a pram (1964-65). When her parents recognised me in the television, she was excited and immediately determined to see Nagaland.

Culture is the results of impacts of history and politics, migration and demographic change, religion and faith, education and technology, art and literature, language and communication, war and conflicts, economy and industries. Nagas had so scripts. Tradition says: They wrote in hides of animals. The dog ate them up; so the script was lost. The invasion of Assam by the Burmese in 1817 was a landmark. 18th century was a period of change. Treaty of Yandabo between the British and the Burmese was signed in 1826. Migration of Ahoms from lower Assam to the upper started. Britishers brought labourers from outside to run tea estates along the border between Assam and Nagaland. The advent of Christianity and opening of modern schools had impacted the cultural pattern of the northeast India.

Exposure to the wider culture of India and of the world, there creeps in cultural change. Example:

Beauty contest; Walking in the ramp in alien dress.

Honesty, hard work and such good qualities giving way to softer way of life (loss of cultural strength).

If such changes are signals of the new cultural pattern of northeast India, how and where will people stand in times to come! Present concept of one country and one language; the education reform in the country; and the looming political uncertainty should attract universities and colleges for serious fearless research.

I am a Christian by faith and a teacher by profession. Let me conclude with prayer in my heart; and wishing and hoping for a well refined culture of the Northeast India. AMEN.

List of Contributors

1. **Aparna Mathur**, Associate Professor, Department of History, North-Eastern Hill University, Shillong, Meghalaya.
2. **Hepuni Liba**, Ph. D. Research Scholar, Department of History & Archaeology, Nagaland University, Kohima Campus, Nagaland.
3. **K. S. Mariam**, Ph.D. Research Scholar, Department of English, Nagaland University, Kohima Campus, Nagaland.
4. **Kedivonu Kharutso**, Ph.D. Research Scholar, Department of History and Archaeology, Nagaland University, Kohima Campus, Nagaland.
5. **Krishna Kumar Sharma**, Ph.D. Research Scholar, Department of History, North-Eastern Hill University, Shillong, Meghalaya.
6. **Lallianzuali Chhangte**, Assistant Professor, Department of History, Government Kolasib College, Mizoram.
7. **Pradeep Kumar Deepak**, Assistant Professor, Department of History, A.M.B.S. Mahavidyalaya Amarpur, Gomati, Tripura.
8. **Roja Ahmed**, Ph. D. Research Scholar, Department of History, North-Eastern Hill University, Shillong, Meghalaya
9. **Sentinaro**, Assistant Professor and HoD, Department of English, Baptist College, Kohima, Nagaland.

10. **Shürhonuo Tsürho**, Ph. D. Research Scholar, Department of English, Nagaland University, Kohima Campus, Nagaland.

11. **Tajen Dabi**, Assistant Professor, Department of History, Rajiv Gandhi University, Itanagar.

12. **Temjenwabang**, Assistant Professor, Department of History, Unity College, Dimapur, Nagaland.

13. **Tsering Yangjom**, Assistant Professor, Department of History, Dera Natung Government College, Itanagar.

14. **Tsutshowe-ü Sekhamo**, Assistant Professor, Department of History, Don Bosco College, Kohima, Nagaland.

15. **Velhou Koza**, Assistant Professor, Department of Sociology, Don Bosco College, Kohima, Nagaland.

16. **Vizovono Elizabeth**, Assistant Professor, Department of English, Baptist College, Kohima, Nagaland.

17. **Vunglunmawi**, Ph. D. Research Scholar, Department of History, North-Eastern Hill University, Shillong, Meghalaya

18. **Xavier P Mao**, Professor, Department of Philosophy, North-Eastern Hill University, Shillong, Meghalaya.

1

Language, Thought and Culture with Special Reference to the Tribes of Northeast

XAVIER P. MAO

In an important sense language, thought and culture go together that is to say one cannot be detached from the other. Can one think of doing effective research on culture without knowing language? The distinction between tribe and non-tribe is very ambiguous or very thin. I wish to point out that the study of tribal languages and cultures has not been given due place till today. It is said that a person is known by the language he/she speaks and writes. The English word mother tongue is really basic and fundamental. Immediate and effective steps should be taken to develop the various languages of the Northeast. Language in mother tongue is in a sense the soul of culture. Tribal languages have not yet been developed; therefore, the cultural traditions of Northeast tribes have not been effectively studied and researched. The Northeast tribes are fast forgetting their languages. Many of their languages are in the danger zone of disappearance. As a result the values and virtues embedded in their languages are also losing its grip from the minds of young people. Hence revivalism and revitalization of the study of various languages of the tribes of the Northeast are urgent and absolutely imperative on the part of the native scholars.

In what follows I wish to raise fundamental and foundational questions about tribes in general and tribes of Northeast in particular. It is sometimes popularly said that Northeast states are tribal states. Anthropology, sociology and history have raised questions about tribes in general and the tribes of Northeast in particular. Even teachers of philosophy have taken interest in the cultures of the tribes. M.Phil and Ph. D. theses have been produced on tribal philosophy and philosophy of tribal culture under the supervision of the teachers of philosophy NEHU. I do not wish to make comments on these Ph. D theses. On the other hand, I am happy to learn that some teachers of NEHU have taken keen and special interest in the study of tribal cultures.

The two terms of Scheduled Caste and Scheduled Tribes were coined after British people came to India. In India throughout the country scheduled caste people were treated as untouchables. But this is not the case with regard to scheduled tribes particularly Northeast tribes as they were historically and politically isolated from the so called present day mainland India. It is interesting to mention that before the British came to India the terms scheduled caste and scheduled tribe were unknown in India. The term Adivasi was very much in vogue beyond Northeast India in the past. Gandhi coined the word Harijan to denote scheduled caste. Harijan is a Sanskrit word which means the children of God. But the Scheduled castes themselves do not like to be called Harijan. Nonetheless Gandhi was very much worried and disturbed at the treatment of scheduled caste people. The so called scheduled caste people were not allowed to enter in

Hindu temples. Further if by chance one touches scheduled caste person he/she has to take bath and wash his/her clothes. There were so many other oppressive restrictions for the scheduled caste. This kind of treatment was not meted out to scheduled tribe people.

It is very interesting to note in this connection that Bhagavad-Gita one of the sacred books of the Hindus does not make any such distinction between touchable and untouchables. According to Bhagavad-Gita 4 (four) types of people were created and this division was based on the qualification (guna) and action (Karma). In other words, according to Bhagavad-Gita caste is not determined by birth: it is determined by action or karma. Accordingly Brahmin, Kshatriya, Vaishya and Sudra are the 4 varnas. Who are the Brahmins? Those who engage themselves in study and research are Brahmins. Who are the Kshatriyas? The answer is those who defend the country at the time of war and aggression they are the Kshatriyas. The Vaishyas are those who engage themselves in business. Sudras are those people who do other types of so called menial work in society. It is important to mention in this connection that the words touchable and untouchables in Sanskrit were not used. The Bhagavad-Gita was composed in 5th century A.D. The idea of touchable and untouchable was not in currency at that point of time. Later on varna was degenerated into very rigid caste system solely determined by birth.

The so called forest dwellers were given high position in Indian Epics. In Mahabharata and Ramayana the so called adivasi or forest dwellers now called scheduled tribes were given very high position. Hanuman is treated as the monkey warrior was considered as the close confidant of Lord Rama. Ramayana is not a historical record but it reflects the then cultural conditions at the time. Sugriva was a forest dweller but close friend of Lord Rama. During 14 years of exile, Rama was in close relation with Sugriva. Further Ekalavya a forest dweller boy became very efficient in archery and he became very close to Drona, the war teacher of Pandava and Kauravas.

It may not be out place to mention in this connection that Lord Jaganath worshipped in Puri temple with his brother and sister is worshipped by Sabaras (forest dwellers). Till date Sabaras play very important role in worship of Jaganath. This clearly shows that culture and civilizations grow out of belief systems entertained by various groups of people and history gets reflected in myths and ritual practices. There is a sense in which it can be said that each of us has tribal ancestry. If we accept this point of view then the distinction between tribal and non-tribal is very ambiguous or disappear altogether. In other words, it is very difficult to draw the exact boundary line between tribe and non-tribe. Some groups of Hindus regard tiger as their ancestor and some others cobra as their ancestor. The so called upper caste Brahmins and others have chosen various seers and rishis or monks as their ancestors. What about the tribes of plain India? They chose various animals as their ancestors. What does Gotra or ancestor indicate? It simply indicates and tells us in nutshell that we have a common ancestor. The ancestor worship is not only prevalent among caste Hindus but also among SCs and STs in India. It is also widely prevalent all over the world.

Let us look to the various tribes of the Northeast India. Each group of people have their own culture and language. With the advent of Christianity, the tribal view of life and culture gradually disappear or the worldview of the tribes are greatly modified or in some cases completely replaced by other worldviews. I am not saying here that the spread of Christianity in Northeast has done damage and destroyed the so called tribalism. On the other hand, I wish to mention in this connection that the advent of Christianity opened up a new chapter in the life of Northeast tribes. The Christian missionaries in Northeast tried to do many good things. They set up educational institutions of various kinds, dispensaries and hospitals etc. They also helped the tribes to develop their languages by way of adopting Graeco-Roman scripts. There is no doubt the Christian missionaries did yeomen service to the tribes of Northeast India. After independence it is late Indira Gandhi the then Prime Minister wanted to improve the educational system in Northeast. Accordingly North-Eastern Hill University the first central university was set up at Shillong in 1973. NEHU has inspired the tribes of Northeast. Many people got advantage of higher education at the door step. But at the same time I wish to point out that the study of tribal languages and cultures has not been given due place till today. Few of the languages of the Northeast are now having separate Department in few universities and colleges to carry on teaching and research on the languages of the region.

It is said that a person is known by the language he/she speaks and writes. The English word mother tongue is really basic and fundamental. Perhaps, nowhere in the world a child in the primary school is taught in foreign language. I am sorry to say that language policy of the Government of India is defective. Up to secondary level a child must be taught in his/her language. English should be taught from class IV onwards. I wish to suggest that there should be provision for learning various languages in schools and colleges. In order to have effective learning, mother tongue should be the medium of instruction up to class 10. Mother tongue should be the first language and English should be the second language. Perception, thinking and understanding effectively take place in mother tongue. Mother tongue should be the solid base. Unfortunately this is not done in India till date. Efforts should be made to commit to writing of oral traditions, values, stories, legends, folklores, folktales, folksongs, myths etc. English should be taught compulsorily. Immediate and effective steps should be taken to develop the various languages of the Northeast.

Language in mother tongue is in a sense the soul of culture. Tribal languages have not yet been developed; therefore, the cultural traditions of Northeast have not been effectively studied and researched. In an important sense language, thought and culture go together that is to say one cannot be detached from the other. Can one think of doing effective research on culture without knowing language? Can one understand the values and morality of a particular community without knowing well the language of that community? For example, the Vedas, Upanishads, Puranas and other various branches of knowledge were composed in Sanskrit; therefore the meanings of such writing cannot be deciphered without knowing Sanskrit. Max Mueller the Indologist did not come to India to study Sanskrit. But he studied Sanskrit in French and wrote sacred books of the East. Most of the times it is said that Europeans came to India for business purpose but Europeans also came to India to collect Sanskrit manuscripts. The reason being Sanskrit contains the scholastic achievements of ancient India. I gave this example to show that study of language is the basis and foundation of interpreting and understanding of culture and tradition. Therefore, I humbly suggest that tribal intellectual should take serious collective effort to study and do in-depth research.

Unfortunately many tribal intellectuals are also fast forgetting their languages. In other words, I have come across many tribal intellectuals cannot speak their languages fluently without mixing with other borrowed languages. As stated earlier language, thought and culture go together that is how I have entitled my paper. I wish to suggest in this paper that tribal culture and tradition cannot be understood sufficiently without knowing their languages thoroughly. Without knowing tribal languages any study of tribal culture will be of no use. The researcher without the knowledge of tribal language will miss the subtleties and nuances of meanings of tribal culture. Therefore I would like to suggest that those who wish to study tribal culture in Northeast should learn tribal languages for the simple reason that without knowing language it is not possible to do genuine research on folklores, folksong, folktales, myths, legends etc. Some scholars without knowing the tribal languages have done research works. In my considered opinion such research work without knowing the language is incomplete and defective.

Language, thought and culture are intimately connected so much so that one cannot be separated from the other without doing damage to the entire research. It is a fact that in spite of western education and culture tribes of Northeast have retained their identities. Tribal people do not necessarily mean forest dwellers as many tribes are not living in the forest for many generations. But the general connotation means honest, simple, straightforward and sincere people. Even this connotation is also changing overtimes. This dimension of tribal people in general and tribal people in particular should be collected and depicted. Therefore, I suggest in this connection that tribal folklores, music, arts, dance, myths etc. should be collected, compiled and published. They should be even translated into English. Tribal intellectuals should make special efforts to speak well their languages when they are with their people. I re-emphasize that language; thought and culture inter-mix and intertwine. Therefore, to understand people we must know language, thought and culture.

Sociologist and anthropologist have been doing research on the various tribes of the Northeast which is praiseworthy. The researchers have forgotten the basic requirement of learning the native language on which research is conducted. Language is the soul of culture. As stated earlier without knowing language we cannot effectively study culture: ipso facto we cannot understand people. Language, thought and culture are closely interwoven we cannot properly understand tribal culture without knowing their languages. To understand people means to understand culture and language. To understand the thought and ideas of a people we need to know their culture. To understand their culture means we need to know their arts, stories, music, folksongs, myths, legends, social practices, beliefs, values etc. Unfortunately many tribes of the Northeast are fast forgetting their languages thereby many of them are endangered as per the United Nations estimate. Subtle thoughts, ideas, moral and spiritual values and virtues are embedded in language. Therefore, with the loss of language other thoughts and ideas will be also lost. Hence there is compelling need to revive consciously the languages of the tribes Northeast.

2

Tantra and Buddhism: An Inquiry into Early Assam

APARNA MATHUR

Assam has been famous for one of the oldest and most important seats of tantra in India. The well-known *Shakti-Pitha* Kamakhya is held in high esteem as the locus of goddess' womb and the home of the supreme 'goddess of desire' (*Kamakhya*). Assam is also known in sources as the very 'manifestation of desire' (*Kamarupa*). It has been identified as the original heartland, 'the principal center', and even the 'birthplace' of tantra in the literal and metaphoric sense (Sharma, 1990: 37). The popularity of tantric traditions in Assam made Mircea Eliade (1971) observes that Assam (*Kamarupa*) is perhaps 'the tantric country par excellence' (p. 305).

Buddhism and Buddhist practices have attracted the attention of scholars worldwide, and consequently, various dimensions of Buddhism have been explored in the studies. Tantric practices representing a diverse aspect of Buddhism have been the subject of inquiry in many works. But anyhow studies on tantric practices of Buddhism missed Assam in their discussions and are mostly Tibet and China-centric. Assam is well-known as the heartland of tantra, which has 'long held a place of deep ambivalence, fear, and embarrassment for both Indian and western observers' (Urban, 2001: 777). Scholars who have worked on the tantric practices of Assam viewed it from a Brahmanical angle, concentrating primarily on the study of *Kamakhya* temple, locating it as a center of tantric rituals, and did not pay much attention to look into the tantric developments in Buddhism in the region. Scholars such as David Gordon White (2003) Gavin Flood (2006) and Charles Orzech (1998) have recently discussed the role of kingship in the development of tantra in the Brahmanical and Buddhist sects in India and China but missed Assam in the discussion. Despite the exoticism and attraction, the tantric traditions of Assam remain generally unexplored in modern scholarship. Buddhism and the development of Buddhist tantric practices in Assam largely remained a neglected area in the available studies. Thus the present paper aims to explore the development of tantric practices among the Buddhist followers of Assam. The article is divided into two parts. The first part is a general overview of the tantric tradition, including discussing the meaning of the term tantra and the critical discussions related to its antiquity and origin. The second part discusses the development of tantric practices among the Buddhists of early Assam up to the thirteenth century CE.

I

The early history of tantricism, its chronology, and initial locale, are difficult to reconstruct. As Padoux has opined that it is also difficult to identify a core of tantric ideas and practices, because of their variety and the secrecy that has always surrounded them (Padoux, 1987: 272-274). Some general features of tantra include the importance attached to energy, rituals, yogic practices, terrifying deities, and sexual rites. During Gupta and post Gupta periods, the impact of tantra was felt not only in Brahmanical sects, but also within the Buddhist fold. Hindu and Buddhist tantra share some broad similarities, but have many philosophical differences.

The word tantra has been derived in several ways. Derived from the root *tan* (to spread), it is taken to mean 'by it, knowledge is disseminated'. Some derive tantra from the root *trai* (to save); it is called 'it protects its followers' (see Williams 1995 and Urban 2010). Tantra considers Godhead as involving the union of a masculine and feminine aspect. Energy (*shakti*) is conceived of as feminine and is central to the Tantric view of the universe and liberation. Tantric practice is usually called *sadhana*. Initiation (*diksha*) into a sect involves ritual initiation, an important part of which is the imparting of a secret mantra by the guru to the initiate. *Mantras* (prayers and formulae) and *bijas* (syllables associated with various deities, believed to have a mystic potency) have an important role. Diagrams known as *yantras*, *mandalas*, or *chakras*, and symbolic gestures known as *mudras* play an important role in rituals. *Hathayoga* postures and meditation (*dhyana*) are also important. All these are supposed to be harnessed towards awakening the *kundalini* energy that lies coiled like a serpent in the body, drawing it upwards towards union with the supreme. Sexual symbolism and magic are other aspects of tantra. The notion of *puja* (worship) in tantra involves transforming the worshipper into the deity. It is often associated with five elements (*panchatattva*) - namely *madu* (alcohol), *mamsa* (meat), *matsya* (fish), *mudra* (generally parched grain), and *maithuna* (sexual intercourse). Scholars with different viewpoints have looked at these tantric traditions from their complex ritualistic understandings as paths to liberation to the widespread associations of these traditions with sorcery and sexuality. Gray has opined that, "tantric traditions are the communities of practitioners who practice, preserve, and transmit through both time and space both the texts and the practices traditionally associated with them" (Gray, 2016: 3).

Defining tantra and tantric traditions is not an easy task as they are diverse and spread across several religious and cultural traditions of various time and space. Thus to come up with an adequate definition, one that is broad enough to apply to all of the tantric practices, is exceptionally challenging, leaving scholars debating on the matter without the agreement of views. The term tantra does not refer to a singular, monolithic, or neatly defined category. Instead, as David G. White has opined, it is a very perplexed and unclear term used to refer to different mysterious/esoteric precepts, and practices followed in the many parts of Asia from the sixth century down to the present day (see White 2005 and Lorenzen 2002). According to Urban, it includes an enormous variety of diverse texts, traditions, and ritual practices followed by the Brahmanical, Buddhist, and Jain communities in the different parts of Asia (Urban, 2010: 4).

While there is very little evidence to suggest that any of the tantric traditions existed before the fifth century CE, there have been attempts to trace back these traditions much earlier, i.e., in the period of Harappan culture or to the time of the Buddha. Some scholars believe that widespread Buddhist tantric practice, namely, *Guhasamajis* existed even during times of Buddha only. But historically, there are no shreds of evidence to support such claims (Wayman, 1977: 97-99). The oldest *Dharanis* of tantric Buddhism is supposed to date from the fourth century CE and G. Tucci is of view that tantra literature originated during the period of Harivarman and Asanga which probably belong to fourth century CE (Banerji, 2007: 14). On the other hand, Winternitz thinks that Buddhist tantra came into being in the seventh or eighth century under the influence of the Saivite Tantras (Banerji, 2007: 14). Thus, how these practices originated in the Indian religions is a debatable issue, and who has influenced whom Buddhist or Brahmanical is challenging to answer.

The tantric form of Buddhism is usually called esoteric Buddhism. The term/name 'esoteric Buddhism' is often used interchangeably with other terms/words, such as Tantric Buddhism, Vajrayāna, Mantrayāna, Kalachakrayāna, and so on. There are two primary views regarding the development of esoteric practices in Buddhism. One set of scholars has seen the development of tantras as evidence of the decay in Buddhism from earlier standards. According to them, tantric practices are a 'degenerate' development of Buddhism. In the tantric rituals, the deeply altruistic motivation and penetrative insight of Mahayana Buddhism were discarded in favour of the expression of baser instincts. Therefore, it was degeneration from high Buddhist practices of morality, compassion, and philosophic insight (Eliade, 1969: 179). The other group of scholars viewed 'tantricism as a frustrated attempt to turn away from monastic celibacy and prolonged practice of the path to immediate gratification in sexual ritual' (Hopkins, 1990: 88). In contrast, David Snellgrove (1959), in the introduction to the translation of the *Hevajra Tantra*, speaks of the tantric tradition as embodying religion and scholarship of the first rank (p.9).

Ronald Davidson (2002) has related the developments of tantricism with the socio-political changes of early

Medieval India. He has argued that tantra emerged out of Indian feudalistic developments and is structured around the metaphor of the *rājādhirāja*, and the systematic use of *abhiseka*, *mandala*, *homa*, and injunctions to secrecy. He has suggested that there was a complex interaction between *tantric* movements and indigenous communities in many parts of South Asia and the development of mature *tantricism* was the consequence of a number of factors. With the decline of the Gupta-Vakataka power in the first half of the sixth century, Indian polities were further divided into smaller units, and newly formed regional powers developed into formidable forces. With these events, the urban centres in the Gangetic Valley experienced population loss, as the trade and markets of the region gradually declined and guild system had suffered a setback forcing population to move once again to agrarian livelihoods and giving rise to a complex socio-economic structure termed as "Indian feudalism" by Sharma (1980).

After the collapse of the Gupta-Vakataka economic base, brahmans and artisans, merchants and politicians started migrating towards new power centres and began to infuse the new regional polities with their skills and their learning (Davidson, 2011: 19). However, during this period, due to the intermingling of people of different regional and social background, the range of religious activities becomes much broader, giving rise to the new iconography that included extraordinary multi-armed deities, sporting weapons of war, and with inscriptional evidence for the valorisation of distinctive local religious practices. As a result, 'new forms of literature were developed to adjudicate, discuss, and (eventually) sacralise practices that included ritual murder, suicide, sexuality, and the ritual employment of polluted substances (bones, blood, semen, urine) and their manipulation or ingestion' (Davidson, 2011: 19). According to Davidson (2002), Buddhist institutions responded to the events in a variety of ways. Internally, they institutionalized a series of intellectual developments that challenged the authority of traditional Buddhist learning. Northern Indian monasteries began to assume fortress identities, and over time they became *de facto* feudal holdings. They exercised police powers, collected taxes, engaged other feudal lords in discussions, received their gifts, and otherwise assumed many of the accessories of *sāmanta* by investing their dominion over a sphere of territory (*mandala*). The feudalization of Buddhist institutions eroded their ideological sphere, so that earlier assimilation that Buddhists had done with the Brahmanical practices of *homa*, coronation, image consecration (*pratiṣṭhā*), mantra recitation, and so on were now engaged in a much more sustained manner.

The earliest form of Buddhist tantricism arises in the first half of the seventh century. It draws strongly from the *dhāraṇī* literature that had already been developed for the previous several centuries. *Dhāraṇī* literature was fully integrated into the idea of bodhisattva, and this is recognized throughout Mahāyānist literature. Outside of Buddhist and Śaiva/Pancarātra literature, the most significant influence on the formation of tantricism was from political sources, including the rituals and ideology associated with kingship. The ritual systems mentioned in the *dhāraṇīs* have thematic analogues in the *abhiseka* rites used in kingship in the sixth and seventh centuries, as well as with rituals drawn from non-Buddhist practices, such as cults to *Cāmuṇḍā* and *Hayagrīva*, as well as rites from the larger *Pañcarātra* and *Śaiva* world (Davidson, 2011: 23).

By the mid-eighth century, tantricism became increasingly radicalized. Due to its involvement with tribal or outcaste spirits such as *yakṣas, vetālas, ḍākinīs, yoginīs, herukas*, etc. usually under the aegis of the greatest *yakṣa* of them all, Vajrapāṇi. Later, Vajrapāṇi, became a marker for the full development of a rhetoric of sanctification of locality and incorporated the associated spirits or gods into the *mandala* by prefacing all their names with the designation *vajra* thus giving rise to *Vajrayana*, the most famous form of tantric Buddhism.

II

Assam has frequently been identified as the original homeland of the tantric practices in the Indian religions. All the early accounts that refer to Assam whether it is Indian, Tibetan, or Muslim (see Shastri 1991; Kooij 1972; Borah 1973) unanimously describe Assam as a land of black magic, tribal superstition, and human sacrifice or more precisely the land of *tantra* practices (Urban, 2010: 8). This association of Assam with the most extreme forms of magic and, above all, sexual rituals continues in the British accounts also. British accounts of this region from the nineteenth century up to the mid of the twentieth century continuously maintained this position (see Wilson 1972: lxi; Eliot 1921: 287-289; Gait 1933: ix; Briggs 1938: 166). *Pragjyotisa* and *Kamarupa* are the terms used in Sanskrit sources to refer to early Assam. The connotation of these terms is not very clear. But most of the scholars agree that the use of term *Pragjyotisa* is earlier and the idea of *Kamarupa* developed in the first half of the Common Era (see Bagchi 1958, 1989; Banerji 2007; Barua 1933; Battacharya 1958; Chaterji 2009).

There are a range of opinions on the meaning of these two terms. According to Gait the term *Pragjyotisa* means 'the city of eastern astrology' and 'the name is interesting in connection with the reputation which the country has always held as a land of magic and incantation and with the view that it was in Assam that the tantric form of Hinduism originated'(see Gait, 2004: 15; Barua, 1933: 13). According to Kakati (1948) *Pragjyotisa* seems to be connected with topographical features of the land rather than any religious cult as opined by Gait following an etymological lead given in the Kalika Purana (39.126). Kakati suggests that the association of Assam to magic and incantation seems to be covered by the term *Kamarupa* which has a religious association and not by *Pragjyotisa* which he interpreted as indicative of topographical elements like mountains, hills etc. The *Mahabharata* mentions *Kamarupa* as a land of *Kiratas*, ruled by the *mleccha* kings (Sukthankar and Belvalkar (Eds.), 1944: 9-10). The *Kalika Purana* (38.130) broadly describes the original inhabitants of *Kamarupa* as *Kiratas* with shaven heads and yellow skins. The Austric and Tibeto-Burman group of Mongoloid trait which were settled here from early period are known as Kirata (see Chatterji 2007; Barua, 1960: 2). The faith and rituals of these Austric and Tibet-Burmans formed the basis of tantra practices in Assam, which gradually mingled into the various religious ideologies that became prevalent in the region (Choudhary, 1959: 390). These tribal groups were associated with phallic cult, magic and charms popularly known as fetishism and this contributed to the origin and development of tantricism (Choudhary, 1988: 14). It is to mention here that female principle which occupies an important place in tantra, widely prevailed among some of the tribes in Assam since earliest period (Sircar, 1948: 15). Buddhist group came in touch with prevailing magic, fertility cult and matrilineal society and developed *tantricism*. Tara emerged as one of the most important female deities in the Buddhist Pantheon and envisioned the female principle in Buddhist ideology of Mahayana and more clearly in Vajrayana (see Mantri, 1971: 152-153; Nakamura, 1987: 443-335). The popular Buddhism that flourished under Mahayanism assimilated the practice of magic, sorcery, exorcism, witchcraft and the associated deities and sublimated them for being inducted into esoteric Buddhism which proliferated into many tantric sects. The Vajrayana, which was the assimilation of the monastic philosophy, magic, and erotics, became popular in Assam. Vajrayana was developed in the agrarian society which required the worship of feminine power as fertility of soil was important for sustenance and nurturing of the society. Aryamanjusrimulakalpa, a famous Mahayani text refers to the development of the tantrika conception and mention Kamarupa as a fertilizing soil for the development of the Tara cult. It reveals that the practices of *Taramantra* at the places viz. Harikela and Kamarupa, achieve good result (see Bhattacarya 1953, 1956, 1958; Kakati 2004: 32; Das 2016). Taranatha also refers about the prevalence of Tara deity by describing that when Asvabhaha came to preach Mahayana Buddhism in Kamarupa; he was attacked by the poisonous snakes and with the help of the spell of Tara mantra he could save himself (Nakamura, 1987: 264 & 274-276; Chattopachaya (Ed.), 1990: 253). The mythical narratives as provided by the Buddhist texts, *Kalika Purana* and Mahabharata as well as descriptions in the inscriptions of early Assam all point towards the interaction and assimilation of brahmanical and Buddhist ideals with the tribal beliefs and practices.

Historically, the Varman dynasty was the first most prominent ruling power in this region that ruled up to the seventh century CE followed by the Salastambhas and the Palas. Literary sources such as Huien Tsang's account and Harshacarita of Bana corroborate the version of the Kamarupa rulers and their alliance with Harshavardhana. The study of the inscriptional evidence between the fifth to the thirteenth century CE by Lahiri helps us in understanding the historical process in early medieval Brahmaputra valley and its peripheral regions (Lahiri 1991). Scholars believe that Brahmanical ideas and practices in the region are visible as early as the fifth century C.E (Sharma 1978). The popularity of the Brahmanical ideology has been unanimously accepted by the scholars but for the prevalence of Buddhism in Assam there is no unanimity. Scholars have put forward the contrasting views in this regard. The traditional view of many scholars is that there is no record of Buddhism in Assam and that the religion of early Assam was some forms of non-Aryan, early Hinduism or Brahmanical or others. The basis for these opinions lie in the fact that neither there is any mention of Kamrupa or Pragjyotisha in the list of sixteen Mahajanpadas as given by Anguttara Nikaya nor this region is included in the Asokan Empire, and any single edict of Asoka has not been discovered here (see Gait 1926: 27; Barua 1951: 185; Majumdar 1952: 270-271; Choudhury 1959: 399).

On the other hand scholars have argued that there are sufficient historical facts to support the prevalence of Buddhism in Assam to at an early date and its continuation till the Ahom period. Most of these arguments are based on literary evidences but few archaeological evidences are there to support the arguments. The testimony of Tibetan scholar Taranatha provided many references to the popularity of cult in the region even before the reign of Bhaskarvarman as he mentioned a Brahman Siddha who was responsible for construction of a vihara called Mahachaitya after he was converted to Buddhism by Dhitika (Chattopahaya (Ed.), 1990: 47). Coincidentally various Buddhist relics discovered in various parts of Assam, especially those of Suryapahar and Bhaitbari near Tura in Meghalaya bear archaeological signs of the prevalence of Buddhism in Assam from early age. Sites like Surya Pahar, Hajo, Pancharatna, etc. are connected by Buddhist elements and trade (see Das and Thakur 2014: 303-313). The inscriptions of Indrapala and Dharmapala clearly proved the prevalence of Buddhism. In the Gauhati grant of Indrapala the word *Tathagata*, occurs in connection with the donated land (The Gauhati Grant of Indrapala, Line 51). Buddhist art remains are recovered from many sites in the region undoubtedly suggest its extensive prevalence. Art remains found at Suryapahar, Pancharanta, Bhaitbari (near Tura) Abhayapuri, Kamakhya area, Da-Parbatya, Golaghat etc. are sufficient to discuss some traits of Buddhist art in the region. Dalton opines that some new shrines had been built with materials belonging to Buddhist shrines (Dalton, 1856: 10).

Buddhist tantricism became well established in Kamarupa with the ascendency of Salastambha dynasty that ruled Assam from around 655 C.E. to 990 C.E (Choudhary, 1988: 330). It has been opined that Salastambha was a non-Aryan ruler (Sharma, 1978: 161) who probably followed the Salistambha Sutra of Mahayana Buddhism (Deka, 2004: 6 and 14). During this period, Kamarupa emerged as one of the main centers among the four-important Vajrayana centers of Hevajra list. Hevajra Tantra, the Buddhist work assigned shortly before 693 C.E (Sircar, 1948: 12) mentions Kamakhya as one of the main centers of Vajrayana along with other three important Vajrayana centers situated in Assam and Eastern India (Bhattacarya, 1927: 733-746). It is evident that under the influence of Rahulabhadra, king Ratnapala was converted to Vajrayana or Tantric Buddhism.

The early history of the religion of Kamarupa is full of myths and legends that developed with the backdrop of the prevailing beliefs and practices. The traces of the introduction of Tara deity and the successive course of the development of Tantricism were recorded in Brahmanical Sakta literatures in the form of myths. Tantric goddess Tara and Ugratara are said to have been discovered and introduced from China or Tibet by Nagarjuna (Walser, 2008: 65-80; Bagchi, 1958: 225; Choudhary, 1988: 303). In the Brahmanical literature, Nagarjuna was replaced by Vasistha and portrayed that Vasistha was responsible for the introduction of Tara deity (see Kakati 1948: 33; Briggs 1938: 280). The Vasistha legends which occupy an important place in Kalikapurana, is associated with the importation of Tara deity (Kakati, 1948: 30). Tara Tantra was adopted by both Hinduism and Buddhism. *Aryamanjusrimulakalpa* suggests that in Kamarupa, Tara deity was associated with Buddhist group much earlier than Hinduism (Briggs, 1938: 279-280). It is to mention here that Buddhist goddess Tara, entered in to Hindu fold as Ugra Tara. Mahacinakrama Tara or Ugratara is a special form of Tara was imported from Buddhist Tantric pantheon into Hindu pantheon (Bagchi 1989: 23; Sastri 1992: 4; Kakati 1948: 19; Buhnemann 1966: 472). Tara is known as Sgrol-ma or Dol-ma in the Tibetan translation of the name. It is to be noted that there is still a temple of Ugratara in Guwahati which is believed to have been built by king Ratnapala after the worship of *Ekajata* was introduced by Siddha Nagarjuna. According to Kalika Purana, Ugratara in Assam is generally identified with *Tiksna-Kanta*, *Eka-Jata* of the Buddhist pantheon.

Taranath speaks of a Buddhist Chaitya in Assam which scholars have identified with the Hayagriva- Madhava temple at Hajo. This temple is visited by the Buddhists from Bhutan, Tibet, and even from Ladakh and Southwest China. The main image of the shrine called *Madhava*, was supposed to be installed from very early date. Buddhist revered this image as *mahamuni*. Dalton (1856) has considered the image as a colossal image of Buddha in stone. This made Waddell to conclude that the present shrine of the temple seems to be the original shrine of an older Buddhist temple, which according to both Buddhist and Assamese tradition, formerly existed here – the upper portion only, is modern. Waddell has observed that some of the rocks in that area bear Tibetan characters of the mystic sentences, like *Om manipadme hum*, *Om Ah Hum*, etc. Probably the famous Buddhist monk *Padma-Sambhava*, who propagated Lamaism, had died here (Waddell, 1895: 310-313). Yogini Tantra describes the Vasinavaite origin of Hayagriva temple at Hajo. According to Kakati, the account of Yoginitantra is an attempt at Vaishnavaising the God who seems to be of a different origin. He remarks that Hayagriva is not a sufficiently famous god in the Hindu pantheon to merit worship and a temple. But he occupies a high reputation in the Buddhist tantras and in the Buddhist pantheon (Kakati, 1948: 73). In Buddhist sadhanas, he is described as a companion of Khasarpana along with Tara and two other deities. He and Tara are also the two companions of Lokanatha. Heruka and Hayagriva are two of the nine males emanating from Aksobhya.

Thus, on the basis of above discussion, it can be concluded that the prevalence of the cult of *Hayagrīva*, and the involvement of tribal or outcaste spirits such as *yakṣas, vetālas, ḍākinīs, yoginīs, herukas*, etc. naturally helped in the evolvement of Vajrayana sect in the region and paved the way for the development of tantra practices among the Buddhist followers of early Assam. In addition to these elements, the emergence of Tara as a female deity which can be worshipped by the *Vamacara* practices especially in the form of Ugratara and said to be followed by Mlecchas helped in the strengthening of the tantric practices in the sect (Chaterji, 2009: 46). The ideals of *mantra*, *yantra* and the *bija* were accepted and Kamarupa emerged as an important centre of Vajrayana sect.

REFERENCES

Bagchi, P. C. (1958). Evolution of Tantra. In Haridas Bhattacharyya (Ed.), *The Cultural Heritage of India*, Vol-iv. Calcutta: The Ramkrishna Mission Institute of Indian Culture.

Bagchi, P. C. (1989). Evolution of the Tantra. *Studies on the Tantras*. (Swami Lokeswarananda, Ed.). Calcutta: The Ramakrishna Mission Institute of Culture.

Banerji, S. C. (2007). *A Companion to Tantra*. New Delhi: Abhinav Publication.

Barua, B. K. (1951). *A Cultural History of Assam*. Nowgoan: Barooah, K. K.

Barua, K. L. (1933). *Early History of Kamarupa*. Shillong: Self Publication.

Barua, K. L. (1960). *Early History of Kamrupa*. Guwahati: Lawyers Book Stall Publications.

Bhattacarya, B. (1927). Origin and Development of Vajrayana. *Indian Historical Quatorly*, iii(1), pp. 733-746.

Bhattacarya, Benoytosh. (1953). Mahayanic Pantheon. In Haridas Bhattacharyya (Ed.), *The Cultural Heritage of India*, Vol-1. Calcutta: The Ramkrishna Mission Institute of Indian Culture.

Bhattacarya, Benoytosh. (1956). Tantrika Culture among the Buddhist. In Haridas Bhattacharyya (Ed.), *The Cultural Heritage of India*, Vol- iv pp.263 - 272. Calcutta: The Ramkrishna Mission Institute of Indian Culture.

Bhattacharya, Benoytosh. (1958). *The Indian Buddhist Iconography*. Calcutta: Firma K. L. Mukhopadhyay.

Borah, M. I. (1973). Five Lectures on the History of Assam as Told by Moslem Historians. In H.V. Sreenivasa Murthy, *Vaisnavism of Sankaradeva and Ramanuja*. Delhi: Motilal Banarsidass.

Briggs, G. W. (1938). *Gorakhnath and the Kanphata Yogis*. Calcutta: OUP.

Buhnemann, Gurdrum. (1966). The Goddess Mahacinacrama-Tara (Ugra-Tara). In Buddhist and Hindu Tantricism, *Bulletin of the School of Oriental and African Studies,* 59(3). University of London.

Chaterji, S. K. (2009). Contributions from different language culture group. *The Cultural Heritage of India*, vol-1.

Chatterji, Suniti Kumar. (1951). *Kirata-Jana-Kirti* (Reprint 2007). Kolkata: The Asiatic Society.

Chattopahaya, Debiprasad (Ed.) (1970). *Taranatha's History of Buddhism in India*. (Reprint 1990). Delhi: Motilal Banarsidas.

Choudhary, P. C. (1959). *History of Civilization of the People Assam to the Twelve Century AD*. Gauhati: Department of Historical and Antiquarian Studies in Assam.

Choudhary, P. C. (1988). *Assam- Bengal Relations*. Gauhati: Spectrum Publications.

Dalton, E. T. (1856). Notes on Assam Temple Ruins. *Journal of Asiatic of Bengal*, (XXIV), pp.1-24.

Das, Boby and Thakur, Amrendra Kumar. (2014). Buddhist Centres of Early Assam Along Trade Routes: A Preliminary Probe. In Mitali Baruah and Jyotima Phukon (Eds.), *Mosaic (A Collection of Research Articles)*. Dibrugarh, pp. 303-313.

Das, Boby. (2016). *Buddhism in Assam: From Earliest Times to 13th Century AD*. New Delhi: Aayu Publications.

Davidson, Ronald M. (2002). *Indian Esoteric Buddhism: A Social History of the Tantric Movement*, Chapter 2. New York: Columbia University Press.

Davidson, Ronald M. (2011). Sources and Inspirations: Esoteric Buddhism in South Asia. In Charles D. Orzech, Henrik H. Sorensen, Richard K. Payne (Eds.), *Esoteric Buddhism and the Tantras in East Asia*. Leiden: Brill.

Debiprasad, Chattopahaya (Ed.) (1970). Taranatha's History of Buddhism in India. (Reprint 1970). Delhi: Motilal Banarsidas.

Deka, Pranav Jyoti. (2004). *Nilacala Kamakhya*. Guwahati: Lawyer's Book Stall.

Eliade, Mircea. (1969). *Patanjali and Yoga*. (trans. C. L. Markhann). New York: Funk & Wagnalls.

Eliade, Mircea. (1971). *Yoga: Immortality and Freedom*, Princeton: Princeton University Press.

Eliot, Charles. (1921). *Hinduism and Buddhism: An Historical Sketch*. London: E. Arnold.

Flood, Gavin. (2006). *The Tantric Body: The Secret Tradition of Hindu Religion*. London: IB Tauris.

Gait, E. A. (1926). *A History of Assam*. Second Edition, 1926, (2004 Reprint). New Delhi: Surjeet Publications.

Gait, E. A. (Reprint, 1933) [first edition1905]. *A History of Assam*. Calcutta: Thacker Spink and Co.

Gray, David B. (2016). Tantra and the Tantric Traditions of Hinduism and Buddhism. *Oxford Research Encyclopedia, Religion* (religion.oxfordre.com). USA: Oxford University Press.

Hopkins, Jeffrey. (1990). Tantric Buddhism, Degeneration or Enhancement: The Viewpoint of a Tibetan Tradition. *Buddhist-Christian Studies*, (10).

Kakati, B. K. (2004). *The Mother Goddess Kamakhya*. Guwahati: Publication Board Assam.

Kakati, Bani Kanta. (1948). *The Mother Goddess Kamakhya*. Gauhati: Assam Publishing Corporation.

Kooij, K. R. van. (1972). *Worship of the Goddess according to the Kalikapurana*. Leiden: Brill.

Lahiri, N. (1991). *Pre-Ahom Assam*. Delhi: Munshiram Manoharlal.

Lorenzen, David N. (2002). Early evidence for Tantric religion. In Katherine Anne Harper and Robert L. Brown (Eds.), *The Roots of Tantra*. Albany: SUNY Press.

Majumdar, R. C. (1952). *Ancient India*. Banaras: Motilal Banarsidas.

Mantri, Naresh. (1971). *Journal of Indian and Buddhist studies*, (1). Tokyo: Japanese Association of Indian and Buddhist Studies.

Nakamura, Hajime. (1987). *Indian Buddhism*. Delhi: Motilal Banarsidas.

Orzech, Charles. (1998). *Politics and Transcendent Wisdom: The Scripture of the Humane Kings in the Creation of Chinese Buddhism*. University Park: The Pennsylvania State University Press.

Padoux, Andre. (1987). Tantrism: An Overview. In Mircea Eliade (Ed.), *Encyclopedia of Religion*,(14). New York: Macmillan.

Sastri, Biswanarayan. (1992). Some aspects of Sakticism in Assam. *Journal of Assam Research Society*, xxxii. Gauhati: Kamarupa Anusandhan Samiti.

Sharma, M. M. (1990). *Religion in The Comprehensive History of Assam*. Guwahati: Publication Board.

Sharma, M. M. (1978). *Inscriptions of Ancient Assam*. Gauhati: Gauhati University Publication.

Sharma, R. S. (1980). *Indian Feudalism*. Delhi: Macmillian.

Shastri, B. N. (Ed. and trans.) (1991). *Kalika Purana*. Delhi: Nag Publishers.

Singh, Lalan Prasad. (2009). *Buddhist Tantra*. New Delhi: Concept Publishing House.

Sircar, D. C. (1948). *The Sakta Pithas*. Delhi: Motilal Banarsidas.

Snellgrove, D. L. (1959). *The Hevajra Tantra: A Critical Study*. London: Oxford University Press.

Sukthankar, V. S. and S. K Belvalkar, Bhandarkar. (1944). *Mahabharata, Sabha Parva*. Poona: Oriental Research Institute.

The Gauhati Grant of Indrapala, Line 51.

Urban, Hugh B. (2010). *The Power of Tantra*. London: I. B. Tauris.

Urban, Hugh B. (Dec. 2001). The Path of Power: Impurity, Kingship, and Sacrifice. In Assamese Tantra, *Journal of the American Academy of Religion*, 69(4).

Waddell, L. A. (1895). *Lamaism*. London: Allen & Com.

Walser, Joseph. (2008). *Nagarjuna in Context*. Delhi: Motilal Banarsidas.

Wayman, Alex. (1977). *Yoga of the Guhyasamajatantra: The Arcane Lore of Forty Verses. A Buddhist Tantra Commentary*. Delhi: Motilal Barnarsidass.

White, David G. (2005). Tantrism. In Lindsay Jones (Ed.), *Encyclopedia of Religion*, (13). New York: MacMillan.

White, David Gordon. (2003). *Kiss of the Yogini: Tantric Sex in its South Asian Contexts*. Chicago: The University of Chicago Press.

Williams, Monier Monier. (2010). *A Sanskrit-English Dictionary*. Oxford: Clarendon Press.

Wilson, H. H. (1972) [First edition, 1840]. *The Vishnu Purana: A System of Hindu Mythology and Tradition*. Calcutta: Punthi Pustak.

3

The Dragon, Sun, Lotus and the Cross: Religious Pluralism in Arunachal Pradesh

TAJEN DABI

Introduction

One of the most plural states in the northeast, religious forms in the mostly mountainous and tribal Arunachal indicates many things: migration of people from different places and cultures to where they are now (Mipun and Nayak, 1999: 17-28); peculiar historical past; hill-plains relations; relative laxity of indigenous tribal religions; competing mainstream religious dogmas at play; etc.

Political relations of the tribes of Arunachal with the Ahom state and later-on the British colonial state were at times hostile but always marked by a mutually beneficial and self-complimentary stance: no territorial annexation by the either state; sporadic military explorations and expeditions into the hills and grant of *Posa* (Jha, 1996 : 446-458; Thakur, 2016: 58); violent quelling of rebellions where the states' strategic interest was threatened (as in the case of the Khampti-Singpho Rebellions of 1839-43; Tani, 2018); exchange of local produce in the *Duars* or the foothill-markets (Yania, 2018); employment of a class of native interpreters known by various terms like *Dobashi*, *Kotoki* and to which was later-on added the government representatives cum local arbiters of disputes called *Jemadar* and *Gam/ Gaonbura*; no missionaries of any hue, etc. From the second decade of the twentieth century, due to strategic reasons, the colonial authorities started to politically define the hills north and east of the Brahmaputra Valley- a process revived during the Second World War crisis with the extension of "control area" up to the Mc Mahon Line (Reid, 1942: 263) within a broad "police-autocracy" (Stonor, 1957: 3) under ICS and military officer level appointees called Political Officers. This arrangement tallies well with a recent analysis according to which, in the Eastern Himalayas, the state agents prioritized the achievement of authority over people against territory (Guyot-Rechard, 2017: 263-4). The period from 1945-48 witnessed hectic official communication for administrative re-organisation and expanding dispensaries and hospitals (Dabi, 2018) - a process carried forward by the new government under Nehru-Elwin era of NEFA's history (roughly from 1950s to mid-1960s, the time when major policy changes were brought in the aftermath of the Chinese aggression). Such developments of pre-colonial and colonial periods clearly indicate that the people of Arunachal Pradesh had political and economic relations with the neighbouring Assam. The trade relations and cultural contacts of Arunachal Pradesh with its neighbours is a well established fact now (*see* Thakur, 2016). Hence, in the historical shaping of the socio-cultural life of the people of Arunachal Pradesh a plural life developed in which the differences were accommodated (Thakur, 2008: 336-358).

Experts have culturally mapped Arunachal, relevant to their times and this still provide introductory yardsticks when trying to comprehend the cultural geography of this extensive and diverse state. Verrier Elwin identifies three cultural zones roughly corresponding to the three major religious groups- Buddhism, Animistic and the Vaishnavism (Elwin, 1958: xiii) while Parul Dutta and Syed Ishteaque Ahmad speaks of two cultural zones- the plains and the hills. Without elaborating this hills-plain binary, they classified the communities of the state into five major tribal groupings (Singh, 1995: xiii-xiv). The ecological variations run from the north to the south and the cultural variations run from east to west (Singh, 1995: 6) since the north-southerly hill ranges discouraged closer interactions between groups in a west-easterly fashion or vice-versa.

The Religions

Buddhism

Both the major doctrinal formats of Buddhism - Mahayana and Hinayana - are practised. In the western and northern parts of the state, the region bordering Tibet, Mahayana forms, variously also known as Tibetan or Lamaistic Buddhism, with further sectarian divisions like Nyigmapa and Gelugpa, is practised. The communities are: the Monpa and the Sherdukpen (in Tawang and West Kameng districts), the Nah (Upper Subansiri), the Memba (Mechuka and Gelling in the Shi-Yomi and Upper Siang districts), and the Khamba (in the Upper Siang district). Among the Monpas and Sherdukpens there is an undercurrent of their pre-Buddhist Bon religion (Dutta and Tripathy, 2008: 89-111) just as Bon deities and sacrificial rituals have been incorporated in the Nyigmapa tradition among the Membas (Tamak, 2016: 232). The pre-Buddhist elements have been integrated into the Buddhist pantheon of Arunachal

Pradesh and are reflected through the arts and paintings (Thakur, 2016: 26-42). Likewise the Nahs (Hiri, 2016: 146) and the Singphos (Geyi, 2015: 189-198) continue to practice parts of their shamanistic rites and rituals even after largely following Buddhism.

The Hinayana/Theravada is followed in the eastern part of the state by the Khamptis, the Singphos, and the Tikhak section of the Tangsas. From where these peoples migrated and brought the religion along with them, it is thus sometimes referred to as Burmese Buddhism. The Khamptis share close cultural affinity with the Thais (Thailand); a trans-continental cultural bonding that has recently found favour in the government for patronage. The Tikhak Tangsas, the earliest among the Tangsa groups to migrate from Burma, who now live in the plains of Miao, Bordumsa, Jairampur and Manmao and the Patkai ranges in Nampong and Namtok bordering Myanmar in the Changlang district, originally did not follow Buddhism. They adopted it after coming in contact with their neighbours, the Khamptis and the Singphos, after having migrated to Arunachal (personal comm.: J. Tikhak, June 6, 2020).

Animistic-Shamanistic Tribal Religion

An animistic religion, marked by a nearly "classic" shamanism (Jones, 1968:333), is the traditional religion of the majority of the people of the state. A visiting colonial military officer has described it as 'polydemonism' (Duff-Sutherland-Dunbar, 1915: 67). All the communities outside the fold of Buddhism as well as the erstwhile followers of Vaishnavism fall into this category. The majority of the people under this group live in what is now commonly referred to as "central Arunachal"- the region roughly from the Kameng in the west to the

Dibang in the east. Even in the 1950s, these communities were reported to be living in Neolithic stage of culture (Stonor, 1957: 2). Parul Dutta and Syed Ishteaque Ahmad (Singh, 1995: 42) describes the tribes like the Mishmis, the Adis and the Tangsas as having anthropomorphic view of nature. This quality may be attributed to all the animistic communities. The myth-origin narratives, lore, the ritual-chants and in day to day life elements of anthropomorphism is noticeable though the religion itself may not be termed anthropomorphic. Another study (Dutta and Tripathy, 2008: 32) has classified the religion of the Noctes and the Wanchos - the two eastern tribes living in the Patkai Hills bordering Nagaland and who are constitutionally recognised as the "other Naga tribes" - under animism while describing the rest of the fellow animist as "hereditary shamanism".

Vaishnavism

Vaishnavism entered Assam in sixteenth century (Eliot, 1910: 1169; Bora, 2017: 53). The process of the Hinduisation of the Ahom court completed towards the end of the eighteenth century (Baruah, 2004: 360). The propagation of Hinduism in areas or among peoples originally not Hindu was thereafter gradually effected - primarily among the tribes (Eliot, 1910: 1155). The history of Vaishnavism in Arunachal Pradesh draws from this ongoing cultural interaction; and it has been a short lived one as both the Akas as well as the Noctes no longer follow Vaishnavism.

Writing about the Aka religion in 1868, C.H. Hesselmeyer, a Christian missionary, said that the concept of *Hori Deo*, a Hindu deity, was introduced by Tagi Raja, the elusive Aka warlord, among his people after being released from imprisonment in the plains. As a captive Tagi became a disciple of a Hindu *guru* who in turn obliged Tagi by giving security of the new convert's future good behaviour before the government (Elwin Ed., 1959: 441). Going by this account, it can be seen that a "civilizing" element was part of the conversion of the menacing warlord. Presently, there are hardly few practitioners of Vaishnavism among the Akas as most of them practice the ancestral animistic traditions (personal comm.: G. Nimasow, June 6, 2020).

The Noctes are believed to have embraced Vaishnavism some 250 years back, under the affiliation of the Shree Shree Chaliahl Bareghar Satra of Nazira in upper Assam, led by one of the Nocte chief, Khumbao, who later on came to be known as Naga Noruttam, abandoning beef and adopting the Sattriya hair-cut in the process (Dutta and Tripathy, 2008: 33). Khumbao's conversion appears slightly different from that of Thagi Raja: weary of inter-group killings, Khumbao, guided by a seminal dream, found his guru in one Shri Ram and was eventually christened as Narottam ("Narottam: A Nocte Saint", *The Arunachal Times*, May 16, 2012; Mishra, 2004: 265-273).

Some recent studies on the influence of Hinduism on the Mishmi (Miso, 2005: 69-70) and Apatani (Naku, 2006: 256, 264) speak about sects like *Jai-Guru* and *Gayatri* cult being followed by sections of the respective community members but these studies does not offer chronology of this process. Some factors suggested for adoption of the new faiths include "lack of spiritual fulfilment" in the indigenous religion and the belief that "if purification is done through practices of other communities, the result would be beneficial" (Miso, 2005: 69-70). Practices such as these are not an aberration as many people in Arunachal privately worship popular Hindu deities like Shiva, Laxmi, Saraswati, etc., in their own convenience without identifying oneself as a member of the particular sect.

Christianity

At 30.2 % (4, 18,732) of the total population of the state as per the last census (2011), from a mere 0.79% (3,684) in 1971, Christianity is the single largest religion in the state. The church has also become "mainstreamed" with rival denominations vying for adherents (Lishi, 2019). One Delhi-based policy think-tank has called attention to the rise of Christian population in the state saying "Arunachal Pradesh joins the Christian northeast" (http://blog.cpsindia.org/2016/02/religion-data-of-census-2011-xiii.html).

The history of the church in Arunachal is recent. French missionary Father Nicholas Michael Krick, who had in 1853 visited Mebo in the Siang valley (Elwin Ed., 1959: 236-48), was on August 2, 1854 murdered, along with his colleague Augustine Etienne Bourri, in the Tibetan border by a Mishmi villager (Mackenzie, 1884: 49). Existing literature suggest the murder as incidental rather than anything to do with their faith; their journey was exploratory, not evangelical. In the 1830s and the 1840s the American Baptist Missionaries from Burma were pressed to work amongst the eastern tribes of the state like the Singphos, the Noctes, the Wanchos and the Khamptis (Bora, 2017: 314-342). After the Khampti Uprising (1839-40), the exercise was abandoned (Downs, 2003: 78).

From the last decade of the nineteenth century, missionary influence among the Adis, the Nyishis and the Mishings living near the foot hills is said to have begun though without much success. By 1950 some youths of the above tribes were converted into Christianity (Sangma,

1980: 271) mainly through the missionary schools in the neighbouring towns of Assam like Sadiya, Jorhat and North Lakhimpur. In July 1947, the Bishop of Shillong offered the services of their Sisters in the running of the hospital being improvised at Pasighat and proposed to open and run schools for the hill tribes of the frontier to work for their "intellectual, moral and social uplift" (Rev. Dr. S. Ferrando to the Governor of Assam dated July 29, 1947, *Medical-B, NEFA Branch*), a proposal declined by the government of the time.

Christianity in Arunachal did not contribute to spread of English education or in the process of unification of tribes neither is there a distinct Christian political identity; this is unlike the experiences in most of the hills of northeast where such developments were associated with the spread of Christianity (Webster, 2012: 93-94). The growth of church in the state has been happening in the absence of a colonial setting, minus missionaries' medical and educational works and it has no association with rebellious voices. Thus, while Christianity is identified as "anti-national" in the rest (Webster, 2012: 94), in Arunachal it currently holds the dignity of being an "alien" faith.

Reformed Religion or the Indigenous Faith Movement

Writing about the contemporary religious reform movement in Arunachal - the only detail scholarly work on the subject so far - anthropologist Sarit Kumar Chaudhuri relates the rapid expansion of Christianity to the awakening among the tribes "in order to protect and pre serve their indigenous religious beliefs and practices." The process has, writes Chaudhuri (2013), "generated new taxonomies, such as "Donyi-Poloism," "Intyaism," "Rangfraism,"... to institutionalize tribal religion by inventing images of gods and goddesses, constructing temples, and textualizing religious chants or oral traditions in a manner very similar to that of Hinduism" (pp. 260-261), .

Religious reform in the sub-continent has one known element, that is, the employment of the tool and techniques of the religion perceived to be a threat in the revised format of the religion considered under threat. In the nineteenth-century, Ram Mohan Roy borrowed congregational worship from the Serampore missionaries (Davis, 1946: 119) and many Brahmo and Arya Samaj leaders, influenced by the idea of Christian piety and Islamic monotheism, re-interpreted and institutionalised their respective orders into a new shape (Panikkar, 1995). The nature of religious reform movement in Arunachal is no different: it has been started by the modern-educated elites who felt a sense of loss and threat; there is debate, exchange of ideas and acrimony- in seminars, workshops and informal settings where, often, the tone is unfriendly and the stance confrontational; there is intellectual and organisational links with similar pan-India organisations; there is production of an entirely new genre of devotional literature in vernacular; and there is this *Jai Donyi Polo* greeting, etc. Chaudhuri (2015) sums up the development crisply: "Many of the images invented are largely Hinduized idols, though an attempt has been made to assimilate some local traits into such images based on their mythical characters. Moreover, in the name of reviving indigenous tribal religion, the way it was institutionalized also reveals or supplements how Hinduized norms were imposed consciously or in disguised ways" (p. 275). The Hindi section of the BBC recently carried a news item titled (rendered in Roman script here), "Naye Bhagwan' ko Pujne ko Lekar

Kyon Asmanjas Mein Hain Arunachal ke Adivasi?" ("Why are the tribes of Arunachal confused about worshiping the 'new god'?") (https://www.bbc.com/hindi/india-51776394).

At least among a section of the followers of the reformed religion the result of institutionalisation has generated a sense of loss, and they are, ironically, the shamans. Some of the shamans, many of who I talked to, have apprehensions about the "survival" of their kind as the devotional element in the reformed religion dim the role of the shaman as the mediator between the mortal beings and the deities. Prayers in place of propitiation, devotional hymns in lieu of ritual-chants, idols in place of omen, healing not taboo/*genna* - the shamans' anxiety is not without valid reasons.

Innocuously placed by the wheels of time before waves of new things the desperation of the followers of the animistic religion is not misplaced. Their ancestral faith was originally not modelled to co-exist with this sort of complexity and competition. Thus, this urgency for reforms the course and results of which is going to be probed by anthropologists, sociologists and historians for a long time to come.

Discussion and Conclusion

A quick survey of religious pluralism in Arunachal generates the following observations. First, all established religions have exerted their influence on the animistic communities so as to recruit converts, irrespective of the means and goals of the conversion. In case of Buddhism, the examples are the Tikhak Tangsas and the Nahs (who, according to one version, embraced Buddhism at a monk's behest in order to escape a deadly epidemic; Hiri, 2016: 146); the Akas and the Noctes in the case of Vaishnavism; and all except the Buddhist communities with respect to Christianity.

Secondly, people from the animistic culture have a tendency to "relapse" to their old tradition. Most Buddhists continue to practice pre-Buddhist rituals; Vaishnavism failed to bring all the Aka and Nocte to its fold and its few early followers are nowhere to be found - only to be replaced by animism and Christianity respectively; and the Christian Church have its own 'backsliders' and returnees to the reformed religion. This interesting development brings back to memory a century-old characterisation about the followers of animistic faith: "The tribesmen have no special preference for their own forms of religion, and take fairly readily to Hinduism in the plains, and to Christianity in the hills. If not for their natural reluctance to abandon pork, liquor and freedom of intercourse between the sexes these tribes would have speedily converted to the either of the two religions" (Allen *et. al.*, 1909: 55).

A related issue is the question of the "alien-ness" of a religion vis-a-vis its indigenousness. Ideally, the animistic religions qualify the standards of being the indigenous religion (Harvey Ed. 2000 and 2002). Within this frame, the Buddhism and the Vaishnavism are established "world religions" without necessarily being "alien". From a protectionist, constitutional point of view Christianity becomes the "alien" religion of the state (the APFRA 1978 Section 2 (c) considers Vaishnavism - and obviously the Buddhism also - as one of the indigenous religions of the state). The standard for the categorisation of what constitutes an "alien" religion is anything but anthropological as much as the cited anti-conversion law was enacted to target spread of Christianity. This notion of an "alien" religion is being driven through a tunnel of animosity in the contemporary protection-of-indigenous-culture debate in Arunachal:

sometimes it assumes the form of posters and banners with insinuating slogans like "Imitation of Alien Faith is Slavery", "Loss of Indigenous Faith is Loss of Identity", "Rituals of Birth, Marriage and Death are Tripod of Your Identity", "Culture Without Indigenous Faith is a Body Without Soul", "Our Faith-Our Guide: Our Culture-Our Pride", etc. - a common sight for weeks during the month of December when the Indigenous Faith Day is celebrated across the state, strategically coinciding with the Christmas festivity. In the study of these complex cultural processes, the definition of what is "alien" about a religion and what "culture" is being supplanted in its wake to put a break to the "loss of identity" is going to attract more scholarly analysis in decades to come. Among such themes, semantic studies on the language and vocabulary being used by the Christian preachers, such as "devil", "evil", "repentance", etc. and its perception, and reactions, in the local animistic world-view; the peculiar appeal of the Gospel and the distinct Christian faith-healing among the animistic peoples of the state, etc. will generate deeper academic insights.

Dawar (2003) has, in detail, tried to understand the question of what he termed as "cultural regeneration" (instead of Chaudhuri's "religious reform") in Arunachal within the Gramscian framework of "cultural hegemony" (Gramsci, 1971), a model of analysis refreshingly and powerfully employed by K.N. Panikkar (1995) with respect to the nineteenth-century India socio-cultural processes. The idea of "hegemony" itself needs to be contextualised while analysing such cultural processes in Arunachal Pradesh. The import of what "hegemony" was in a nineteenth-century colonial metropolis may not fit the situation in a frontier about which the isolation-assimilation discourse was hotly debated in policy circles right in the 1950s and whose administrative philosophy (Elwin, 1957) was initially guided by a sympathetic, protectionist regime.

The defining features of religious pluralism in Arunachal are two: one, the spectacular rise of Christianity and the extra-ordinary effort of the indigenous religious reform movement that has generated a powerful network of activists, intellectuals, temples and organisations (within and beyond the state). Good or bad, apt or misplaced the greatest contribution of the reform movement is in its ability to make the notion of the "loss of culture" popular and create an un-ending debate around it. The second important feature is the sweep of devotional element in the religions of Arunachal- Buddhist, Christian and the reformed religion's devotion; the animistic propitiatory rituals has become the casualty of this march of organised, worship-based religions. A detached observer might view the development as ominous: across all of tribal India, Arunachal, being the terrain where the contest of culture is intensely being fought, will enter the pages of history as India's most interesting cultural laboratory in the post-independent era.

REFERENCES

Allen, B. C., Gait, E. A., Allen, C. G. H., Howard, H. F. (1909). *Gazetteer of Bengal and North-East India* (reprint 2012). New Delhi: Mittal Publication.

Arunachal Pradesh Freedom of Religion Act, 1978 (APFRA 1978).

Baruah, Chandan. (2004). Hinduisation of the Ahom Court in the Medieval Assam. In the *Proceedings of the Indian History Congress*, 65th session, pp. 357-361, https://www.jstor.org/stable/44144751

Bora, Simashree. (2017). Recurrence of neo-Vaishnava Faith: Emergence of Srimanta Sankaradeva Sangha in Assam. In the *Indian Anthropologist*, 47(2), 53-68, July –December, https://www.jstor.org/stable/10.2307/26494031

Bora, Shiela. (2017). American Baptist Missionaries' Ethnological Writings: The Singphos and the Namsang Nagas. In the *Pre-Colonial History and Traditions of Arunachal Pradesh* (Sudhir Kumar Singh and Ashan Riddi Eds.), pp. 314-342. Guwahati: DVS Publishers.

Chaudhuri, Sarit Kumar. (2013). The Institutionalization of Tribal Religion: Recasting the Donyi-Polo Movement in Arunachal Pradesh. *Asian Ethnology*, 72(2),259-277. http://www.jstor.org/stable/23595479

Dabi, Tajen. (2018). Medicine in British Frontier Policy: Disease, Epidemics, and Dispensaries in Arunachal Pradesh c. 1912-1947. *Indian Historical Review*, 45(I), 124-150.

Davis, George W. (April, 1946). Some Hidden Effects of Christianity upon Hinduism and Hindus. *The Journal of Religion*,26(2),111-124.http://www.jstor.org/stable/1197324

Dawar, J. L. (2003). *Cultural Identity of the Tribes of North-East India*. New Delhi: Commonwealth Publishers.

Downs, Frederick S. (2003). *History of Christianity in India, Vol. V, Part 5*. The Church History Association of India.

Duff-Sutherland-Dunbar, George. (1915). Abors and Gallong: Notes on Certain Hill Tribes of the Indo-Tibetan Border. *Memoirs of the Asiatic Society of Bengal*, V, Extra No.,1-91.

Dutta, Sristidhar and Byomakesh Tripathy. (2008). *Buddhism in Arunachal Pradesh*. Akansha Publishing.

Eliot, Charles N. E. (October, 1910). Hinduism in Assam. *The Journal of the Royal Asiatic Society of Great Britain and Ireland*. pp.1155-1186. https://www.jstor.org/stable/25189782

Elwin, Verrier. (1957). *A Philosophy for NEFA* (Reprint 2006). Government of Arunachal Pradesh.

Elwin, Verrier. (1958). *Myths of the Northeast Frontier of India*, xxii, 448. Shillong: North East Frontier Agency.

Elwin, Verrier (Ed.). (1959). *India's Northeast Frontier in the Nineteenth Century*, xxxii, 473. Bombay: Oxford University Press.

Geyi, Goken. (2015). *The Singphos of Arunachal Pradesh: A Study in Historical Perspective from 1800-1947*. (Unpublished Doctoral Dissertation). Rajiv Gandhi University.

Gramsci, Antonio. (1971). *Selections from the Prison Note Books*. Ed. and Trns. by Quintin Hoare and Geoffrey Nowel Smith. New York: International Publishers.

Guyot-Rechard, Berenice. (2017). *Shadow States: India, China and the Himalayas, 1910-1962*. Delhi: Cambridge University Press.

Harvey, Graham (Ed.). (2000). *Indigenous Religions: A Companion*. London: Continuum.

Harvey, Graham (Ed.). (2002). *Indigenous Religions: A Reader*. London: Continuum.

Hiri, Sanjay. (2016). *The Traditional Institution of the Nah of Arunachal Pradesh: An Ethno-Historical Study*. (Unpublished Doctoral Dissertation). Rajiv Gandhi University.

Jha, B. N. (1997). Politics of Posa: A Case Study of Pre-and Post-Independence Scenario in Arunachal Pradesh and Assam. In the *Proceedings of Indian History Congress*, 57th session, Madras, 1996, pp. 446-458. Kolkata: Indian History Congress.

Jones, Rex L. (May, 1968). Shamanism in South Asia: A Preliminary Survey. *History of Religions*, 7(4), 330-347. http://www.jstor.org/stable/1061796

Lishi, Tado. (2019). *Contemporary Christianity in Arunachal Pradesh: Intra-Extra Conversion Issues*. Indian Society for Promoting Christian Knowledge.

Mackenzie, Alexander. (1884). *The North East Frontier of India* (reprint 2004). New Delhi: Mittal Publication.

Medical-B, NEFA Branch, File No. 80/6(c) of 1947. Itanagar: State Archives, Government of Arunachal Pradesh.

Mipun, B. S. & Debendrak Nayak. (1999). A Geographical Background to Peopling of North-East India: A Study in the Dynamics of Identity and Inter-group Relations. In Kailash S. Aggarwal (Ed.), *Dynamics of Identity and Inter-group Relations*, pp.17-28. Indian Institute of Advanced Studies.

Mishra, Ajay Kr. (2005). Religious Practices of the Noctes of Arunachal Pradesh: Exposure and Response, in *Proceedings of North East India History Association*, 25th Silver Jubilee Session, (Manorama Sharma Ed.) 2004. pp. 265-273. Shillong.

Miso, Rajiv. (2005). *Priesthood among the Idu-Mishmis.* (Unpublished M.Phil. Dissertation). Rajiv Gandhi University.

Naku, Hage. (2006). *Beliefs and Practices of Apatanis- Study in Continuity and Change.* (Unpublished Doctoral Dissertation). Rajiv Gandhi University.

Panikkar, K.N. (1995). *Culture, Ideology and Hegemony: Intellectuals and Social Consciousness in Colonial India.* New Delhi: Tulika.

Reid, Robert. (1942). *History of Frontier Areas Bordering on Assam from 1883-1941* (Reprint 1983). Delhi: Eastern Publishing House.

Sangma, Milton. (1986). Attempts to Christianize the People of Arunachal by the American Baptist Missionaries (1836-1950). *Proceedings of the North East India History Association*, J.B Bhattacharjee (Ed.) 7th Session, pp. 263-272.

Singh, K. S. (Ed.). (1995). *People of India: Arunachal Pradesh, Vol. IV*. Calcutta: Anthropological Survey of India.

Stonor, C. R. (1957). Notes on Religion and Ritual among the Dafla Tribes of the Assam Himalayas. *Anthropos*, Bd. 52, H. 1./2,1-23. http://www.jstor.org/stable/40453996

Tamak, Chera. (2016). *The Memba of Arunachal Pradesh: A Historical Study*. (Unpublished Doctoral Dissertation). Rajiv Gandhi University.

Tani, Rubu. (2018). *Resistance Movements in Eastern Arunachal Pradesh: The Khamptis and the Singphos, 1825-1843*. (Unpublished Doctoral Dissertation). Rajiv Gandhi University.

Thakur, Amrendra Kumar. (2008). Pre-modern Accommodation of Differences and Modern Innovations: Religion and Society of Arunachal Pradesh. In *Religious History of Arunachal Pradesh* (B. Tripathy and S. Dutta Eds.), pp. 336-358. New Delhi: Gyan Publishing House.

Thakur, Amrendra Kumar. (2016). Cultural Development in Buddhism of Arunachal Pradesh: Probing Through Arts. In *Pre-Colonial History and Traditions of Arunachal Pradesh* (Sudhir Kumar Singh and Ashan Riddi Eds.), pp.26-42. Guwahati: DVS Publishers.

Thakur, Amrendra Kumar. (2016). *Pre-Colonial Arunachal Pradesh: Society, Technology and Trade*. New Delhi: Akansha Publications.

Webster, John C.B. (2012). *Historiography of Christianity in India*. New Delhi: Oxford University Press.

Yania, Taw. (2018). *Duars in Arunachal Pradesh: Study of Hill-Plain Symbiosis in Sixteenth to Nineteenth Century*. (Unpublished Doctoral Dissertation). Rajiv Gandhi University.

4

The Cultural History of Tripura: An Overview

PRADEEP KUMAR DEEPAK

Introduction

It is not denying that many scholars have researched the socio-cultural life of the people of Tripura earlier. However, some of the earlier writings are too specialised to understand for general readers and researchers. They are much specialised researches on the developments of pre-colonial or the colonial periods or even the post-1947 period dealing with a particular set of people. In my previous researches on historical aspects of Tripura, I have provided a survey of literature too (see Deepak, 2011, 2014, 2017, 2018). Based on the secondary sources and my observations of more than a decade of Tripura, this article of mine tries to present an overview of socio-cultural life of the people of Tripura. At the outset, I want to make it clear that, I am aware with the formulations of Eric Hobsbawm regarding the changing character of festivals and the emergence and acceptability of new features in the socio-cultural life of people of a society as tradition (see Eric Hobsbawm and Terence Ranger (Eds.), 1983 and Eric Hobsbawm, 2013). Considering the limitation of a paper in an edited book, the analysis of some of the festivals on the lines suggested by Hobsbawm and some other scholars has been avoided in this paper. On another occasion this exercise will be done.

The glory of the Tripura kingdom is known from the Puranic period and much before the *Ramayana* and the *Mahabharata* (Debbarma, 2006: 1). The earliest history of Tripura is still shrouded in obscurity. No records in the shape of documents or monuments of the Autochthons people of the land belonging to the pre-historic or proto-historic periods have survived (Palit, 2004: 10). Culture plays a significant role in moulding the destiny of one's own country. Tripura witnessed the emergence of secular identity as the people of different religions, just like Hindu and Buddhists, walked together to form a common cultural identity.

During Pre-Colonial Tripura, the dwellers in the hills of Tripura belonged to the following tribes: (i) Tripuri (ii) The Jamatia (iii) The Reang (iv) The Halam divided into twelve sub-tribes and (v) The Kukis divided into two major groups, namely, the Darlong and the Dusai (Mizo).

Tripura was known as 'Hill Tipperah' in the Colonial period. Since the beginning of the 15th century A. D., the lunar dynasty of members ruled it with Manikya ending names. The British Govt. gave Tripura the status of 'Native State' under the general supervision of a political agent. It was merged with India on October 15, 1949, and became a full-fledged state on January 21, 1972. The scholars believe that the name of this land as 'Tripura' is the Sanskritised form of Tipra, a tribe to which the ruling family belonged. Territorially, Tripura, a hilly state in the North-eastern region of India, is the homeland of different tribes. Altogether there are nineteen tribes in the state. These tribal communities have been classified into the following two broad groups.

1. Mongolian comprises 15 tribes,
2. Non-Mongolian comprises 04 tribes.

No doubt, the maximum number of tribals in the Indo-Mongloid group and their ancestors came from the "Bodonome" in Central Asia (Palit, 2004: 20). According to the order of the President of India in 1956 A.D. on the SC's and ST's in Tripura, there are 19 Schedule Tribes in Tripura just as Tripuri, Reang, Jamatia, Noatia, Halam, Chakma, Mog, Lusai, Kuki, Garo, Chaimal, Khasia, Bhutia, Munda, Orang, Lepcha, Santhal, Bhil and Uchai.

Tripura illustrates the co-existence of Hinduism and tribal religions. The Hindus worship fourteen deities- Hara or Shiva, Uma (the spouse of Shiva), Hari or Vishnu, Lakshmi, Saraswati, Brahma, Prithvi (Goddess of Earth), Samudra (God of Ocean), Ganga, Agni (fire), Kamadeva (Cupid), and Himalaya. The list has some unusual features: Brahma's worship has been discontinued elsewhere (except a few small pockets) in Hindu society. Those listed after Brahma does not figure among the gods and goddesses worshipped in northern and peninsular India (Roychoudhury, 1983: 99).

The cultural link between Bengal and Tripura was well established. The royal family's liking and attachment to the Bengali language dates back to the first decade of the 18th century when Dharma Manikya II got the great epic the Mahabharata translated into Bengali. It is significant to note that in one of his instructions to his minister Maharaja Radhakishore Manikya (1897-1909 A.D.), who was a great patron of art and literature, asked his minister to take care that the use of Bengali as a state language did not suffer because of the highbrow attitude of English educated people.

It was during his time that the Tripura State Gazette was first published in Bengali. By the process of Sanskritisation, the tribal community of Tripura tried to prove themselves to be a part of Hindu society. Sanskritisation occurred sooner or later in those castes which enjoyed political and economic power in Tripura.

Religion and the Festivals of the Tribes

So far as the religious aspect is concerned, the Hinduisation of tribals is an example of religious Sanskritisation in Tripura. Due to the growing process of Sanskritisation, many temples were constructed in Tripura during the 15- 16th centuries. Mention may be made that Dhanya Manikya built the Tripura Sundari Temple in 1501 A.D. There are four predominant communities in Tripura professing different religious beliefs-Hindus, Muslims, Buddhists and Christians. Most of the tribal people have their tribal customs and ideas. Still, in the broader sense of religion, they are believed to be followers of Hinduism. The Mogs and the Chakmas are Buddhists. The Lushais and some people of the Kuki and Garo communities embraced Christianity. The Hindus as a whole have occupied a significant place commanding an overwhelming majority of the population. Next to the Hindus, the Muslims occupy the second position in the State. The majority of tribal people follow the religion of Hinduism as well as Animism. It is stated that the old Gods of tribal people have not yet been ousted, and they are worshipped along with Hindus by tribal priests. They worship the elements, such as the God of fire, the God of forests and the Gods of earth etc. Even their old fate is found in the worship of Kharchi puja.

As per the views of Dr. Suniti Kumar Chatterji (1974), "The Tipras, like the other Bodo groups, had their tribal religion much modified by Hinduism. But among them and under the aegis of the ruling house of Tripura, a good deal of their old pre-Hindu religion and its rituals is preserved as part of the state religion. For several Centuries the Tipra, Comtawas (as the Assamese writer called them in 1724) or Cantais (As they are now called) or high priests and the Tipra Deodhais or Deodhairs (Deoris) have ministered to the old gods, holding a position in society almost as exalted as that of the Brahmans, Cantais and Deodhais on the one hand, and brahmins on the other- the former preserving the old gods (though sometimes under new names) and the old rites- these are the custodians of Tipra religion; a dual arrangement which is still in vogue" (pp. 135-136).

The Temple of Tripura Sundari

Maharaja Dhanya Manikya, one of the greatest Manikya king of Tripura had built the temple of Tripura Sundari in 1501 A.D. Of course, this temple occupies the best place in the history of Tripura and the Indian Peninsula. This temple is one of the 51 holiest shaktipeeths (Shrine of Goddess of Power) in India as per Hindu mythology. There are two images in the temple, one called Chhoti maa and the other of Tripura Sundari. This Pithasthan (centre of pilgrimage) is also known as Kurma pith because the shape of the temple premises resembles that of Kurma or Tortoise.

The Temple of Fourteen Gods

The temple of fourteen gods is also known as Chaturdas Devata Mandir. It is located about fourteen km away from Agartala at a place called Old Agartala. Maharaja Krishna Manikya built this temple in the middle of the 18th century. It is believed that this temple was initially situated at Udaipur, the old Capital of Tripura. As per the local tradition preserved in the Rajamala, the fourteen gods were first worshipped by king Trilochana, a contemporary of Yudhisthira, the legendary king of Mahabharata (Raychoudhury, 1983: 99).

The massive idols of these fourteen gods and goddesses, according to a legend, were in possession of the king of Burma. The king of Tripura sent his army, which fought a battle and, after defeating the king of Burma, decided to bring back only the heads of the fourteen idols as it would have been difficult to carry home the very heavy statues. They are made of stone; thirteen of them are covered with gold, one with silver. All the priests are tribal Tripuris, not Brahmans. The head priest is known as Chantai; his four principal assistants are known as Narayan. They have eighty junior priests called Galim. The heads are kept in an iron safe, and each day three of them are worshipped in turn. Only on the occasion of the Karachi festival, held in June July for a week, they are lodged in a hut open on all sides, and all fourteen are worshipped. On these days, many goats are sacrificed by the Galim on behalf of the worshippers. In a separate hut is kept the idol of another goddess-Burma. During the Kharchi festival, women desiring children make her the offerings of vermillion and light candles in the shrine. All worship this tribal goddess; she also receives her share of sacrifices. Tripura illustrates how tribal tradition is assimilated with the Hindu heritage and the two-function together in harmony. This situation needs to be known better (Dubey, 2016: 13).

Bhuvaneswari Temple

The Bhuvaneswari temple is situated on the southern bank of the river Gomati at Udaipur. This temple is located close to the ruins of a big palace built by the Maharaja Govinda

Manikya in the 17th century (Roychoudhury, 1983: 114). Rabindranath Tagore's famous novel 'Rajarshi' and Drama 'Visarjan' have depicted the inside story of this temple. It is said that human sacrifices were performed in this temple by the Tantric priests. It was Govinda Manikya who probably abolished it in the latter half of the 17th century.

Regarding the human sacrifices in Tripura, Rev. James Long remarked, "Human sacrifice prevailed at an early period in Tripura and even of the late years is strong suspicions have been entertained at the shrine of Kamakhya and Kalighat in Calcutta. But in no part of India where more human teams of heard than in Tripura, which appears to have been one of the strongest holds of Hinduism" (Roychoudhury, 1983: 101-102).

Unakoti Tirtha

The Shrine Unakoti, which means 'one less than a crore, is situated between Dharmanagar and Kailashahar, the two Subdivisional towns of North Tripura. This hilly place is at a distance of about 110 miles from Agartala. Numerous excellent specimens of sculpture are found scattered on either side of the meandering hill tract, up and below the basin on the rocky walls of the hill slopes, amidst bushes, some hidden beneath the rich underground and others half-buried in the ground. Both the rock-cut figures and the stone images can be found here. Among the numerous rock-cut figures, the central Siva head and the gigantic Ganesa figure are the first objects to arrest the visitors' attention. The images of Hindu deities like Siva, Durga, Vishnu, Ram, Lakshmana, Ravana, Vricha, including some of the heroes and deities of Ramayana and Mahabharata, bear the silent testimonies of India's past heritage (Roychoudhury, 1983: 102).

As per *Tripura District Gazetteers*, "Among the rock-cut figures, the Central Siva head and the gigantic Ganesa figures deserve special mention. The Central Siva head, known as Unakotisvara Kal Bhairava, is about 30 feet high, including the embroidered headdress, which is 10 feet in height. Three enormous images of a bull are found half-buried in the ground. On each side of the headdress of the Central Siva, there were two full-sized female figures. The figure of Durga standing on a lion and another female figure are found carved on the rocky wall above. Two other gigantic heads of Siva and Durga attract notice if one stands on the terminus of the new road leading to Unakoti. Among the images, particular mention of the two Chaturmukha and one Trimukhalingas, the former found on the bank of the stream and the latter at some height on the hill, may be made for their fine execution. At the top of the hill images of Vishnu, Panchamukha, Ravana, Hara-Gouri, Narasingha, seated Ganesa, Hanumana etc. are found."

Pilak

Pilak is a place where we find the treasure house of Hindu and Buddhist sculpture and architecture. It dates back to the 8th and 9th centuries. Beautiful images scattered in an area of about ten sq. Km. Have been found. The images, terracotta plaques, and sealing found here reflect existence in remote antiquity of heterodox creeds and sects representing Hinduism and Buddhism. Colossal stone images of Avolokiteshwar and Narasimha have been found here.

Mangal Chandi Temple

The 'Mangal Chandi' temple in the heart of Amarpur town in South Tripura is no less important or attractive as a religious place. This historical temple was built by Tripura's erstwhile princely ruler Amar Manikya (1577-1586), blending traditional Hindu-Buddhist architectural style. The presiding deity in the sanctum sanctorum of the temple is 'Devi Mangal Chandi', but there is also the figure of a cow built within as a vehicle of Lord Vishnu besides images of minor deities. Despite conflicting interpretations of the architecture and nature of dedication to deities, 'Mangal Chandi Temple' is a centre of pilgrimage to devotees and tourists of all hues keen to perform religious rites and acts pieties (Palash, 2010: 155).

Tirthamukh

In the Amarpur subdivision, Tirthamukha is so-called as it is near the Dumbur falls, which is the source of the river Gomati- considered as the holiest river by the tribals. Every year thousands of pilgrims visit the place - about 117 Km away from Agartala - on the occasion of Uttarayan Sankranti for a holy dip. A mela is held on this occasion, and the tribals make their annual purchase there.

Jagannath Temple

Situated near the Kunjaban palace, the temple attracts the Hindus and many others because of its peculiar structure, which is octagonal at the basement and has an excellent pradakshinapatha around the sanctum. "Every pillar of the octagon is crowned by a square pyramidal cone rising above a multifoil niche which comes at the level of the terrace. The Sikhara is a stepped octagonal pyramid rising in four storeys above the vertical portion over the terrace. An elevation like this reminds A construction like this would perhaps suggest a snowy Himalayan origin, as in these parts it would have no meaning in the physical environment." Many other temples were also erected during the middle of the 15th century to the middle of the 16th century. Their names are as follows: Tripureshsiva temple, Hari temple, Vishnu temple on the bank of Dhanyasagar, Jagannath temple of Daityanarayan, Visnu temple of Hirapur etc.

So far as the religious aspect is concerned, the Hinduisation of tribals is an example of religious Sanskritisation in Tripura. Due to the impact of Sanskritization, human sacrifice was stopped as we know that human sacrifices also prevailed in Tripura from very ancient times. Durga Puja, Shiv Puja, Kali Puja, Laxmi Puja and other festivals of the Hindu religion were celebrated with great zeal & pomp like indigenous tribal worships of Kharchi Puja, Ker Puja, Garia Puja & Ganga Puja.

Due to the impact of Sanskritization, a bond of love and faith was developed among the tribal and non-tribal people and lived in an atmosphere of peace and tranquillity in Pre-Colonial Tripura. Due to Sanskrtization, Tripura was culturally linked with other parts of India and a sense of Integrity developed among indigenous people of this land.

Festivals of Tripura

Kharchi Puja

The worship of the fourteen gods, popularly known as Kharchi Puja, is celebrated in July every year. This Puja (worship) is celebrated for a week. It is held in the temple of Chaturdas Devata or the temple of fourteen gods. The sacrifice of many goats and pigeons at the altar of gods is a special feature of this festival. Though initially a tribal festival, devotees of all classes of people, both tribals and non-tribals from every corner of Tripura, participate in this festival (Roychoudhury, 1983: 100).

Ker Puja

Another important festival in Tripura is the Ker puja which is celebrated generally fifteen days after Kharchi Puja. This Puja (worship) is performed to ward off all dangers. The Ker puja is held within a boundary specially marked with previous notice. During the Puja, nobody is allowed to enter or come out of this specified boundary. The festival continues for two days and a half.

Garia Puja

The tribals of Tripura perform Garia Puja on the seventh day of the month of Baisakh (April). The people believe that this puja makes for their prosperity and enjoyment for the whole year. Cocks are sacrificed, and after the puja, people start dancing.

Ganga Puja

After Navanna, the festival of new rice, Ganga Puja, is celebrated in March-April every year. This is another excellent tribal festival. Ganga, it may be recalled, is one of the fourteen deities of the land. Like Garia puja, this is a community festival; about four to five tribal villages join together to celebrate the occasion. People gather by the streamside, pare three pieces of bamboo into beautiful flowers; the villagers then build a temple with bamboos in the middle of the stream, and the ageless rituals take place amidst joy and splendour. God is appeased by the sacrifice of goats, buffaloes and ganders to save the people from any epidemic.

Pous-Sankranti Mela

Since ancient days Tirthamukh has been a holy place of the Hindu Tripuri Tribals. On a specific day, people flock to the site to shave their head in their ancestors' names and worship Hindu deities and perform individual sacrifices and rituals to appeasing the souls of departed ancestors. It is on this occasion that a two-day long fair is also held.

The Mela held near the source of the river Gomti in an area known as Tirtha Mukh, and the accompanying festival attracts a large number of devotees from all over the state. Both tribal and non-tribal people assemble every year on the occasion of the Uttarayan Sankranti for a holy dip in the lake.

Buddha Poornima

Though the number of Buddhists living in the state is minimal, Lord Buddha's birthday is celebrated on a grand scale every year. People of all communities enthusiastically take part in this festival.

Reforms of Maharaja Bir Chandra Manikya: The reforms of Maharaja Bir Chandra Manikya were very much pivotal for the cultural impact in Tripura.

Abolition of Sati System in Tripura: Another landmark in the State's history was the abolition of the Suttee in 1888 (Sur, 2010: 74). Sati was legally forbidden in British India. However, the practice continued in Hilly Tipperah till the end of the 19th century. Suppose we have a glimpse over the Rajmala. In that case, we find that three decades back, Sati was prevalent among the royals during the first half of the 16th century. The Rajmala mentions that after the death of Maharaja Dhanya Manikya, his wife Kamla Devi committed Sati. Reference to Sati among the royal family of Tripura is also available in Tripura Desher Katha Likha or Tripura Buranjis, written by Ratan Kandali Sharma and Arjun Das Bairagi during the first half of the 18th century.

Abolition of Slavery in Tripura: Maharaja Bir Chandra Manikya stopped the heinous Sati System from Tripura by enacting the law in 1877 A.D. The system of slavery was a common practice in Tripura from a very early period. The rulers of Tripura brought slaves from the adjoining states. Most of the eunuchs of the palace were selected from among the slaves. Whereas in India the slavery was abolished by ACT V of 1843 A.D., the same was abolished in Tripura in 1877 A.D. Regarding the abolition of slavery in Tripura, Mr. Bolton, the officiating political agent of Tripura, reported, "With regard to the subject of domestic slavery, I am glad to report that since the close of the year the Maharaja has issued a proclamation forbidding the sale, purchase, receiving in pledge, or forcible detention and a slave, of any human being under penalties to be awarded by the criminal courts, but authorising the making of contracts of service for a period not exceeding three years. The proclamation, I think, deals effectively with the custom of domestic slavery (Bhattacharya and Deepak, 2014: 65-66)."

Towards a Composite Culture

Tripura has a mixed population of Tribals and non-tribals. Of the former, the Tripuris, the Reangs, the Jamatias, the Chakmas, the Hamlas, the Noatias and the Mogs are important. The non-tribal population consists mostly of Bengalees. But what is unique in Tripura is that here one finds elements of the culture of different sets of people, each unique in its way mingled together. In the process, a composite culture is embracing the different strands of faith.

In any assessment of a particulars culture or way of life, one generally looks at what is best in that culture or way of life. There may be higher points of aspiration of those who want to live by the culture. A meeting point of two different ways of life – a point where two cultures meet without loss of identity and individuality-is not only quite possible but seem the only possible way towards what many of us call 'integration'. The term in our context broadly refers to a situation in which the tribals can retain their languages, myths, religion and social customs while at the same time allowing themselves to a process of change in these matters (Guha, 1986: 81).

The famous dances of Tripura such as – Garia Dance, Hozagiri Dance, Bizu Dance, Hai-Huk Dance, Lebung Boomani Dance present a sense of composite culture in which all people of Tripura celebrate these dances with great happiness. Many fairs are celebrated in Tripura such as Paus-Sankranti Mela, Buddha Purnima, Garia Puja, Ashok Astami Fair, Gari Puja, Ashok Astami Fair, Garia Puja, Dolyatra and Rashleela, Karchi Puja, Ker Puja and Durga Puja. All these fairs demonstrate a composite culture of Tripura.

Conclusion

The cultural and religious aspects of about 19 different tribal communities make Tripura a wonderful amalgam of cross-cultural diversity. Though each ethnic community enjoys its cultural strengths, this meeting point is often referred to as a laboratory of exotic cultural synthesis. Last but not least, we can say that Tripura is making quantum progress in the sphere of peaceful co-existence of the people professing different religions, cultures and languages. It is an emblem of the all-round development of Tripura. Maharaja

Bir Chandra Manikya is known as the 'Father of Modern Tripura'. He had abolished the Sati practice and institution of slavery. He made the judicial reforms in a better manner by which equality can be observed in Colonial Tripura. We find that their religious, cultural, social, and judicial impacts formed a pivotal role in making Tripura a modern one.

REFERENCES

Bhattacharya Ruma & Deepak Pradeep Kumar. (2014). *Tripura.* New Delhi: Vikas Publishing House Pvt. Ltd.

Chandramani, Debbarma. (2006). *Glory of Tripura Civilization.* Agartala: Parul Prakashani, Agartala.

Deepak, Pradeep Kumar. (2011). The Mughal Inroads in Tripura: An Overview. In Amrendra Kumar Thakur (Ed.), *Proceedings of North East India History Association*, 32nd Session, pp.612-261. Agartala.

Deepak, Pradeep Kumar. (2014). History of Tripura - Land, People, Settlement, Pre- Colonial State Formation, Sanskritization, State Structure (Unit 2). In Tripura, *Book for M.A.(History)*, Directorate of Distance Education, Tripura University, pp.25-56. New Delhi: Vikas Publishing House Pvt. Ltd.

Deepak, Pradeep Kumar. (2017). Tripura: The Land, the People, Religion and Language, State Formation in Ancient Tripura, History of Tripura Raj: Ancient and Medieval Period. In *Administration and Politics in Tripura, Book for M.A. (Political Science),* Directorate of Distance Education, Tripura University, pp.1-34. New Delhi: Vikas Publishing House Pvt. Ltd.

Deepak, Pradeep Kumar. (2017). The Military Expedition of the Mughals in North East India: Some Aspects. In Amrendra Kumar Thakur (Ed.), *Proceedings of North East India*, 38th Session, pp.254-261. Mirza, Assam.

Deepak, Pradeep Kumar. (2018). Sanskritization and its Impact on Pre - Colonial Tripura. In Amrendra Kumar Thakur (Ed.), *Proceedings of North East India*, 39th Session, pp.131-143. Shillong.

Dubey, S. C. (2016). *Indian Society*. New Delhi: National Book Trust India.

Guha Thakurta, S. N. (1999). *Tripura*. New Delhi: National Book Trust.

Hobsbawm, Eric and Terence Ranger (Eds.). (1983). *The Invention of Tradition*. Cambridge: Cambridge University Press.

Hobsbawm, Eric. (2013). *Fractured Times: Culture and Society in the Twentieth Century*. New York: New Press.

Kumar, Chatterji Suniti. (1974). *Kirata-Jana-Kirti*. Guwahati: Assam Publishing Company.

Kumar, Palit Projit. (2004). *History of Religions in Tripura*. New Delhi: Kaveri Books.

Palash. (2010). *Tripura Year Book 2010*. Agartala: A Tripura info Publication.

Roychoudhury, Nalini Ranjan. (1983). *Tripura Through The Ages*. New Delhi: Sterling Publishers Private Limited.

Sur, Hirendra Kumar. (2010). *British Relations with the State of Tripura 1760-1947*. Agartala: Naba Chandana Prakashani.

5

The Cultural Life of the Thembang Monpas of Arunachal Pradesh: Exploring through Hoi-Si-Na

TSERING YANGJOM

Introduction

The Monpas are one of the major tribes of Arunachal Pradesh. The Monpa people profess their faith in the Vajrayana School of the Mahayana Buddhism and live in the westernmost part of Arunachal Pradesh, mainly in the districts of Tawang and West Kameng. The Monpas are broadly identified with the geo-political area: Tawang Monpa, Dirang Monpa, Thembang Monpa and Kalaktang Monpa (see Thakur, 2006). Broadly, the history of the Monpas can be divided into two phases: Pre-Buddhist and Buddhist. The early social formation can be termed as the pre-Buddhist. The advent of Buddhism marks the phase that followed and its influence on Bonpoism practised among the Monpas. In fact, Bon and Buddhism have complemented each other and evolved, influencing each other. The major areas in which the influence of Buddhism is prominently visible is the rituals and arts. This aspect of the socio-cultural life of the Monpas has been studied in the past. However, the emphasis is on the Tawang area (see Thakur, 2016), and the Thembang area has not found its deserved place. Thus, this paper aims to fill the gap in the historical reconstruction of the Monpas of Arunachal Pradesh. One such ritual is the Hoi-si-na which is associated with the evil spirits of Assamese people that has been incorporated into the ritual landscape of the Monpas of the Thembang Dzong. This paper explores this ritual, origin and addresses the interaction between Buddhism and the Bonpoistic ritual Hoi-si-na.

The Monpas and the Arrival of Buddhism

The Monpa habitat, known as Monyul, has been directly influenced by Tibet as a cultural zone from time immemorial. The occupation of the Monyul by the Monpas may be traced back to the early days of the Christian era, and this Buddhist community had trade relations with Bhutan in the west, Tibet in the north and Assam in the south (Chakravarty, 1973: 22). Tawang, the sacred place of Nyingmapa and Gelugpa sects, till 1950 was connected with the monastery of Lhasa and functioning as a prominent pilgrimage centre for the Buddhists of this region.

The origin and migration of the Monpas to their present habitat in Arunachal Pradesh are by and large obscure. Certain myths are associated with it, and it seems that the forefathers of the Monpas were either Tibetan or Bhutanese. As a matter of fact, for a very long time till 1950, Monpas were under Buddhist politico-cultural dominance with far-reaching impact administered by religious heads. It is generally believed that Guru Padma Sambhava, locally known as Lopon Pema Jungne (Lopon Rimpoche), sowed the seeds of Buddhism among the Monpas (Chhomu,

2013: 82). The legend of Guru Padma Sambhava spreading Buddhism in Monyul reveals that the Nyigmapa sect was the first to have entered in Monyul. Guru Padma Sambhava lived during the 8th Century C.E. It is improbable that Buddhism spread to Monyul during his lifetime. Besides, there are no records of any kind to prove otherwise. Bibash Dhar (2005) has pointed out that the Monpas were starting adopting Tibetan Buddhism in the 12th century.

Before the advent of Buddhism among the Monpas, they were nomadic and followed Bon faith that believed in the forces of nature and worshipped mountains, rivers, trees, jungles and wild animals. The believers of Bon propitiated several gods and spirits thought to be responsible for various calamities and disasters. These supernatural powers were and are still considered to be powerful. They have been influencing the lives of the Monpas. As pointed out by Chhomu (2013: 76), "for various diseases, calamities, epidemics, death, miseries, illness and misfortunes, the Monpas blame the evil spirits. Hence, they try to please the spirits and gods by offering prayers and goods with the assistance of the priest called *Bonpo.*"

Since the construction of the Tawang Monastery in 1681 CE, Buddhism was firmly established in Monyul; the socio-religious, political and economic life of the people of the area have been highly influenced by Tibetan Buddhism. As such, the history of the Monpas is associated with the monastery. With the establishment of the Tawang monetary, the Gelugpa sect gained supremacy over other sects (Sarkar, 1980: 14). The dominance of the Gelugpa became hegemonic after the birth of the VI Dalai Lama in Tawang in 1683. Thus, Tawang was brought under the ambit of Buddhism centered in Lhasa, whose political, socio-economic and religious institutions were replicated in Tawang Monastery, having "supervising rights over administration of the several *Gompa*s erected in various places" (Dutta and Tripathy, 2008: 206). From then on, the Monpas had to pay taxes to the Tibetan government and the monastery officials.

After the popularisation of Buddhism in Tawang, a series of migration took place, especially from Bhutan who mainly settled in the western part of the area and "from there, after a period of cultural synthesis, the movement turned towards south and resulting in the establishment of different settlements in the southern and eastern part of the Monpa country" (Duarah, 1990: 7).

Since its arrival, Buddhism has been a dominant force among the Monpas, anchoring every aspect of life, engulfing even those rituals that do not change easily. Despite this, Bon remained an active religion in the Monpa regions. In fact, Bon and Buddhism, as rightly argued by Mizuno and Tenpa (2015: 95), have "contributed to the development of both the religions... Buddhism and Bon have never been mutually exclusive in their relations to each other." This paper explores the Hoi-si-na, which presents a finest example of this interaction between Bon and Buddhism, especially among the Monpas of Thembang. The Hoi-si-na, at first glance, looks like a pre-Buddhist ritual. However, the beginning of it cannot be earlier than the 17th century, when the Ahom king Pratap Singha (1603-1641) introduced the *Posa* system- an economic appeasement policy to avoid raiding of plains of Assam by the hill tribes. According to this system, the Monpas, among other Buddhist tribes, also enjoyed tax privileges, and this ritual is connected to the *Posa* System (see Jha, 1996).

The Thembang Dzong and the Bapus

The Hoi-si-na ritual is unique to the Monpas of Thembang Dzong- a tentative UNESCO World Heritage site listed in 2014. It is an administrative circle located approximately 55 Kms northeast of Bomdila, the headquarter of West Kameng District. The Thembang Dzong or commonly known as Yuchho Pema Chen is a medieval fortress covering an area of approximately 3.2 acres and is governed and inhabited by the Bapus comprising of four royal clans, namely Khochilu, Sharchokpa, Atjepu and Dirkhipa. These four clans are named after their respective forefathers, who were princes of the king who once ruled the village. They are called the Bapus (Hindi word for fathers) because of their great-great-grandfather, King Wongmei Palder, who was called by that epithet to acknowledge his superior power by the king of Darrang in Assam (Mizuno and Tenpa, 2015: 19). The village was first established in the $16^{th}/17^{th}$ century, but the construction of the current fortress is estimated to be in the 17th to 18th Centuries after a fire accident broke out in the same century (Mizuno and Tenpa, 2015: 26-27). Not much is known during which Ahom ruler, the Bapus were granted the *Posa* privilege, but it is clear that they used to collect taxes from Udalguri and Mazbat of the present district of Udalguri in Assam. These towns were among the many that functioned as marketplaces since the time of Ahom king Pratap Singha. Presently, Udalguri and Mazbat are 176 Kms and 184 kms southwest of Thembang, respectively, while both these towns have a distance of approx.40 km with each other. In the pre-modern times, the route of these two towns from Thembang Dzong may have been shorter, but the duration most likely to have been longer. Of these two towns, which one is associated with the Hoi-si-na is not known, but it is widely accepted by the inhabitants of the Thembang Dzong that it is connected with the collection of taxes in *Lego* a Monpa word denoting the plains of Assam.

There is a frightening story prevalent among the Thembang Monpas of one such visit to Mazbat for tax collection. When exactly the incident took place is lost in time. However, the story reveals that the collection of the Posa system was already a regular practice done usually by the experienced and abled senior Bapus. For once, two young Bapus were assigned the task of collecting the taxes. Owing to some miscommunications, the two Bapus were killed by the people of Mazbat and buried there with a memorial stone. With this, it was believed that the Bapus would be cursed if they visit the area. Hence, still today, the Bapus avoid visiting the site where the two young are laid to rest.

When did Buddhism exert its influence in the Thembang Dzong is difficult to ascertain. However, it can be safely inferred that Thembang Dzong owing to its greater distance from the seat of Buddhism, i.e. the Tawang Monastery, Buddhism reached Thembang relatively late, or its influence was later than other places such as Dirang Dzong. Keeping this in mind, it can be argued that the Hoi-si-na ritual characterised by human/animal sacrifice originated when the people of Thembang Dzong had not embraced Buddhism (Pre-Buddhist Thembang). It can further safely attribute the early 18th century as the period in which Buddhism exerted its influence in Thembang. It must be pointed out here that even after the arrival of Buddhism, Bonpoism existed, and it still is, as a parallel religious tradition. As pointed out by B.N. Jha, Buddhism, "instead of seeking to wipe out the indigenous completely believes and practices and the attempt was made coalesce and syncretise or even to allow the two cultural traditions of Buddhism and Bonpoism to coexist and share a common platform in the shape of sacred centres (Jha, 2006: 232). The prevalence of this non-Buddhistic ritual in the Thembang Dzong, which can be considered a periphery of the Buddhist Monyul spare headed by Tawang Monastery, clearly shows the lesser influence of Buddhism there in comparison to the enduring Bonpoism.

It is worth noting, which further lends support to the proposition mentioned above, is the fact the Bapus profess their faith in the Gelug sect of Tibetan Buddhism. In the history of Buddhism among the Monpas, the Gelugpa was a late entrant compared to the Nyigmapa. The Gelugpa became a force to be reckoned with only after establishing the Tawang Monastery in 1681 CE. At least, a generation must have lapsed for the Gelugpa to reach and exert its influence on the Bapus of Thembang Dzong. A plausible date would be the early 18th century for the spread of Buddhism in Thembang Dzong. This fits perfectly well with the Hoi-si-na ritual, rooted in taxation rights given to the Bapus. This could not have taken place before introducing the Posa system in the early 17th century (see Thakur, 1997 and 1998).

The Origin of the Ritual

Hoi-si-na is not a Monpa word. Hoi-si-na is an abbreviation of distorted Assamese colloquial phrase, *Hoi- se-na- nai,* which literary means "are you done or not?" However, in the ritual context, it forms the question asked to the Assamese evil spirits, "are you satisfied or not?" of the offerings given to them. Mizuno and Tenpa's (2015) understanding of Hoi-si-na is rooted in Tibetan Buddhism. For them, Hoi-si-na is *Hosina,* with Tibetan transcript *lhosrid nag,* which implies it is rooted in Tantric Buddhism given the word *nag*- a term which has a negative connotation. Since it originated in Assam, it is beyond doubt that the Hoi-si-na is derived from Assamese language. This is further supported by the Assamese phrases, which are shouted out by the villagers during the rituals.

This explains how the ritual started and how it is connected to Assam and serves us with an example of how external forces could influence a culture. In this case, Assamese and Buddhism were crucial- the former in the inception of the ritual, and the latter is changing the nature of it. The ritual started during the Ahoms in Assam when Thembang Bapus visited the plains of Assam to collect tax. After one such visit, when the Bapus returned to Thembang, it is believed that they were accompanied by the evils spirits of Assamese people, thereby causing an epidemic that decimated the population of Thembang. To get rid of the epidemic, a ritual was performed in which offerings were made, and the spirits responsible were asked if the offerings satisfied them or not by asking them in distorted Assamese, "*Hoi se nanai?*" If they were satisfied, they were ordered to leave the place at peace.

Since then, this ritual is performed between April and May every year. The ritual is officiated by the *Phrami* or the village lama, and traditionally, "a human body from which the internal organs have been removed was necessary as an offering to the evil spirits"(Mizuni and Tenpa, 2015; 104). The Chants in localised Assamese are one of the most interesting parts of the ritual. In this ritual, villagers paint their faces in black colour and visit all the houses in the fortified village of Thembang. When they walk down the lane, they loudly shout three phrases in Monpaiized Assamese: "*Pet bimarhuamanu* (men ridden with Stomach disease)," "*soukubimarhuamanu* (conjunctivitis ridden man)" and "*haathbimarhuamanu* (man ridden with hand disease)" followed by repetitive word *Hoi-si-na? Hoi-si-na*? (Short form for asking *Hoi se nanai*, are you done or not?) These phrases reveal the exact nature of the diseases inflicted on the inhabitants of Thembang, which they believe were brought to Thembang by the evil spirits. Rationally, it can be surmised that the people of Udalguri and Mazbat were reeling under an epidemic of some stomach, eye and hand diseases. When the Bapus travelled to these places to collect taxes, they contacted the diseases and brought them to Thembang Dzong and spread these diseases to the people. The superstitious mind blamed some evil spirits of Assam responsible for the epidemic. What kind of stomach, eye and hand diseases they were suffering is difficult to ascertain. The eye disease may be conjunctivitis, although it is not life-threatening. Alternatively, there may have been some other deadly eye disease that further research can reveal.

Once the black painted gang steps out of a house, family members throw assorted grains of maize, barley, millet and beans at them from inside the house, thereby symbolically throwing out the spirits. The family members then quickly wipe the fallen grains off from the porch. Later, the villagers assemble in one place and go for the symbolic sacrifice.

Now, what have been sacrificed shows that Buddhism had not reached the Thembang Dzong or at least, its influence was not substantial enough. Initially, the ritual involved sacrificing human, as mentioned earlier. However, with the advent of Buddhism, animal sacrifice was put to an end as it propagated *ahimsa* or non-violence among the Monpas. Since the interference of Buddhism, the animal sacrifice of the Hoi-si-na ritual has been substituted with animal dough edifices made of millet or barley and coloured them with red symbolic of blood previously involved in human and animal sacrifice, it must be mentioned here that in 2006, Venerable Tsona Gonpatse Rinpoche, popularly known as T. G. Rinpoche who was much adored as a political leader, dissuaded the people of Thembang from practising this ritual. The devout Buddhist of Thembang complied for a year, but soon, many people died for unknown reasons. After the break of a year, the ritual was resumed by the people of Thembang Dzong.

The Hoi-si-na Ritual and its context

Unfortunately, this ritual has completely eluded scholars and researchers alike, and the ritual remains unstudied. The ones, who have addressed it, however scantily, are Kazuharu Mizuno and Lobsang Thenpa. In their *Himalayan Nature and Tibetan Buddhist Culture in Arunachal Pradesh, India* (2015) Mizuno and Tenpa have dealt with the Hoi-si-na ritual very briefly. They are correct to describe the ritual and background of the ritual, which they say is "complex." However, there are many inconsistencies, contradictions and misinterpretations. First, they have classified the ritual as a "festival", which is misleading because it is not a festival in the conventional sense. Although the inhabitants of the Thembang Dzong observe this as a community enterprise, however, there is no point in celebrating the evil spirits of Assam, which had brought epidemic causing much pain, grief and misery irreplaceable loss to the people of Thembang. The involvement of blood or the substitute of it lends much to the fear psychosis of the people who observe the ritual and the belief of evil spirit so deeply ingrained in the minds of the people that categorising it as a festival seems farfetched. To prevent this, the ritual is observed every year. Secondly, they have connected the ritual with the sacred festival of Losar (New Year), which is wrong because there is no connection between Losar and Hoi-si-na whatsoever. If at all, it is because of the coincidence of dates. Taxes were usually collected at the end of the year called *Chungnyipa* (the twelfth month), after which the Losar (New Year) was celebrated during *Dawadangpo*, the first month usually falls in February and March as per the Tibetan lunar calendar.

It is rather disappointing that they have regarded Hoi-si-na as a part of the Bon religion. The Monpas who practised Bonpoism before the advent of Buddhism continued to retain elements of Bon religion even after they embraced Buddhism. Even the mighty Buddhism could not overthrow it but could only alter the ritual in toning down the violent parts involving the sacrifice of animals and human. The ritual originated in Assam, and Buddhism had already established in the Monpa areas, refutes that the ritual has a part of Bon, although it looks like it. The Buddhist inheritors of Bonpoism had to deal with the evil spirits of Assam in the ways best known to them- conducting a Bon ritual in Buddhist sensibility. Luckily, (Mizuno and Tenpa, 2015: 104) reproduced the ritual manual or at least the diagram called *Sangchen Gudrai Rimo* specifying the required ritual paraphernalia such as ornaments made from a human skull, arm, breast and hipbones, which has been stolen.

Mizuno and Tenpa have pointed out yet another interesting aspect of the ritual. They state that traditionally "in this sacrifice, three men wearing the traditional Miji animist costumes and four men dressed as soldiers dance around a boy tied down to the ground in the small plaza in front of the community hall and killed him with their swords. Nowadays, a human figure is used to represent this (Mizuno and Tenpa, 2015: 103)" in the form of *torma*. The association of "three Miji animist costumes" is fascinating and points to the strong possibility that the representation of the Mijis in the ritual is a different story altogether. This can be brought to light by further study. The story, which has been narrated earlier, has no mention of the Mijis.

Conclusion

This exploration shows that the ritual of Hoi-si-na observed by the Monpas of Thembang Dzong is one of the finest examples of internationalisation non-Buddhist elements into the fold of Buddhism. Rooted in the economic aspect of the *Posa* system in Assam, the ritual forms a unique feature of the socio-religious and cultural life of the residents of Thembang. Arguably, the ritual originated in the Pre-Buddhist phase of Thembang, during which human was sacrificed initially and later shifted to the animal. However, with the influence of Buddhism in Thembang, the sacrifice of human/animals was done away with and substituted with edifices made of millet/barley dough. This ritual may look like a Bon practice, but the background and the Assamese phrases uttered during the ceremony to ward off the evil spirits point that it has no connection with Bonpoism. The Thembang Monpas, as one of the inheritors of Bonpoism sought to address the crisis in the ways best known to them. Even when they embraced Buddhism, they could alter only a minor part of the ritual rather than eliminating it.

ACKNOWLEDGEMENTS

I thank the residents of Thembang Dzong for being hospitable and resourceful. I want to acknowledge the contribution of Mr Wang Tsering Dirkhipa (Gaobura), Mr Tashi Wangchu Dirkhipa

(Public Leader), Mrs Tsering Choizom Dirkhipa, Mr Tenzin Chopel Atjepu (Teacher), Mr. Lobsang Tsering Sharchokpa (Teacher) and Mr Lungten Khochilu (Public Leader)- all from the Thembang Dzong for providing me with necessary information on the rituals during my fieldwork at the village. I have gained enormous knowledge from Mr. Dorjee Tsering Lhoupa, Bod-Yig Teacher at Govt. Secondary School, Thembang. I am deeply indebted to Professor Amrendra Kumar Thakur, Department of History, North-Eastern Hill University, Shillong, for his perennial support and motivation to pursue in-depth research in the Monpa areas of Arunachal Pradesh. I am grateful to my colleague Mr Duli Ete, Assistant Professor of History at Dera Natung Govt. College, Itanagar, for his comments and valuable inputs. For any errors and mistakes, I am entirely responsible.

REFERENCES

Bansal, B. L. (1994). *Bon: Its Encounter with Buddhism*. Delhi: South Asia Books.

Biswas, Ashok. (2006). *Mystic Monpas of Tawang Himalaya*. New Delhi: Indus Publishing Company.

Chakrabarty, L. N. (1973). *Glimpses of the Early History of Arunachal*. Shillong: Directorate of Information and Public Relations.

Chhomu. (2013). *Socio-Economic and Cultural Life of the Monpas of Arunachal Pradesh*. (Unpublished Ph.D. Thesis), Department of History, Gauhati University.

Dhar, Bibhash. (2007). *Arunachal Pradesh: The Monpas of Tawang in Transition*. Guwahati: Geophil Publishing House.

Duarah, D. K. (1990). *The Monpas of Arunachal Pradesh*. Itanagar: Directorate of Research, Government of Arunachal Pradesh.

Dutta, D. K. (1999). *The Monpas of Kalaktang*. Itanagar: Department of Cultural affairs, Directorate of Research, Government of Arunachal Pradesh.

Dutta, S and Jha, B. N. (1999). British Colonial Design Behind the Udalguri and Doimara Fairs and its Impact over the Monpas and Shertukpens of Arunachal Pradesh. In Amrendra Kumar Thakur (Ed.), *Proceedings of North East India History Association*, XX Session, pp. 305-316. Dibrugarh University.

Dutta, S and Tripathy, B. (Eds.), (2006). *Buddhism in North East India*. New Delhi: Indus Publishing Co.

Dutta, S and Tripathy, B. (Eds.), (2008). *Sources of the History of Arunachal Pradesh*. New Delhi: Gyan Publishing House.

Jha, B. N. (1996). Politics of Posa: A Case Study of Pre and Post-Independence Scenario in Arunachal Pradesh and Assam. In the *Proceedings of Indian History Congress*, 57th session, Madras, pp. 446-458.

Jha, B. N. (2002). *British Colonial Intervention and Tribal Responses in the North East Frontier of Assam*. (Unpublished doctoral dissertation). Arunachal University, Doimukh.

Jha, B. N. (2006). Buddhism, Buddhist Monasteries and the Societies of the Monyul: A Historical Study. In Sristidhar Dutta and Byomakesh Tripathy (Eds.), *Buddhism in North-East India*, pp. 229-240. New Delhi: Indus Publishing Co.

Mizuno, Kazuharu and Tenpa, Lobsang. (2015). *Himalayan Nature and Tibetan Buddhist Culture in Arunachal Pradesh, India*. Tokyo: Springer.

Nanda, Neeru. (1982). *Tawang: The Land of* Mon. New Delhi: Vikas Publishing House Pvt Ltd.

Norbu, Tsewang. (2008). *The Monpas of Tawang of Arunachal Pradesh*. Guwahati: Bhavani Offset and Imagining Systems.

Norbu, Tsewang. (1997). Status of Monpa Women, in B. B. Pandey (Ed.) *Status of Women in Tribal Society, Arunachal Pradesh*, Itanagar, pp. 298-310.

Sarkar, N. (1980). *Buddhism Among the Monpas and Sherdukpens*. Directorate of Research, Government of Arunachal Pradesh.

Thakur, Amrendra Kumar. (1997). Peasantisation and State Formation in Early Arunachal Pradesh. In the *Proceedings of the Indian History Congress,* 58th Session, Bangalore, pp. 303-12.

Thakur, Amrendra Kumar. (1998). State Formation in Arunachal Pradesh. *N E H U Journal of Social Science and Humanities* (new series), 1(1), 73-87.

Thakur, Amrendra Kumar. (2006). Polity of Pre-Colonial Arunachal Pradesh: Interactions in Trade, Culture, State and Buddhism. In S. Dutta and B. Tripathy (Eds.), *Buddhism in North-East India*, pp.241-63. New Delhi: Indus Publishing Company.

Thakur, Amrendra Kumar. (2016). Cultural Development in Buddhism of Arunachal Pradesh: Probing Through Arts. In Sudhir Kumar Singh and Ashan Riddi (Eds.), *Pre-Colonial History and Traditions of Arunachal Pradesh*, pp.26-42. Guwahati: DVS Publishers.

6

Non-Buddhist Elements in Buddhism of Sikkim

Krishna Kumar Sharma

Su-Khyim (*Limbu/Lepcha*) or Drenjong (*Tibetan*) or Beyul Demazong (*Bhutia*), or as we have commonly known Sikkim is a multicultural and landlocked Indian mountain state in Eastern Himalayas, which has a glorious history. China/Tibet bounds it in the north, Nepal on the west, Bhutan on the East, and West Bengal on the south. Kanchenjunga (the third highest peak in the world) is worshiped by the indigenous people of Sikkim as it is of mythological significance for members of the pre-Buddhist community.

The people residing in this area were of different races, such as Indo-Mongoloid, Tibetan, and Nepalese (Bhalerao *et al.* 2016: 7). Himalayan Sikkim is a cultural mosaic constituted by almost 22 Indo Tibetan and Indo–Āryan groups residing therein (Arora, 2009: 54). There are three major communities in the Sikkimese society. The first is the Lepchas or Rongpa, living in the North Sikkim. The second group is called Bhutia, or Khampas, in the west. They are the people of Tibetan origin and are the followers of a form of Buddhism called Lamaism, a Mahayana form including non- Buddhist

Indian elements and pre-existing 'Bon shamanism' (Raj *et al.* 2015: 291). The third community of Nepalese (Limbus, Magar, Rai, Gurung, Murmi, etc. are allied races that belong to the Kirati sub-cultural stock of the Nepali race) settled in the south practicing Hinduism. Approximately 60.9 percent population (Mostly Nepali) professing the faith of Hinduism, which Buddhism follows with 28.1 percent of the people, Christians with 6.7 percent of the people, mainly consisting of Lepcha and Nepali Hindus converted to the faith due to the influence of Christian Missionaries in the nineteenth century. It is going on at present also. There is also a Muslim population with 1.4 percent of the people.

Buddhism (which has the second largest population in Sikkim) dominates the culture and lifestyle of Sikkim even in the present day, and the main reason behind it is its significant cultural past. In the 7th - 8th century, Buddhism took hold in Tibet. During the 8th to 20th century, the Eastern Himalayas past have a complete illustration of cultural and religious assimilation in the arts and ritualistic practices of different sects of Buddhism, Hinduism, and Animism (see Thakur, 2016 & 2020). Before the introduction of Buddhism, Tibetan religious life was made up of primitive or folk religions comprising supernatural beliefs and myths, magic, shamanistic practices, songs, music, riddles, legends, stories, etc., there was a Bon religion, the pre-Buddhist lha-chos or religion of the Gods (Tewari, 1987: 138). According to R.C. Tewari, "when we closely examine the features of Himalayan Buddhism, most of the Gods and demons, rites and customs, fairs and festivals, dance and music, etc. which give distinctness to Tibetan or Himalayan Buddhism originally belonged to the indigenous little tradition." Marlene Erschbamer (2019) writes, "according to mythological accounts, during the 8th

century, the Indian Buddhist master Padmasambhava was invited to Tibet by the Tibetan emperor as demonical forces hindered the establishment of Buddhism as a state religion. He pacified and converted some of these entities, which were part of the pre- reformed Bon belief." Local ritualism, such as animal sacrifices, clashed with newly established Buddhism. Cuilan Liu (2017) mentioned that "There were efforts to purify Buddhist monastic practice in Medieval Tibet by advocating strict observance of Monastic regulations, including abstinence from Song, dance and Instrumental Music" (p. 76). We can imagine how Buddhism, which has blossomed in Sikkim in a long time, is replete with various non-Buddhist elements such as Dances, Music, etc., of Lepcha, Bhutias, and other indigenous people.

Sikkimese history starts from three tribes of prehistoric times – the Naong, the Chang, and the Mon (Ahmed, 2005: 129). After some time, the Lepcha people arrived from the south of the Brahmaputra valley. The pre-historical tribes who were already living with their naturalistic beliefs, the Lepchas, also got mixed up entirely due to their nature and animist–shamanistic beliefs. The Lepchas give place to mountains such as Kanchenjunga and Yab bdud (located in southern Sikkim) in their historical thoughts. These pre-Buddhist beliefs of the Lepcha people also had to be accepted in Sikkim's Buddhist tradition and culture. Bhutia people, who spread from Tibet to Nepal, Bhutan, Sikkim, and the surrounding areas in the 13th -14th century, also spread the local tradition of Tibet. In Sikkim, they also started the pastorals and semi-settled agricultural practices.

Along with Sikkim's changing socio-cultural dimensions, the Lepcha and Bhutia people also accepted and recognized each other. With the help of the Monks of Nyingma-pa sect

(Red hats), who was expelled from Tibet by the Gelugpa sect (Yellow hats), Bhutias established the kingdom of Sikkim in 1642 under Phunstok Namgyal. He recognized Mahayana Buddhism as a state religion. For the political ambition, spread and the promotion of Buddhism, the non-Buddhist elements of the Lepcha people needed to be respected and accorded a place in the tradition of Buddhism. In this way, the Non–Buddhist elements of the Lepcha people became an integral part of the Mahayana Buddhism of Sikkim. With the arrival of the Nepalese people to Sikkim in the mid of eighteenth century, a new campaign began in the history of socio-cultural assimilation in the state. Hindu belief, indigenous ritual, customs, and philosophy of the Himalayas influenced Sikkim's Buddhism to a great extent.

As a history researcher, when we analyze the expansion of all religions globally, we find that the philosophy of all the circulating religions and their prophet recognizes the cultures and beliefs of the local creeds, or they contain those indigenous beliefs within themselves according to their convenience. Although this process does not happen suddenly, this adjustment goes on continuously. For example, when we do a comparative study of Christianity and Buddhism, one thing clearly states that even though both of them are theoretically sticking to their fundamental principles, they are also practical in agreement with local beliefs. It is a suitable means of proving its legitimacy in society by any religion or philosophy. Those who follow local creeds also have no reason to resist.

We have an example of natural worship, i.e., mountains of the Lepcha and Lhopos peoples, which was entirely connected to their beliefs and culture; secondly, animal sacrifices which had no place in the Buddhist faith but gradually, both non-Buddhist elements became an integral part of the Buddhist authority in Sikkim.

The indigenous Sikkimese beliefs that the mountain deities inhabited the peak of mount Kangchendzonga (*gangs chen mdzod lnga*) (Denjongpa, 2002: 5) and they worshipped this deities. During the initial phase of Buddhism in Sikkim, Tibetan and Sikkimese Lama generally ignored the mountain deities as they do not belong to the Buddhist monastic lineage. In the interval of changing time, Bon religion had acquired a place in society with its modified form as per the need. It was included in the daily lifestyles and rituals of Lepcha and Lhopos people and also influencing Buddhism. Kangchendzonga, as Pholha (*father god or lineage protector*), has various identities as he is considered the chief of all supernatural beings of Sikkim, the owner of the land, the warrior God, the witness deity, the provider of sons. It is believed that the deities Pholha molha (*father godmother god*) have all the power to bless their followers, such as provide sons and good harvests, to avert death in case of illness, to sort out all disputes, and to protect members from curses. However, a similar pattern is observed about Dzo-nga. Some recitations related to ancestral deity considered as a Bon tradition are also included in Buddhist rituals. All rituals related to Bon based on the *khalen* oral ritual text chanted during the performance.

There is another mountain deity Macong (*Pholha or lineage protector*), residing on the mountain range separating the Bhutanese valley of Ha and the Tibetan valley of Chumbi close to Sikkim, who is the provider of sons. The head and the back leg of an ox are offered to show reverence towards the sun deity. There are others mediator deities, such as Pawo, who assist local supernatural beings. It believes that Kangchendzonga's five peaks are the repository of five treasures: the first contains salt; the second gold and turquoise; the third Dharma scriptures; the fourth has arms and the fifth medicine and different types of seeds. It is believed that all these treasures will be made available to the Sikkimese people in times of need (Denjongpa, 2002: 12). The importance of Dzo-nga among Sikkimese people can be gauged by the fact that it is also remembered as a witness deity. A blood brotherhood was sworn between the Tibetan Kye Bumsa and the Lepcha Thekong Tek where the local deities of Sikkim were invoked to witness their alliance, and many animals were sacrificed to cement the alliance (Denjongpa, 2002: 19). In later time Dzon-nga came to be worshipped as a witness deity by the Pemayangtse lamas. It is worth noting that Buddhist lamas who did not like animal sacrifices advocate such rituals later. This suggests a gradual change in the identity of Kangchendzonga as it is transforming from a local deity to a Buddhist deity. This clearly shows how the Buddhist religion of Sikkim was acquiring local culture keeping because of own legitimacy. The subjugation of the spiritual inhabitants is a significant part of the Buddhist conversion of the people who believed in their existence (Denjongpa, 2002: 21). We can clearly understand from some mythology of Buddhist tradition how Buddhist promoter assimilated the lineage protector of local belief such as Kangchendzonga –"*when do-nga was subdued by Guru Rinpoche and appointed keeper of the land and its treasures, he was not to let anyone enter and discover Sikkim's sacred sites. When Lhatsun Chempo (chief propagator of Buddhism in Sikkim) arrived from Tibet, it is said that Dzo-nga first tested him before appearing to him in the form of a while goose and giving him the permission to open the gate to the hidden land.*" There are also village-level rituals performed by village lama and believers in which Dzo-nga is represented as the higher territorial deities of Sikkim. The *Nesol* ceremony is the most important and performed ritual of Sikkim as much in the Pemayangtse monastery of Nyingma sect. *Nesol* belong to the Buddhist tradition of the land. Another is *Chirim* ritual which is the annual ritual where Bon specialists and Buddhist village lama jointly participate.

In consequence of the acceptance of Bon or local traditions by the Buddhist Lama, we see Buddhist legitimacy was also accepted in the everyday life of the indigenous people. In later centuries, Bon ritual specialists were invited to participate in state functions. There were some state-sponsored rituals, i.e., Yangku held to increase a person's or a household's yang, the element which is thought to be beneficial for the production of wealth. The second is called Sinen (*Sri mnan*), a ritual performed to suppress the arising of opposing forces; another was Pang Lhabsol, the national ritual of the land, held at the palace's chapel and at different monasteries. We can say *cham* dances by the Pemayangtse lamas were the way of legitimating indigenous traditions in the Buddhist fold where Dzo-nga and Yapdi were the central deities.

There are other non – animistic elements in the Lamaism of Tibet and Sikkim Buddhism, such as the intermediate state – Bar-do, where people's souls wander after death (Hummel, 1967: 21). According to non – animistic conception, a human being turns into a beast or a beast into a human being. Non – animistic ideas can be seen as Lamaistic mask ceremonies and cult dances. The human being becomes a divine or demoniacal being or a particular animal by wearing the corresponding mask (Hummel, 1967: 25).

Animal sacrifices have been part of pre and post Buddhist Himalayas. Even in India, sacrificing animals is an integral part of indigenous people from the Vedic period practice. We have many examples of Tibetan Buddhist masters who traveled to Sikkim and tried to prohibit the practice of animal sacrifices, while local peoples had found their own way to deal with these ancient rites, which theoretically contradict Buddhist principles. Lepcha and Lhopos belong to the original inhabitants of Sikkim, and they show similarities in their shamanic traditions. They fear severe consequences if they stop worshipping supernatural beings. As is well known, the recognition of early local rituals and beliefs by a new religion and incorporating within own custom has been the tradition in history. It is noteworthy that several Buddhist masters have spread their teaching in Sikkim, but original and indigenous practices never eliminated. According to common belief, local deities prefer "red offerings" such as blood and meat. Nearly every mountain is said to be populated with supernatural beings. The Sikkimese shamans are the ritual specialists responsible for keeping good relations with the households and the lineage's ancestral Gods. *Pawo* and *Nejum* maintain good relations with the ancestors and the lineage protectors, while the *bongthing* is responsible for good relations with supernatural entities of the locality. The sacrificing of animals was practiced as part of rituals to show loyalty and worship supernatural beings. Shamanistic tradition in which animal sacrifice was part of religious rituals was followed by people of Tibetan origin and Lepcha. However, they were gradually influenced by Buddhist thought of Tibetan masters, but they never renounce ancient pre-Buddhist rituals.

The practice of animal sacrifices sometimes creates problems as many people in Sikkim define themselves as Buddhist, whereby the principle of non-violence is an essential part of Buddhist thought. However, ignoring ancient practices does not seem to be an option for them, here we see, both shamans and Buddhist masters interact and co-exist in daily village life. The practice of animal sacrifices was really a challenge for newly established Buddhism. At the time of Padmasambhava, non-Buddhist followers of ancient local traditions (Bon) carried out animal sacrifice. Padmasambhava was probably the first Buddhist master who tried to prevent people from performing local practices. It can be said that the prohibition of animal sacrifices was a sign of Tibetan Buddhist dominance over local pre-Buddhist deity cults. It was a legitimation of the new religious system. Based on some chronicles, it can be concluded that how two religions fighting for supremacy. According to a local myth, a magical contest took place in North Sikkim during the 8th century. The two main protagonists were Padmasambhava and a Lepcha, a member of the original inhabitants of Sikkim. Even though Lepcha won the competition, Padmasambhava showed his power with several prophecies. Scared by his power, the locals began following him (Erschbamer, 2019: 6).

Animal sacrifice was a point of tension between local shamanic and Buddhism in Sikkim, and that this balance was upset from time to time by the arrival of a charismatic Tibetan master who advocated the prohibition of animal sacrifices. After the enthronement of the first Buddhist ruler of Sikkim, dkon mchog rgyal mtshan (1601-1687) traveled to Sikkim – a place that he described as being a land of darkness, where people showed harsh behavior and where the animal was killed. Dkon mchog rgyal mtshan helped locals by providing infrastructure. In this way, he also benefited traders and pilgrims. He banned killing animals and thus rescued many fish and wild animals. Several decades later, another Tibetan master traveled to Sikkim. Bsod nams chos dzin providing infrastructure to locals and rescued many animals. Both masters conducted activities for the welfare of humans and animals. But their attempts to prohibit animal sacrifice only lasted for a short time as it was against bon rituals. In later centuries, Buddhist masters continued to preach prohibition on animal sacrifice or "red offerings." For example, third Lachen Gomchen, a local Buddhist leader criticized practices like animal sacrifices. The arrival of Buddhist leaders and their activities in Sikkim can be seen as a wave of Tibetanisation. For example, 16th Karmapa (1924-1981) came to Tingchim to find that people still sacrificed animals. He replaced these practices. Due to the influence of the Karmapa, people from Tingchim abandoned animal sacrifice for some time, although they secretly started the practice again.

Among the Lepcha, animal sacrifice was part of their rituals, especially to avert diseases (Erschbamer, 2019: 9). Elements of Tibetan Buddhism and ancient local rites are strongly interconnected and are not interpreted as a contradiction by local community (Erschbamer, 2019: 10). The Nyingma master Rig'dzin gar gyi dbang phyug (1858-1930) composed a text on animal sacrifice and called it evil customs. His authorship shows that, to a large extent, Buddhist philosophers also harmonized with the non-Buddhist elements of indigenous rituals. Meat from animals that died of natural causes was acceptable. According to Marlene Erschbamer animal sacrifices can be divided into rituals to show loyalty and practices to tame and please supernatural entities. An example of the first category can be observed in Sikkim; a shamanic ritual was performed during the Namgyal dynasty to legitimize kingship where Lepcha shows loyalty towards the Sikkimese monarchy, a pig was offered at the shrine of Tsugphud Namgyal, even though Sikkim was Buddhist kingdom and the practice theoretically contradicts Buddhist principles. Second, blood sacrifice is one method to calm or tame supernatural beings that live in the environmental surroundings and have a strong influence on welfare. In southern Tibet, animal sacrifice is mainly widespread as a form of worshipping mountain deities. Apart from this, animal sacrifice was an essential part of oath-taking ceremony in Tibet. Buddhist monk ministers had to swear by smearing the blood of animals on their lips. Some similar cases were found in Sikkim in 1877, where people from two valleys met against the rude behavior of the lama of Chungthang monastery. The two bulls were slaughtered; men dipped their hands in the warm blood and swore to obey the Chungthang lama no longer. Chungthang lama had escaped due to fear of people. Local rites and beliefs such as animal sacrifices were the way to show loyalty to supernatural entities by indigenous people of Sikkim. Buddhist masters also had to compromise their rules and, to some extent, accept these non-Buddhist elements.

Some wooden documents were from Miran and manuscripts from Dunhaung which tell us about non-Buddhist rituals and beliefs. These are discussed as Buddhist practices as bad religion (chos ngan pa) or little religion (chos chu ngu). On the other hand, Buddhism is a good religion (chos bzang po/chos legs pa) or Buddha religion. Wooden documents discussed funeral rituals where libation offering was the central element of ritual practices (Schaik, 2013). These local rituals are directed towards local deities like *yul lha*. We find some instances from funeral rituals records dealing with Bon Po's involvement, or Buddhist monks participate in the same kind of funeral rituals associated with Bon Po. Records shows in certain rituals Bon Po, and Buddhist clergy worked together. These examples show substitution in which Buddhist elements replaced traditional non Buddhists elements of the practices (Schaik, 2013: 29).

The Hinduism of Nepali communities has greatly affected the rituals and lifestyles of the Buddhist community of Sikkim. According to S. Radhakrishnan, "Buddhism, in its origin at least is an offshoot of Hinduism" (Nandan, 2013). Padmasambhava established the first community of the lamas, which was the mixture of Mahayana Buddhism with local mythology and mysticism. Like Hindu funeral rituals, when someone dies, Buddhist calls to the lama who conducts prayers for thirteen to fourteen days. In Sakya tradition, the elder son is considered the successor of property, the same as a Hindu tradition. Lay people believed in multiple gods. There are three main Gods; first, Sangey (Buddha), second is Guru Rinpoche, and third is Cherezi. Same as a Hindu tradition, there is no concept of divorce in the Bhutia Buddhist community. In marriage rituals, similar to Hindu Kundli, the *loh* of the couple is consulted. Lama decides the date and time for the marriage ceremony. The bride's family performed *Yanku* (Laxmi) puja. During the naming ceremony of a child, lama performed *namkaran* ceremony and conducts prayer for his/her health, same as pandit of Hindu community. Lama performed a death ritual when someone dies in a Buddhist family. People hoist flags of five colours representing earth, water, fire, wind, and space, respectively, are also important in Hinduism. Buddhist prayer wheels, *Om Mani Peme Hun* are similar to Hindus' *Om Nama Shivay*. The murals and paintings inside monasteries relate to various avatars of the Gods like God of fire (leads the right way), just similar to Naga Panchmi of Hindu. Influenced by Hinduism, Buddhism has also suffered from caste-specific practices. Sikkimese architecture is complex as it shows the influence of its neighboring regions, with effect from Nepal and Bengal, Bhutanese and Tibetan had a more serious role to play which is visible in its monastic form and in the more elaborate kothis (Chopel, 2011: 62).

A new class of people has emerged in recent years in Sikkim, who cut across the boundaries of caste, ethnicity, language, and religion. Due to the effect of modernization, the socio-cultural behavior and lifestyle of the Buddhist people of Sikkim also changed (Choedon, 1995: 74). Modernization has a severe impact on the traditional folk music of ethnic communities of Sikkim (Amit, 2015: 61). The modern education system of Sikkim created awareness among people, and males and females of different classes or communities come close to each other without any religious-cultural apprehension (Sharma, 2019: 16).

Conclusion

Due to indigenous habitants and Hinduism, cultural assimilation has profoundly impacted the Buddhist sects living in the society of Sikkim. With the point view of assimilation, the Buddhist community reciprocated the culture embedded in the language values, rituals, law, and perhaps even religion of their homeland. The Buddhist culture of Sikkim was affected by three different waves

- giving legitimacy to the indigenous practices of Lepcha and Lhopos; second, being influenced by Hinduism propagated by various Hindu sects of Nepal; third, the influence of conversion by Christian missionaries in the 18-19th century. If we talk about the pre-Buddhist Bon culture, then the local people are never disillusioned with the Bon culture. Buddhism in Sikkim has assumed different characteristics by amalgamation with Bon religion practiced by the Lepcha in the pre-Buddhist period. Buddhist thinkers and Bhutia leadership had the notion that the Lepchas and other autochthonous groups could assist into dominant modes of production and consumption, which was more critical from the economic and political point of view. It was seen as a way to enhance the social mobility and religious-economic opportunities of new entrants into the Sikkim and contribute to the social and economic stability of the newly established Buddhist nation. In the Buddhist kingdom of Sikkim, the reactions had started among Buddhist fuglemen when Lepcha, Lhopos, and other indigenous inhabitants carried and tried to continue their non-Buddhist ritualistic practices. Some Buddhist leadership wanted to abolish non-Buddhist practices through social welfare works, but as written sources informed us, indigenous non-Buddhist ceremonial practices never gave up by inhabitants.

Conversely, Buddhism took the golden means with assimilation and legitimating the primitive local practices into the Buddhist fold. The arrival of Nepalese Hindus in the 18-19th century posed a tremendous challenge to Buddhism, the effect of which is reflected in the changed general life of Buddhist cults. Even after Guru Pandmasambhava propagated Buddhism in Sikkim in the 7th - 8th century or after strengthening the Bhutia monarchy in the 14-15th

century or attempts by Buddhist missionaries to consolidate their hold in society, through several monasteries, non-Buddhist elements continued to influence Buddhism. Whether it is the worship of supernatural powers or native mythological deities, or ritualistic acts like animal sacrifice, all these non-Buddhist primitive practices have influenced Buddhism till the present. The social composition of Sikkim's civilization is such that all communities are interlinked. On the one hand, the indigenous habitants are dedicated to their primitive rituals; on the other hand, Buddhism is also confronted with people of new creeds in Hinduism and Christianity. All these have been things that have accommodated non-Buddhist elements in Buddhist solemnity and community too.

REFERENCES

Ahmed, Syed Jamil. (May, 2005). When a People Do Not Need to Remember: Witnessing the Death of Pangtoed 'Cham in Sikkim. *New Theatre Quarterly*, 21(2), 127-147. DOI:https://doi.org/10.1017/S0266464X05000047

Amit, Manger. (2015). Understanding Modernization and Cultural Resistance in Sikkim: A Sociological Analysis of Folk Music. *International Research Journal of Social Sciences*, 4(5), 59-66.

Arora, Vibha. (2009). Framing the Image of Sikkim. *Visual studies*, 24(1), 54-56.

Bhalerao, A. K., Bagish Kumar, A. K. Singha, P. C. Jat, R. Bordoloi, A. M . Pasweth, Bidyut C. Deka (Eds.). (2016). *Agricultural Folk Songs of Sikkim*. Meghalaya: Indian Council of Agricultural Research, Meghalaya.

Choedon, Yeshe. (1995). Cultural evolution of Sikkim: A Survey. *Bulletin of Tibetology*, Seminar volume,73-77.

Chopel, Gary. (2011). Historic evolution of the Sikkimese Monastery. *Bulletin of Tibetology*, 47(1 & 2), 57-64.

Denjongpa, Anna Balikci. (2002). Kangchendzonga: Secular and Buddhist perception of the mountain deity of Sikkim among the Lhopos. *Bulletin of Tibetology*, 38(2), 5-37.

Erschbamer, Marlene. (March, 2019). Taming of Supernatural Entities and Animal Sacrifice. The Synthesis of Tibetan Buddhism and Local Shamanistic Traditions in Northern Sikkim (India). *Etudes mongoles et siberiennes, centrasiatiques et tibetaines*, 50, 1-12. https://doi.org/10.4000/emscat.3915

Hummel, Siegbert, *Non – Animistic elements in Tibetan Buddhism*, Bulletin of Tibetology, vol 4, no.1, Sikkim, 1967, pp 21-31.

Liu, Cuilan. (2017). Regulating the performing Arts: Buddhist Canon Law on the performance and Consumption of music in Tibet. *Revue d' Etudes Tibetaines*, No.40, Juillet, 55-91.

Nandan, G. B., Nasir Ahmed M. Jangubhai. (May, 2013). The Comparative study between Hinduism and Buddhism. *International Journal of Humanities and Social Science Invention*, 2(5), 27-31.

Raj, Richa, Alice Rai, Maxine P. Mathew, Naina Johnson, Neethu Mathew, Magu, Shivangi Singh, Srishti Gupta, Supriya Sinha, Tanya Ranjan, Urvashi Bhardwaj. (2015). Buddhism in Sikkim: A study in Cultural Syncretism. *Journal of undergraduate Research and Innovation*, 1(2),291-302.

Schaik, sam van. (2013). The naming of Tibetan Religion: Bon and Chos in the Tibetan imperial period. *Journal of the International Association for Bon Research*, vol 1, Inaugural issue, 227-257.

Sharma, Krishna Kumar. (2019). Women in Eastern Himalaya with special reference to Sikkim, *Samvedna*, Vol-1, 13-21. Delhi: Maitreyi College.

Tewari, Ramesh Chandra. (1987). Pre Buddhist elements in Himalayan Buddhism: The Institution of Oracles. *The Journal of the International Association of Buddhist Studies.* 10(1), 135-155.

Thakur, Amrendra Kumar. (2016). Cultural Development in Buddhism of Arunachal Pradesh: Probing Through Arts. In Sudhir Kumar Singh and Ashan Riddi (Eds.), *Pre-Colonial History and Traditions of Arunachal Pradesh.* pp.26-42. Guwahati: DVS Publishers, Guwahati.

Thakur, Amrendra Kumar. (2020). Techno-Culture of Northeast India: Some Aspects. In Sikhamoni Konwar (Ed.), *Overview: North East India.* pp.5-15. Guwahati: E B H Publishers (India).

7

Clothing of the Kukis of Manipur: A Study in Cultural Progress

VUNGLUNMAWI

Introduction

Jules Prown postulates that cultural expression surpasses material objects. In tune with this, especially in northeast India, clothes and their designs are not just randomly made; rather, they are attached with a profound meaning. The comprehension and understanding of the uniqueness of their rich culture are essential to have a better grasp of the cultural progress of any society. Therefore, it is indispensable to study clothes and accessories to reconstruct their cultural life, mainly explaining the technological advancement of the society (Thakur, 2018: 5). C. A. Mawlong posits material culture embodies the abiotic environment of a culture that generate and remodel it through culturally determined rules (Mawlong, 2019: IX). When we observe at cultural expressions in terms of material cultures like clothing, technology etc., the technological differences between societies regarding innovation and invention become the deciding factor (see Rafael, 2013). Subsequently, the more advanced the technology is, the higher the culture (see Grant

& Skovira, 2008). Consequently, social determinists opined that society shapes technology as opposed to the idea put forth by technological determinism theory (see Bastable, 1992). For all these reasons that the material culture of a particular tribe creates unique niche and distinct cultural identities for the people. Recently, development with issues relating to "gender, personal identity, consumerism" (Thakur, 2018: 29) etc. had spurred this branch of material culture into a unique position in social history. The intimate relationship between culture (humans) and technology (things) is in sync with the entanglement theory proposed by Ian Hodder. His entanglement theory is based not only on the interdependency between humans and things, but it includes other things as well, i.e., "humans depend on things, things depend on other things, things depend on humans, and humans depend on humans" (Hodder, 2012: 122). Thus, illustrating how the interdependence of humans and things functions like a food web; their relations are entangled. In the case of northeast India besides various articles, a book is impotant to be consulted. Thakuria (Ed.) (2019), Eli Doye (Ed.) (2019), Thakur, (2017) is important to be consulted for future researches on the problems of culture. These have been consulted in the preparation of this paper.

To start, it is crucial in any study that a comprehensive understanding of any subject requires a proper evolutionary based insight, i.e. how it began, how did it evolve and how much progress it has achieved. From this proposition, it is vital to highlight and understand the concept of technology and its evolutionary theories. The study of technology and its role in shaping the culture or vice-versa is one of the latest and most innovative methods in social science and form a significant object of scientific inquiry. Technology as a tool of analysis can help unravel the basis on which human thoughts and ideas flow. This idea is not entirely new. It is reflected in the Marxist praxis on society and in the writings of Lewis Henry Morgan. Later, Irwin Thompson and Lewis Mumford have extensively developed the concept, which a modern thinker, Neil Postman, explicitly validified. In general, the economic determinism of history gradually paved the way for the approach to the study of history, which is known as 'Technological Determinism'. The aspects of the study of technology of the tribes of northeast India has been done extensively by Amrendra Kumar Thakur (see Thakur, 2017). The theoretical discussions and the references cited in the book have been used by me in the preparation of this paper.

However, the study of technology is guided by the application of Technological Determinism towards the same. It is also significant to discuss the cultural construct of the problem. However, it is not out of context to mention that in most of the studies dealing with technology in India, technological determinism is adopted by scholars. In this manner, the role of technology in the developments of society and states is evaluated. Such an approach can be called one-dimensional. In this paper, an attempt has been made to explore the connections between technology and human culture over time and space in Northeast India. This paper will also enable us to understand the social significance of technology.

Archaeologists, anthropologists, cultural historians, and many social scientists have been studying the technological progress of the past from their perspectives. While most historians of archaeology have focused on the significant conceptual differences between nineteenth century evolutionists and early twentieth century culture historians, oddly enough, both paradigms shared an implicit definition of technology. Whether one believed that: (1) culture was best defined by the evolutionary stage of its technology; (2) technology was but one of many normative traits comprising a cohesive individual culture; or (3) technological innovation and the diffusion of inventions were core indicators of cultural change-what defined technology was the same; hardware (Dobres, 2009: 104; also see Olsen *et al.* 2009).

To V. Gordon Childe, "The outstanding common features" to the many Neolithic societies are "wood-making, pottery manufacture, and a textile industry" (Childe, 1951: 52). Verrier Elwin observes these developments from other perspectives (Elwin, 1988: 258-59). To quote him,

> The same may be said of the music, the dance, the wood carving, the ornaments. They are part of the heritage...The song and the dance of the hills are simple; they are the very expressions of the spirits, as are the patterns of the cloth they weave. Their industry is, necessarily, a home-industry; ... But they sing and dance and weave their homely designs for their own pleasure, the pleasure of their family members and the pleasure of their fellow-villagers- in a sense, the truest of artistic pleasures.

Bruce Bimber writes that "Marx must be informed by an interpretation of his account of the forces of production. There is little doubt that for Marx, whatever significance technology has derived from its relationship to economic activity - its role as a productive force - rather than from any other social influence it might have. The connection between technology and productive forces is the central factor in the problem. As a focus, this much should be uncontroversial" (Bimber, 1990: 335). In this background, an attempt has been made in this paper to study the material culture relating to the traditional weaving techniques of the Kukis.

By 16th and 17th centuries, the history of cotton cultivation was widely known in Southeast Asia. The people have usually worn unsewn strip of cloth around their bodies and most of the time were naked from above the waist (Reid, 1988: 91). These features share some common traits with that of the Kuki men who wore a strip of cloth tied around their waist in front to about a foot or more above the knee. They went nearly naked except for the shawl thrown over the shoulders. On the other hand, women wore a kilt of blue cloth, extending from the waist to just above the knee and another cloth from the breasts to the waist (Soppitt, 1887: 6).

Manipur enjoys a special place in the handloom industry and has a legacy of craftsmanship (The Northeast Window, 2017). The traditional cloth materials for weaving are produced from natural fibres like silk and cotton. In his work, C.A. Soppitt briefly mentioned that the Kukis did not practise silk rearing (Soppitt, 1887: 6). However, it was believed that sericulture came to be known to them later through government initiative works. They cultivated their cotton in the jhum lands, plucked and dried in the sun. Followed by the ginning process using home-made gin known locally as *Pat-kheh*. After which, they use a bow like an instrument made of bamboo *Patkapna/Patsai* to teased the cotton to become clean. This process is called carding. The teased cotton is then placed on a smooth plank and rolled with a long thin stick made out of bamboo or even just the cotton to form the sliver. This whole process is called *Pat-tul/Patchon-huol*. The spinning wheel called *Mui* transform cotton into thread or yarn for weaving.

Dyeing: Colours play a vital role in the textile tradition (Medhi, 2018: 147). This process includes both natural and synthetic dyes. Natural or vegetable dyes are mostly from barks of trees, leaves and roots, etc. Some of the natural dyes include the bark of bitter bean (*Parkiaspeciosa*), onion skin, pomegranate,marigold flower petals, orange peel, lemon peel, sunflower petals, bamboo leaves, banana leaves and bark, *Lac, Morinda augustifolia, Dolthing (Tectona grandis linn)*, Turmeric *(Curcuma longa), Assam indigo (Strobilanthes flaccidifolius Nees), Anjangkha (Solanum incanum), Gelthing (Pasaniapachyphylla), Naolukoppah (Melastoma malabathricum), Gulta usitata, Phyllanthus embellica, Carthamus tinctorius, Bixa orellana, Berberis manipurana Ahrendt, Vaupah (Bauhinia purpurea linn), Tuilheng (Amoora spectabilis miq), Achyranthesaspera linn, Jonglha neo silneh (Acacia catechu willd), Clitoria ternatea, Clerodendrum, Zouzampah (Celosia argentea)* (Potsangbam *et al.* 2008 : 146), *Garcinia xanthochymus, Indigofera tinctoria,* etc. The techniques of dyeing among the hill tribes of Manipur do not vary much with that of the plain areas. With the arrival of synthetic dyes in the Imphal market in 1905, the traditional technique of dyeing was abandoned (Chandam, 2012: 106). Synthetic dyes are more common since it is readily available in the market in the form of powder and soaps. Synthetic dyes enhances the choice of the Kukis in addition to the natural dyes.Prior to dyeing process, the yarns are first degummed using soda ash and soap (Weavers' Service Centre, 2020) by boiling or immersing in water for a wholenight and later parched in the sun. Salt is basically used in the process to avoid the colours from fading. As a result of their skills in dyeing, the Kukis have rich and vibrant colours of clothes.

The most common type of weaving is backstrap loom or loin loom as it can be made from readily available materials found in the surrounding natural environment. As a result of its intricate designs and the nature of portability, it is quite popular among the households. Traditionally, it is woven by women folks and the knowledge is passed on from one generation to the next. In the entire Northeast India where weaving is practice, typically, it is considered as an inherent duty of women and her dignity lies in the quality of work she produces. Thus, women play an active role in the economy by weaving. Weaving is a long and enduring process and it requires a lot of dedication on the part of the weavers which is extremely commendable. It is considered as a taboo on the part of the Kuki men to weave or in extreme cases touch the loom especially for hunters as it is considered a bad omen. However, it is usually men who collected all the instruments needed for weaving. The post-weaving of this loom involves joining together two straps that are already woven to obtained the desired width (Khatoon *et al.* (Eds.), 2014: 598-99), The raw materials used for weaving includes: bamboo, wood, cane and iron. The following instruments are mainly used for backstraploom:

Kongdop (backstrap) is usually made of leather strap or a piece of cloth which support the hips at the same time keeping the warp taut and is attached at both sides of the extremities with *Tainam*. *Taalha'ang* is the bar that is attached to the wall or pole at the top. Cords are tied against a wall or post and *Chungkam* (warp bar) is inserted in these cords to fixed the thread from unnecessary movements. *Tumbi* and *Tana* (long thread in a loom) raises the thread of the warp and using *Lhem* (used for ramming), it open a space and allow *Patphei/khothei* (bobbin) to form the weft. *Thilbukang* passes over *Tumbi*, two or three *Thilbukang* supports *Tumbi* from unnecessary movements. *Ponkam* is a bamboo bar pointed at both ends and attached with the weaved yarn to get perfect straight result. *Tuhdet* is a comb-like bar to balance the thickness and thinness of the threads of the warp and spread out evenly. Rice water is used to damp the interlaced yarn which is called *Pat-twinu* in rough translation and the bowl or small gourd for keeping the rice water is called *Pat-twinunabel* and the brush for damping the interlaced yarn is called *Pat-twinuna/pona. Tumbineo/khajuum* is a bamboo bar sharpened at the end point. *Sakuling*, a porcupine quill is used to re-adjust the uneven weft (Lianhmingthanga, 2020: 68). Any varieties of *Thingbong* (wooden block) were used to support the legs while weaving. The fly shuttle loom was introduced in Manipur during the Colonial period and it was more popular among the plain areas since the hilly tribes were more engaged in their *Kon* (traditional loom) (Chandam, 2012 : 106).

In the case of designs and motifs, twill and simple weave along with dobby patterns were mainly used. This technique is followed even today by both the two looms. The Kuki textiles are usually of a single colour with intricate designs along the borders. They give a lot of importance to motifs and most of their textiles are named after the motifs to which interesting legends and folklores are attached. Any colours could be use in the textiles but the motifs cannot be altered (Longjam, 2014: 73). It is believed that the reason why loin loom was more popular than any other looms among the hill tribes was mainly because the loin loom meets the suitable requirements of the weavers. As a result of weaving, they produced traditional indigenous textile arts like *ponve* (wrap around), *boitong* (waistcoat), *pheichom* (dhoti loin white cloth), plain shawls, a girdle for carrying babies, traditional handbags, *delkop* (turban), *lukop* (used by women to cover their head), *ponlhe* (cotton bedspread), *phoipi* (cotton blanket) and many more. They also bury the dead with woven cloths which is associated with their belief system or myth (Longjam, 2014: 12-15). Efficiently, making them self-sufficient and self-reliant, thereby making them unique and distinct from the rest of the tribes in Northeast India and the rest of the world.Originally, the Kukis have a number of *nampon* (traditional attire). Each tribes within the Kukis also have their own *ponve*. It will be misleading to universalize the whole Kukis as "a single cultural pattern"(Thakur, 2018: 2).

In recent trends people modified the *nampon* by adding two or more designs and motifs according to their own personal choices. However, it still cannot replace the uniqueness of the original *ponve* and is still in vogue for a much more longer period and they are preferred to be worn on important occassions. The price of these modified *ponve* will vary depending on the number of intricate designs woven, the more designs it has, the higher the cost. Nowadays, traditional *ponve* are high priced since weaving of these intricate designs requires traditional skills and artistry which is lacking among the new generations. The following *nampon* common among the Kukis can be listed below:

Saipikhup simply means *saipi*=elephant and *khup*=knee in Thadou-Kuki. In the olden days, it was worn as a shawl. Two types of *saipikhup* are designed for men and women. Women *saipikhup* is weaved with twill weave pattern. Its name is given from the design which are placed at both ends of the shawl. The designs are weaved with pattern similar to dobby style and has *saipikhup* and *changmaimu* (cucumber seed) as motifs. Whereas, *saipikhup* for men is a male variant black shawl weaved with twill weave pattern, having a particular design on both ends. The motifs design weaved with dobby style resembles elephant knee in the centre, surrounded by *changmaimu* (cucumber seed), *sumtung* (pestle), and *goshemjang* (gourd musical instrument) design.

Nowadays, it is commonly worn as wrap around. Typically, this shawl in red is mostly considered prestigious indicating status for men folks and is usually gifted to honour men in the society. *Thangnang*, a shawl weaved with twill weave pattern, having two designs at the end borders. The motifs design weaved with dobby style is known as *Goshemjang* (gourd musical instrument) and geometric python belly pattern. The border designs generally use red, green, yellow and white colours. Originally, it was a shawl but now even women started wearing them as *ponve*. *Thadou Pondum* is weaved by a simple plain weave with two warp colours of blue and black and dobby design. Traditionally worn by both men and women. This is typically worn for funeral programme even today. *Mongvom* is simply woven with dobby pattern and twill weave. At first, it was a shawl for men and was usually customized as *delkop* (turban). In recent times, it has been woven as *ponve*. *Khamtang* which is originally the only *ponve* for women. Myth has it that its design is believed to have been inspired from a python. *Khamtang* and *saipikhup* is associated with similar beliefs that one should not wear it during *twisolai*, meaning during flood or heavy rainfall seasons, else the python will sweep them away. It is a plain weave with dobby design patterns. Just as *saipikhup* is prioritized by men, *Khamtang* is to honoured women with dignity and grace. *Nihsan* means red slip/skirt in Thadou-Kuki. In ancient past life of the Kukis, women wore it underneath their *ponve*. It is woven with a plain weave and dobby design. Lengtejem is a traditional design *ponve* with a plain weave and dobby pattern with a number of geometric designs with the weft and warp yarn of different colours. *Vagulmit* whose design is created from the inspiration they got from the eyes of a wild bird called *vagul*. It is a plain weave with dobby pattern of geometric designs. *Nineljem* is inspired from the mythical association from the sun. It was a shawl for women which was customized as *ponve*. *Maijapjem* inspired from hand held fan made of bamboo and cane. Initially woven as a women shawl but later it was customized as *ponve.*

Ponve is very much significant among the Kukis as a result of which several other collection includes : *Pahchapon, Ponloupi, Pongeisan, Ahsijem/Valpajem* inspired from the stars or constellation, *Bipahjem* (bi, a kind of plant species), *Aizawlsinel, Kamsajem, Sonpah, Vankotchabi* (key to heaven's door), *Linglukhuhjem, Aipah/Aikengjem* (crab), *Pahpijem, Sineljem, Chohcholjem*, etc. Some of the *ponve* are also available without any motifs. Some motifs used by the thadou tribe is also common with those of the Aimol, Chothe, Chiru and Kom tribes. Culturally, the Kukis has a unique artistic skills and their designs and motifs are influenced from their surrounding environment – animals, birds, insects, flowers, rivers, vegetables, weapons, musical instruments, etc., (Longjam, 2014: 61).

In olden days, due to the animistic belief system weavers woven products were rarely sold as selling the product would mean selling off the weaver's soul (Longjam, 2014: 15). However, with their conversion into Christianity the outlook towards life changes, people can now acquire the woven textiles easily from the market. Popularity of loin loom is fast declining with the introduction of fly shuttle loomwhich is less time consuming and could produce more and meet the market requirements. Yet, the price of cloth woven from loin loom is much costlier than that of fly shuttle loom.

Conclusion

Textile weaving technology uplift the Kukis mainly because material objects like clothing are the means and ways in which they can express themselves. It is through their unique and creative artistry which is shown in the intricate designs and motifs with interesting legends and myths evolving around them that made them distinct from the rest of other tribes. Thus, it contributed in unfolding and understanding their way of life, their traditional belief systems, social customs and traditional values, ethnicities,etc. which laid the very foundation of their identity. Consequently, with the effort of a large number of an educated and intellectual minds in the society,even the least uneducated person started developing a sense of cultural awareness and understanding its material culture thereby, appreciating and valuing the work of art, in this case weaving technology. This gives them a sense of belongingness, a sense of security and nationhood among the Kukis. Significantly, the advancement in technology too provides them a platform to share their identity in cultural forum,their values and aspirations in various global media circuit. Eventually, breaking down all previously unimaginable barriers. Now, the Kukis are known world wide as a result of their unique identity and distinct culture.

REFERENCES

Bastable, Marshall J. (April, 1992). From Breechloaders to Monster Guns: Sir William Armstrong and the Invention of Modern Artillery, 1854- 1880. *Society for the History of Technology*, 33(2), 213- 247. http://www.jstor.org/stable/3105857.

Bimber, Bruce. (May, 1990). Karl Marx and the Three Faces of Technological Determinism. *Social Studies of Science*, 20(2), 333-351. http://www.jstor.org/stable/285094.

Chandam, Victoria Devi. (January, 2012). Women in Informal Sector in Manipur: A Sociological Study. *Indian Journal of Traditional Knowledge*. https://shodhganga.inflibnet.ac.in/

bitstream/10603/58599/13/13_chapter%204.pdf, accessed on 30th August, 2020, p.106.

Childe, V. Gordon. (1951). *Man Makes Himself*. New York: The New American Library. (Revised edition with a Foreword by Professor Glyn Daniel).

Dobres, Anne. (2009). Technologies, in B. Cunliffe, C. Gosden and Rosemary A. Joyce (Eds.), *The Oxford Handbook of Archaeology*, 115-141.

Doye, Eli (Ed.).(2019). *Cultural Heritage of Northeast India*, New Delhi: Aayu Publications.

Elwin, Verrier. (1988). *A Philosophy for NEFA*. Itanagar: Directorate of Research, Government of Arunachal Pradesh (*passim*).

Hodder, Ian. (2012). *Entangled: An Archaeology of the Relationships Between Humans and Things*. London: Wiley- Blackwell Publication.

Information collected from Weavers' Service Centre (WSC). (2020). Imphal, Ministry of Textiles, Government of India.

Khatoon, Reshma, A. K. Das, B. K. Dutta and P. K Singh (Eds.). (July 2014). Study of Traditional handloom weaving by the Kom tribe of Manipur", *Indian Journal of Traditional Knowledge*, 13(3), 596-599.

Lianhmingthanga. (1998). *Material Culture of the Mizo*. Calcutta: Firma KLM Private Ltd.

Longjam, Nivedita. (2014). *A Study on the Motifs, Colors And Designs of the Traditional Tribal Woven Textiles of Manipur*. (Unpublished doctoral dissertation). Mumbai: National Institute of Fashion Technology.

Mawlong, C. A. (2019, Keynote address). In Tilok Thakuria, *Perspectives on the Material Cultures of Northeast India*, pp.xiii-xxiv. New Delhi: Lakshi Publisher & Distributors.

Medhi, Satyabati. (2018). Traditional Handloom Culture Products and Practices A Socio Cultural study in Hajo Circle of Kamrup District, Assam.

https://sg.inflibnet.ac.in/bitstream/10603/225998/14/14_chapter6.pdf/, accessed on 9th August 2020, p.114-178.

Olsen, J. K. B., S. A. Pedersen and V. F. Hendricks (Eds.). (2009). *A Companion to the Philosophy of Technology*, 115-141.

Potsangbam, Lunalisa; Ningombam Swapana; S warjeet and Warjeet Laitonjam. (February, 2008). Natural Dye Yielding Plants and Indigenous Knowledge of Dyeing in Manipur, Northeast India. *Indian Journal of Traditional Knowledge*, 7(1), 141-147.

Rafael, Erwin F. (July - December 2013). Technology as a Social System: A System Theoretical Conceptualization. *Philippine Sociological Review*, 61(2), 319-347.

Reid, Anthony. (1988). *Southeast Asia in the Age of Commerce 1450-1680*. London: Yale University Press.

Soppitt, C.A. (1887). *A Short Account of the Kuki-Lushai Tribes on the North-Eastern Frontier: A Comparison of Lushai with other Dialects*. Shillong: Assam Secretariat Press.

Thakuria, Tilok. (Ed.) (2019). *Perspectives on the Material Cultures of Northeast India*. New Delhi: Lakshi Publisher & Distributors.

Thakur, Amrendra Kumar. (2017). Material Culture and the Historical Reconstruction of Northeast India. In the *Proceedings of North East India History Association*, 37th session, Gangtok, 2016, pp. 17-23.

Thakur, Amrendra Kumar. (2017). *Technology of the Tribes of Northeast India*. Guwahati: DVS Publishers.

Thakur, Amrendra Kumar. (2018). Apatani Clothing: A Window To History. In *Reading in Culture & Tradition Souvenir*, pp.1-5. Itanagar: Capital Complex Dree Festival Committee.

The Northeast window. (2017). https://www.thenortheastwindow.com/2017/09/weaving-manipur-rich-cultural-heritage/, accessed on 13th August 2020.

8

Rites and Rituals with Special Reference to Death and Disposal of Death Bodies of Poumai Naga Tribe before the 20th Century

HEPUNI LIBA

Introduction

Every tribe, caste or creed performs its traditional rites and rituals of any events like birth, death, etc. The word 'Rite' is derived from the French word 'Rites' and Latin word 'Rifus' which means a solemn act of religion or an act performed in divine solemn service'. According to Oxford Advanced Learner's dictionary, 'rite' is a religious or other solemn ceremony and 'ritual' is the action that is always done at a fixed time and in the same way, especially as part of a religious or other ceremony. According to the New Encyclopedia Britannica, in any sacrificial rite a number of goals or intention may be expressed, yet the ultimate goals of all sacrifice is to establish a beneficial relationship with the sacred order, to make the sacred power present efficacious sacrifice' (Vol. 16, 1974: 132).

Rites and rituals are practiced by any society since time immemorial to express their sense of gratitude and for the favor of their god and deities or spirits in times of need. According to Sinha (1977) "the rituals are to appease god, to secure their blessing of thanks giving, to mark supremacy in kinship as well as in atonement of some wrongful act. It forms a kind of communication between man and god" (p. 68).

Like any other group of people, the Poumai Nagas has its unique rites and rituals for various occasions and events. Poumai Naga tribe is one of the major tribes belonging to mongoloid race mostly inhabiting in the District of Senapati, Manipur. Some Poumai Nagas are in Chakhesang area of Phek District, Nagaland. The geographical area in Manipur inhabited by the Poumai Nagas extends to about 1500 sq.km and is divided into three areas called Paomata, Chiliivai and Lepaona. Thus, Poumai region is bordered with Nagaland in the north, Thangal villages of Saikul sub-division of Senapati District in the south, Tangkhul villages of Ukhrul District in the east and Mao and Maram sub-division of Senapati District in the west.

Like any other tribal groups of the North East India, the Poumai Nagas has its unique traditional practices of performing several rites and rituals on any occasion. Rites and rituals are very significant components of Poumai Naga traditional and religious life. Its main purposes and intentions are presumed to appease god and pray for well-being, multiplication of population on both human and domestic animals, fertility of soil, good harvest, success in warfare, protection from sickness and death, etc. Among many religious and traditional practices of the Poumai Nagas, rites and rituals especially of the death and its disposal of death bodies are less documented and less researched. This paper therefore, attempts to elucidate the nature of such rites and rituals performed during the death, and disposal of death body by the Poumai Nagas before the advent of Christianity.

Death

The Poumai Nagas have different views on the definition and meaning of death as far as the literary term and other metaphysical term are concerned. It can be seen in various aspects of knowledge generation and its advancement. The Poumai Nagas like many other tribal groups also believed in life after death. They believed that death is just a moment or a particular time period when one's soul leaves the body. Death is therefore, considered as a journey to the land where our ancestors have gone before. Since the Poumai Nagas believed in life after death, and the existence of soul, when someone dies, proper rites and ritual and offering were made for the soul.

Poumai Nagas classify deaths into two types; natural death and unnatural death. Every death is not treated equal for burial rites and rituals. Some deaths were highly regarded whereas others are not. In the natural death, for instance a person who died of diseases, from accident, due to old age, etc. the death body will be buried in the village near the house or in the garden. Villagers shared the sorrow and show sympathy to the bereaved families' by coming to the house and observe genna together with them. For unnatural deaths, that is, deaths due to suicide, hang, killed by wild animal, death by fire, drowning in river, death in child birth, etc., due respect is not given and the opportunities for burial inside the village is also denied. Instead the death bodies are taken outside the village boundary without coffin. They are treated with outmost contempt and humiliation and their souls are supposed to be death forever. It was also a taboo to cry on those dead bodies and the young people are not allowed to touch. This denial was made so that it is not repeated in future. Besides, unnatural death is considered to be a bad omen for entire villagers. (personal comm.: R. Hepuni, 2018).

When a person is near his/her death due to terminal sickness or due to any fatal injuries or because of its old age, he or she shall be removed from the dying bed and laid on the floor so as to avoid the death pollution upon the bed. This practice is also found practicing in most of the other Naga communities. Once the person is about to breath his last, people of male gender standing nearby him usually howl and called out the name of the dying person to revive back the passed away life. Ornaments such as necklaces, bangles, bracelets and earring were generally removed from the person. When the struggle and breathing completely stopped, eyes were closed followed by taking out his personal belongings and utensils for cooking rice, curry, rice beer and yeast outside the house.

As soon as the person was declared death, relatives and friends who are close by cried out and call out the name of the person to wake up. Then the priest Napao, generally a male gender entered the room where the death body is lying and he sprinkled water over the death body. Nepuni (2010) Then the death body will be taken for washing. It is a must for everyone after the death (pp. 90-91). Normally, the dead body is washed by the Napao or by an elderly person. In some peculiar situations, washing of death body used to be delayed till the next day, believing that once the dead body is washed, the person will never rise again. After the death body is washed, it will be kept in the open bed and then covered with his personal clothing especially his favorite shawl. Articles such as plates, cups, bag, daos, spears, and his favorites were laid above his head. Besides, all the luxury items were also displayed to show the wealth and riches of the deceased. The whole villagers observed genna for the deceased person and people usually kept aside the festival, marriages or any merry making. Ngupani (2010) "It is an obligatory on the part of the bereaved family to observe five days genna for the death of every family irrespective of age" (p. 111). Villagers bring gifts such as rice, wine, meat and money as a sign of sympathy to the bereaved family.

When a person dies at night, youngsters from village gathered at the residence of the deceased to keep vigil and show solidarity. Then in the morning young people were sent to give information to the neighboring villages about the death of the person. If the deceased is rich or an elderly man, blank fire of the gun was made to announce the death of a person to the villagers and nearby villages. But the gun fires were not meant for the woman. One thought that struck the mind of the people after hearing the fire of gun was; "Oh! a rich person must have died" (Nepuni, 2010: 91).

Disposal of death body

For the purpose of disposal of death bodies, Poumai Nagas treated natural deaths differently from unnatural deaths. For disposal of natural death, certain rituals were performed with due respect and honor. Generally, the death bodies are buried in a properly dug grave. Ngupani (2010) observed that, "To dispose of the death body, certain set of rites and rituals are to be performed for burial procedures in which the Napao played a vital role. It is the Napao who inaugurates digging the grave and then other male members join especially relative and friends of the deceased person (p. 111).

Like in the present days' funeral, a close friend or relative will narrate the life history of the deceased person by means of 'Dirges' (Kulili) in Poumai Naga dialect - recalling and remembering of life history). These Kulili are either in the form of speech or lamenting song. A close friend or relative will perform the Kulili and it usually mentions about the good deeds and achievements of the person in his lifetime. Not everyone is well versed in Kulili. It is believed that if the Kulili is not performed well, it is a disgrace and death may come again to the family. Therefore, it is a must to properly perform the Kulili.

Salonii Poukai observed that, "After the Kulili is performed, gunshots are fired. For some instances, gunshots were fired which continue for two days if the deceased person is from a noble family. The cloths which are to be buried with the death body are sprinkled with water by the Napao. Then the clothing is cut with knife and the knife used for cutting those cloths is also buried with the death body in the same grave" (personal comm.: Salonii Poukai, 2017).

Once the procedure of performing Kulili is over, certain rites are to be performed again by the responsible persons from the family. Such rites are generally performed by the eldest son of the deceased person or the closest male relative if the person does not have any son. About such rituals performance, S. Pinii observed that, "The eldest son or the close relatives who dig the graves will take a bundle of thatch fire, move around the grave and throw the burnt pieces into the dug grave. Putting of the burning thatch fire signifies purification of the grave and also it is believed that it gives light and warmness to the dead man's soul because the grave is cold and dark for the soul to dwell" (personal comm.: S. Pinii, 2018).

As death happens to everyone regardless of rich or poor, when one died in other place, the death body is taken to their native place for burial ceremony. A day of village genna is observed on the death of a man and woman of honor. Domesticated animals were slaughtered on funeral with the belief that the soul of the slaughtered animal will accompany the departed soul as it goes to join those who have gone before. Generally, some domesticated animals were also slaughtered for funeral. As per their belief the souls of the slaughtered cattle will accompany the departed soul. Hutton (1968), for a hunter, usually a dog is killed in order that its soul will guard him from the attacks of the soul of the beasts he killed when he was alive (p. 71).

Personal belongings and items of the deceased persons are considered important and carefully collected once a person is declared death. Children below 15 years of age were restricted to touch any such belongings and items of the deceased person. Such personal belongings and items were also supposed to be buried with the death body. P. L Maikho observed that, "Once the grave is ready; the Napao will bring thatch fire inside the grave before the coffin is lifted down. Personal important items such as Spear, Shield, Dao, Male Basket, Cloths, etc., are normally buried along with male corpse. In case of women, cotton, spinning and weaving implements, carrying basket, cloths iron staff, rain protection sheet, etc. are buried" (personal comm.: P. L. Maikho, 2017). For a chief or a man of honor, a live rooster is usually buried within a cave like space dug along the side of the corpse with an air passage pipe projected above the ground. "They believed that at times crowing of the buried rooster is heard through the pipe" (personal comm.: S. Thaili, 2018). The Poumai Nagas believed that dead men continued to live another life with the materials that are buried with them. Shimray (1986) "the concept of Nagas' heaven was that all the worldly riches, garments, weapons etc, would go to heaven along with the dead person and that they would meet all those who were already dead and would pass on news of their respective families when he/she met them and would be made some presentations which were sent by the living" (p. 230).

When a child dies within five days of its birth, it is wrapped in cloths and put in an earthen pot and buried under the floor of living room without any special ceremony except the family observed genna. Such disposal of death body is called 'ngaih re' meaning forgotten. Nepuni (2010) the grave is usually 5 feet in length and 2 feet in breadth. Flat stones tiles are of 2'x3' breadth and length with the thickness of 3 inches to place over the corpse. Generally, the number of piles to cover were around 6-8 pieces, (p. 93). In the circumstances when stones were not available good quality of wooden planks were used. The dead bodies were laid with the head facing towards the east out of the four cardinal directions. The main reason for laying head towards the east is that since the sun rises in the east, so the body should receive the first light of the day. It is considered to be a good sign of new hope to see new life.

Once the death body is buried, Napao will cut some bitter plant, smash it and then wash his hand with the bitter plant juice. Washing with the bitter plant juice signifies that no more of such death will happen in the family again and spirit of dead may not disturb nor sad memory lingers on in their minds. (personal comm.: S.Thaipei, 2018). After this ritual, the priest Napao comes back to the house of the deceased and cleans the hearth by removing the old stone oven. Then, he erects a new stone oven and sets a new fire in it. The family's cloths are flipped over the fire. Sha (1999), these acts of cleaning and sanctification signify the sanctification of the house so that dead may not occur again in the family (p. 28).

Genna was observed for over certain period of time and the family members of the deceased abstained from taking part in any social entertainment program and other festivities unless it is a cultural sanctioned rites and rituals related to death. L. Shiliru observed that; "A village genna is observed, which continues for 5 days for the bereaved family members irrespective of their age. From the day of the death, the family members of the deceased were not allowed to partake in any of the social activities till the completion of one year" (personal comm.: L. Shiliru, 2018).

Koh (farewell to departed souls)

With a unique way of belief in life after death, life after death is another form of life which the departed souls will be living in the village of deaths (Thaimai Ngu). Therefore, certain rituals called 'koh' (Bidding farewell to departed souls) is performed as a ritual ceremony to bid farewell to all the departed souls of the particular year. This ritual is performed once in a year particularly at the ending month of Dohkhou which falls in November/December. Until this month arrives, the bereaved families avoid from participation of any activities like festival, celebration or any entertainment. It is the time period where the families remain in lamentation and grief for the lost. On the day of Koh, relatives and friends of the deceased offer rice liquor to the departed soul. And the villagers pay their last respect to the departed souls. While performing this farewell ceremony, every villager comes out of the house of that deceased in order to get away and free from all evil spirits.

Then all the leftover food, rice liquor and water are thrown away. This signifies freeing the family from all impending sickness and deaths. It is believed that unless this ritual is performed the souls of the death persons continue to live with the family members. As such, food and rice liquor are usually served for them on all the special occasions. Once the ritual is performed the souls are believed to have gone permanently to the land of death and therefore no food and drink are necessary to serve nor is any other ritual required to be performed.

Conclusion

Poumai Nagas have a strong traditional religious belief and accordingly its traditional practices were strictly observed and followed since time immemorial till the advent of the 20th century. Religious rites and rituals with respect to death and its burial were deeply rooted to its nativity and not just only the events of observing genna by the villagers, but also it directs and gives meanings to various aspects of the society; its unique culture, traditional and religious belief systems and other practices. Poumai Nagas believed that physical death is not the real death but a journey to the land of soul called "Thaimaingu". Therefore, when someone died, proper rites, ritual and offerings were made for the living soul. Death also reminds the achievement of the individual while he/she is alive and it often brings relatives and friends closer. Today, with the advent of western culture and Christianity, they have slowly abandoned most of their old traditional religious beliefs and practices. Only a handful of elderly people who don't embrace Christianity continue to practice the old aged religious beliefs and practices.

REFERENCES

Hutton, J. H. (1921). *The Sema Naga.* (1st Ed.). London: Macmillan & Co. Ltd.

Nekha, K. N. (2015). *The Nagas: Culture and Education.* Dimapur: Heritage Publishing House.

Nepuni, William. (2010). *Socio-Cultural History of Shiipfomei Naga Tribe.* New Delhi: Mittal Publication.

Ngupani, R., M. C, Arun, Tao. (2005). *The Poumai of Manipur.* Directorate of Tribal Welfare: Government of Manipur.

Ngupani, Raoping. (2010). *Socio-Cultural and Political Changes among the Tribes of Manipur: A Case Study of Poumai Naga Tribe.* (Unpublished Doctoral Dissertation). Manipur University.

Sha, David. (1999). *Influence of the Traditional Rites and Rituals of the Poumai Nagas on Christianity in Manipur.* (Unpublished Doctoral Dissertation). Serampore University.

Shimray, R. R. (1985). *Origin and culture of Nagas.* New Delhi: Pamleiphi Shimray.

Sinha, Raghuvir. (1977). *Religion and Culture of North East India.* New Delhi: Abhinav Publications.

The New Encyclopaedia Britanica, Micropaedia. (1974). Sacrifice. Vol. 16.

Venuh, N. (2004). *Naga Society: Continuity and Change.* Delhi: Shipra Publication.

Personal interviews with

L. Shiliru, village elder person who personally performed some of the rites and rituals. 19.5.2018.

P. L. Maikho, social worker, a person the community members always refer for any traditional practices. 12.8.2017.

R. Hepuni, an educationist, who has some, documented papers on cultural and traditional practices among the Poumai Community. 16.5.2018.

S. Pinii, member of a village authority board. 19.5.2018.

S. Thaili, an elderly person and Ex Councilor, who is instrumental in promoting and preserving traditional and cultural practices within the community. 23.6.2018.

S. Thaipei, politician, who travelled far and wide within his constituency and well versed with traditional practices. 23.7.2018.

Salonii Poukai, retired bureaucrat who reportedly has thorough knowledge about the traditional and cultural practices of certain communities. 6.7.2017.

9

Oral Tradition as an Itinerary to the Past: A Reflection on the Socio-Cultural Values of the Nagas

SHÜRHONUO TSÜRHO

Oral tradition can be discovered as the foundation of knowledge, tradition, social life, or of a nation's history or heritage. To understand the relation between writing and oral tradition, the earliest form of tradition in the history of English literature especially from the Anglo-Saxon settlers who conquered Britain in the latter half of the fifth century is to be anatomized first. In the words of Arthur Compton-Rickety (2009) on oral tradition of the Anglo-Saxon:

> The earliest English literature is unwritten. It consists of songs and legends, heroic and stirring in character, sung to the harp by the minstrel and gleeman, and handed down from one generation to another. Parents taught these tales to their children, and the younger learned of the elder singer" (p. 4).

The Similarity between the European and the Naga Oral Tradition

Picking up the European-English literature as the base for oral tradition and literature, there are similarities to the Naga oral literature as well. We find "songs and legends" passed and narrated in every generation about heroes or of their heroic deeds. These are trends found in all the Naga tribes and communities. Of course, there may not be a shared legend for all the tribes because people lived in hostility towards each other. Yet, these were things which people kept as treasures. Clearly the Naga society did not have the gleemen or the minstrels as entertainers. Unlike the agile entertainers mentioned above, they had the inactive and motioned speakers, the elders of the community who dealt in the impartment of these age-old wisdoms and legends. On its delivery, we find the Nagas engaged in music and instrument to some extend just as the English entertainers delivered. The difference here once again is mainly on the themes. These songs carried more of their own stories, experiences and legends than of another supreme mortal. These are songs which carried their pain, sorrow, regret, envy, happiness and joy. In short, these songs were the most genuine expression of their emotions which they skilfully employed to their songs. Lastly, on the technical artistic form, there are certain rules and guidelines maintained by the singers or poets. This we see especially in the poems among the Angami-Naga tribe who use a set of uniform syllables for a single line. This fixation is upon the number of syllables in a line which is nine. The syllables cannot be more or less than the number nine. For this, though there are no stressed or unstressed syllables to create patterns, the number of syllables themselves forms as the uniformity to its sound. Again, the work of oral tradition is at work here as these poems are part of the narration, both in giving the guidelines and in passing the classical poems are in their original form without losing or altering a letter till date.

Reasons for Diversity

The situation among the Nagas has always been of a tumultuous environment. There are two main reasons as to why the Nagas have, though not strictly divided but not wholly united. Firstly, their apprehensive attitude towards each other because of their 'Kill and Be Known' nature has led to a total detachment among the different villages. In *U Niedimia* (Liezietsu, 2010), it is pointed out that the constant fear and enmity existing among each other led to complete zilch in communication and that the only known history on communication was through the barter system of the Salt Trade which was popularly executed in Golaghat. During the pre-independent period of our nation India, East India Company further extended its area by making a pact with the Ahom king and from which the Nagas starting calling the Britishers as "Company People". It was from the Salt Trade that they communicated with the outsiders for the first time and received this information of the "Company People." Besides the ignorance of the existence of the 'outer world,' the feeling of detachment, isolation and mistrust between inter-tribal, inter-village and inter-clan also existed.

Secondly, the British Company brought in their strategy of "Divide and Rule" with which they established their hold on the North-Eastern parts of India, or for the sake of history, the whole of India. Thus, division was one of the features of the Nagas for history to remind us.

Thus, both the internal and external factors led to the division of the Nagas which led to a clearer language barrier. Delving into the diversity of language, the Nagas with its several tribes had several languages. However, with diversity and division in its best union, it further gave birth to several other dialects.

On the Legend of its Script through Oral Tradition

Before the coming of the British "company", there was no written script to be used by the Nagas. However, there are myths on the formation of Naga script and how it was lost. This is recorded in Temsula Ao's poem, "The Old Story Teller" (2011) with the narrator in a state of regret and frustration over the change in society and how people were failing to acknowledge the importance of oral tradition. Oral tradition, emerging as one of the most prominent features of culture and myth, we find Temsula Ao's works as most befitting for this point. The poem "The Old Story-Teller" itself informs the reader of the theme through its title not only in revealing the act of the person but also indicating that the story teller is indeed 'old' and that the practice of storytelling is dying with the old people. While the narrator is in awe of her grandfather's skill and considers it her "primary treasure," her grandsons consider it as "ancient gibberish". The poet stresses on the art of storytelling and also reveals the 'myth' of the "Original Dog" who had eaten the skin of the animal on which the Naga script was written by their ancestors. It can also be noted that the poem through the form of the myth survives from oral tradition.

In the following lines, the speaker narrates her desire to retrieve the script only if time were to take her back to the past. "To wrench the thieving guts/Out of the Original Dog /And consign all my stories/To the script of his ancient entrails" (Ao, 2011: 83).

Here, the narrative poem highlights on the existence of a written script and how it was eaten away by the "Original Dog" according to the myth of the Ao-Nagas. One of the largely accepted conclusions is a myth similar to this. While this second myth holds everything alike with the myth of the

Ao-Nagas; one additional detail added here is on the material used for writing the script. Several scholars have opined the theory that the script was actually written of an animal skin. According to this legend as recorded by D. Koulie (2006) the people were actually blessed by God with a script which was treasured for years as it was used for learning the script. One day as the family was working in the field with the script kept in a bag; the dog came and took the scroll for its meal.

The third theory again bears resemblance with the two myths mentioned above but only this time the culprit is no longer the dog. It was the children who took the script to be burnt and eaten as they were hungry. Whoever the culprit was or whether the identical theories were true, one can never know. One could only accept it as the closest consolation to the explanation as to why the Nagas do not have a script of their own.

On Origin through Oral Tradition: The Ao and Angami Legends

Oral tradition has paved way for the several theories on man's origin. We find this in the myth of the Ao-Naga culture, which traces the originality of life and mankind itself through stones. Again, in the poem "The Stones of Lungterok" by Temsula Ao (1992) we find the history, the origin and birth of men. The word "Lungterok" in Ao dialect literally translates to "Six Stones." In their belief, their forefathers created from the earth at a place called Lungterok where three men and three women were formed from the stones. These were the six stone people who were "Born/ Out of the womb/of the earth" (A0, 1992: 48). They were individuals with all the qualities or that they were the embodiment of mankind with artistic qualities as well as the quality to judge, kill and control as they were "The poetic and politic/Barbaric and balladic/Finders of water/And fighters of fire" (A0, 1992: 48). These people were in all the form of being human as they were close to nature, both as its master and its keen observer. They were also individuals who were acquainted with all sorts of skills and knowledge necessary for their living. They were "potters", "weavers", "Planters", "Hunters", "singers" and also carried both their "Gentle" sides in loving and creating a home while "savage" in their killings. All these qualities, the six individuals carried according to the Ao-Naga legend. They were human in their behaviour and living. Yet, the very genesis of their creation seems inhuman. However, for any historical findings or brave defence to be made on this legend, the focus now is not on its credibility but rather on the source, which is oral tradition.

Keeping the Ao-Naga legend and the myth of the Angami-Naga in a frame, there is a striking similarity between the two. While the Ao-Naga legend claims on the source of stones as the origin of its people, the Angami-Nagas hold a claim with its legend sticking to a tale quite similar to the story found in the Bible about the Tower of Babel. Again, the credibility or reliability of these legends cannot be completely accepted as these are from oral tradition which at some point should be given due appreciation. According to the legend shared mostly among the Angami-Naga, its people claim to have once gathered hands to build a mighty tower which could reach the heavens. This act was however halted as their once universal language was suddenly divided and differences entered among them. In the words of J. H. Hutton (2003) we read:

> In the story of the Angami Tower of Babel Kepenuopfü causes the men who are building a tower up to heaven to

> speak different languages, because she is afraid that she will have to give them all gifts if they succeed in arriving" (p. 181).

This legend is one that had existed even before the coming of the American Baptist Missionaries in the late nineteenth century. Though this can be a mystery confounding people, the fact that the story had existed even before the exposure of the Naga land or that the Nagas had always lived in isolation and hostility especially towards outsiders, it does not give any reason as to how they could have any verbal communication for Sunday Bible narration.

Coming to the comparison once again, the conclusion can be drawn from the fact that both the tribes and their legends hold similarities even remotely close to the authorship of the Bible or the very genesis of the man itself. While the Ao-Naga legend holds the myth of the six individuals with three unions as the utmost beginning of mankind bearing resemblance to the three unions of Noah's sons after the great flood, the Angami-Naga legend bears the similarity on the Tower of Babel. Thus bringing in the connection of all the myths to the very form of the Bible.

On Migration

While the above-mentioned literature is mythical in its nature, there are several accounts on the origin of the Nagas or their seedbeds which are based on similar patterns or rather striking coincidences from the orally transmitted stories passed from generation to generation. Through the accounts and findings maintained by Shürhozelie (1982), there are some locations which may have been the possible places from which the Nagas migrated. Again, though the authenticity of these theories cannot be absolutely accepted, there exists and provides sufficient evidence to support the possibilities. The first location mentioned is of the place called "Hedzümiarüna" or 'the place of the Hedzü people.' The term "Hedzü" is a Tenyidie word and is so-called because the place is believed to be one, untouched or uncovered by the sky and thus resulting to extreme coldness. There are three main points gathered from the oral legends which lead to the theory that the place is actually referring to Russia.

According to the oral tradition it is said that the inhabitants there are men with long beards. This was a trend which ended only after the revolutionising change brought by Peter the Great of Russia (1682-1725) who took up measures to curb the culture of its nation with the intention of doing away with conventional social systems while charging taxes upon those who maintain their beards. Secondly, these inhabitants were said to wear long and lengthy clothes which again bears close and remarkable resemblances to the Rubakha (oversize shirts), Sarafan (long dresses) or the Kaftan (coats) used by the Russians until the reign of Peter the Great. Lastly, it is from the claim of its extremely cruel climate conditions for which the name of the place and the need of its inhabitants' mighty clothes and use of furs arises from. Apart from these three points, the available accounts also add that the Nagas were people who lived and also participated in barter system with the inhabitants. The Nagas were people who valued metal or any of its products with such veneration, since the claim proves that the Nagas were not acquainted with the art of processing metal, they used their livestock in exchange with these essentials. Though the Nagas have had a history of peaceful living with everyone, the need for these metals must have stemmed from the purpose of agriculture or weapons to protect their livestock from wild animals. The place of the Hedzü people is part of the oral tradition Yet on the theory as to why the Nagas left the place must be based on the fact that the harsh climatic condition prompted them to leave the place and migrate elsewhere leading to the second location, China.

Several accounts can be collected and mounted for the theory that proves that the Nagas either migrated or originated from China. The first analysis comes from the earlier mentioned source where he propounded that the very Tenyidie word 'bagei' is a term for 'vehicle' which is not a borrowed word. Though the very first car in the world was made accessible for the public only in the year 1908, it can be understood that the civilisation of China was advanced and that it had its own efficient ways through the usage of vehicle or what the transmitted word 'bagei' contributed to its people. From this view, one can also understand the importance of the origin of words and how oral tradition has kept these words or the language in general 'alive' all these times. The very word 'zoumei' is a word whose meaning is lost but finds itself stringing back to China. From this, the legend of the Naga leader who possessed extraordinary aura and luck can be seen again. The possession of this valued object was supposedly the reason for all the success or victory he made. This created enmity between the Nagas and the inhabitants of China and finally through some schemes, the Nagas had to leave the place as they were no more tolerated by the inhabitants and because they were defenceless and vulnerable without the 'zoumei'.

Thus, oral tradition is a form of preserving one's ethnicity and identity as these words act as the key to unlock the doors behind legends and myths which can lead to the deeper understanding of meaning itself.

The existence of Classical Poetry through Oral Tradition even without it Authorship

Though they were never recorded or documented, the songs of yesteryears still live and exist amongst the Nagas through the words as the agents, carrying memories of the past. In any Naga tribe, songs and myths of lovers; of bravery; of wit; and all kinds of tales were shared and celebrated. There are several Tenyidie classical oral poems which have survived till date through documentations. The old but anonymous poem "Our Love" translated by D. Kuolie (2013) brings to the reader the meeting of the two lovers at the "festival of Khruonyi" after years of their separation as they were compelled to sacrifice their love for the sake of their families as seen in the lines, "When the villagers were celebrating the festival of Khruonyi, /I took my child for a parental visit;/My beloved came that day" (p. 8). The lovers are able to meet only because of the festival which was an act of peace between their respective villages which also shows the practice of strengthening their bonds in spite of the long-lasted wars that had initially led to the separation of the lovers. As the lovers prepare to separate once again from the crowd, the man pulls out his "best carnelian beads" and knots the chain on her daughter's neck as the last sign of his love for her. His devotion can be understood through the passage of the beads as these ornaments, especially the ones used on festivals, were considered their prized possessions. The poem stands as a true product of folk poetry, passed down even without its authorship through oral tradition.

Alteration through Written Culture

As many scholars have opined, may it be once again added that oral tradition was best practiced through the education imparted to the youngsters with the existence of institutions like Morung. Through these channels, the youngsters are given life skills, knowledge and most importantly the art of narration through poetry and folklores. These institutions were, however destroyed with the intrusion of the outsiders who changed the society and its tradition at large. Their arrival led to the departure of the rich Naga oral tradition especially poems which are mostly forgotten while folk tunes inscribed with stories and narrations were considered as heresy by some of the newly converted Christians. Thus, the old spoken tradition disappeared as the new written culture entered the lands of the Nagas.

The Naga society has progressed a long way from oral tradition to a culture of writing with the age of time and progress in literacy as introduced to us by the American Missionaries. In Temsula Ao's (2012) perspective as observed,

> What we, the so-called scholars are doing regarding the 'Oral Tradition': is this: we have converted it into the written world! And that too, in a language not ours! This, I suppose, is the most telling evidence that we have travelled a long way from the days of Lungterok into the 21st century (p. xi).

This is the true sign and an appropriate statement to validate that the culture of inheriting literature has shifted from oral narration to documenting them into written form, both through the Second language and the Mother Tongue.

REFERENCES

Ao, Temsula. (1992). *Songs That Try To Say.* Calcutta: A Writers Workshop Redbird Book.

Ao, Temsula. (2011). The Old Story Teller. In T. Misra, *The Oxford Anthology of Writings from North-East*, pp. 83-85. New Delhi: Oxford University Press.

Ao, Temsula. (2012). *The Ao-Naga Oral Tradition.* Dimapur: Heritage Publishing House.

Hutton, J. H. (2003). *The Angami Nagas.* Kohima: Directorate of Art and Culture Government of Nagaland.

Kuolie, D. (2006). *Structural Description of Tenyidie: A Tibeto-Burman Language of Nagaland.* Kohima: Ura Academy Publication Division.

Kuolie, D. (2013). *Tenyidie Literature: Traditional and Modern.* New Delhi: SahityaAkademi.

Liezietsu, S. (2010). *U Niedimia.* Kohima: Ura Academy.

Marak, C. R. (2007). Relevance of Oral Literature. In S. S. Kharawphlang, *Orality and Beyond: A North-East Indian Perspective,* pp.13-19. New Delhi: Sahitya Akademi Publication.

Pou, K. B. (2015). *Literary Cultures of India's Northeast: Naga Writings in English.* Dimapur: Heritage House Publication.

Rickett, A. C. (2009). *A History of English Literature.* New Delhi: UBS Publishers' Distribution Pvt. Ltd.

Shürhozelie. (1982). *U Tsiepfumia Rüve.* Kohima: Ura Academy Publication Division.

Tsuren, E. V. (2017). *Insider Perspectives: Critical Essays on Literature. Norway*: Barkweaver.

10

Cultural Values of the Aos in Temsula Ao's Collection of Poems, *Songs from the other Life*

SENTINARO

'Culture,' is a comprehensive term as it includes the following: Pattern of modes of behaviour; secondly, techniques and technologies for production, social organization, and institutions for the promotion of the arts and the sciences, education, health and other services. Thirdly, basic postures, values, beliefs, world views that are represented in art, music, literature, philosophy and religion.

Culture also refers to the patterns of thoughts and behaviour of people. It includes values, beliefs, rules of conduct, and patterns of social, political and economic organisation. These are passed on from one generation to the next by formal as well as informal processes. Culture consists of the ways in which we think and act as members of a society. Thus, all the achievements of a group life are collectively called culture.

Over the last decades there has been a burgeoning interest in the concept of culture. Unfortunately it has not been put into a precise use. As a result, the concept has been used in different ways. To quote Smith, "A society is a group of people who have a common culture. Culture exists because people are able to share creations pass knowledge from one generation to the next, and thereby change the very conditions for existence" (Smith and Preston, 1997: 19).

Culture has also another dimension. Literature reflects the society and the culture of an age. Literature especially that of the post-colonial countries is a reflection of their once cherished and lost culture. There is a loss of identity and a quest for new meanings in the old culture. In the Ao culture too, there is this recurring theme. Culture is closely related to society and literature. Thus every national literature gives its own interpretation of social communication corresponding to its cultural ethos. While doing so it reflects a normative identity of its culture, in which it is rooted (Paniker, 1997: 158). Accordingly literature becomes an effective projection of the reality of a particular cultural region. It provides a form of distinctive knowledge about society.

To quote Bakhtin (1986), "Literature is an inseparable part of the totality of culture and cannot be studied outside the total cultural context. It cannot be severed from the rest of culture and related directly to Socio-Economic or other factors. These factors influence as a whole and only through it and in conjunction with it, do they affect literature. The literary process is a part of the cultural process and cannot be turned away from it" (p. 140).

The Nagas fall under the Indo-Mongoloid group of people residing in the Northeastern Hills of India, with different tribes each speaking different languages and dialects. Though the Nagas are of Mongolian stock, they are completely different from the rest of the easterners like the Chinese, Indonesians, Burmese etc, in their language, customs and religion. They are unique on their own. The Nagas do not have a written script of their own. Their written customs, laws, practice and treaties were treasured over the years by means of oral narration passed on from one generation to the next.

Among the major tribes of Nagaland, the Aos is a prominent tribe. The Ao tradition states that the ancestors of the tribes came out of the earth at *Lungterok*, which means 'six stone', which was laid at the top of a spur on the right bank of the Dikhu river. Although the Nagas as a whole exhibit a general similarity of culture and have much in common in their way of life and their customs, there are many individual characteristics that differentiate the culture of one Naga tribe from that of another. The most absorbing ethic unit which presents several characteristics not found in other Naga communities is the Ao Naga tribe.

A society or a tribe without a cultural background can be termed as a society without roots or identity. The Aos are fortunately blessed with a rich cultural heritage, which is worth appreciating. As Ao puts it, "the fountain head of everything in Ao folklore is the belief that the ancestors of the Aos emerged out of the earth at *Longterok* (Ao, 1999: 1). The primary reason why the Naga origin myth is perplexing and unclear is because the Nagas do not have a written record. As a matter of fact, scholars and researchers cannot treat these myths and legends as factual but must be clear that it gives us a hint of the past and should therefore understand the word, 'myth' in its totality. It should be made use as a point of reference.

Clan system is very strong among the Aos. The Ao clan system is divided into two major sub-classes: The Jungli Phratry & the Mongsen Phratry. Among the class, there are varied opinions regarding their origin. But the most widely and commonly accepted view is that of the origin of the Aos from six stones. Of the six stones it was believed that three were males and three were females. The oral tradition started with the origin of the Aos from *Longterok* (six stones) at *Jungliyimti* village (The village where the Aos are believed to have taken their first settlement). In fact nothing has really been recorded in written, and everything that we know today is what has been handed down to us through oral narration from our forefathers. The oral tradition plays the all-important role in defining good citizenship and maintaining a harmonious social fabric because all the subtleties of social structure and interaction are encoded in the tradition. Thus Ao literature is inscribed in its oral literature itself.

The Aos like any other tribe have their own rich culture. They make use of a number of traditional oral narratives like proverbs, saying, myths, metaphors, etc., which convey the rich cultural heritage handed down by forefathers from one generation to another. As N. I. Jamir (1997) states that 'the glory of a race is manifested by its culture' (p. 1). The Aos were fond of social and community life. They were a singing and dancing people in times of both joy and sorrow. Their social life was marked with feast of merit, traditional games and festivals. But however the contact of the Aos and the Nagas in general brought many changes in their lives.

In Ao society, a man's wealth and status in the society was determined by his dress, ornaments and the land he owned and the feasts he gave in the village, where a number of animals were killed. Such a man is regarded as a wealthy man. Bell necklace and *takar sü* (a rich man's dress) is worn by them to signify their status in the society.

The Ao society is basically a patrilineal society. Every man after a certain age becomes an administrator or a member of the *putu menden* (village council). All issues relating to property are taken over by the men folks. In a clan's meeting, a man has the right to stand up and speak his mind out but the women are deprived of this right. Though women folk are excluded from areas like inheritance and the freedom to speak in the village council, nevertheless, she is not subordinated in any way by the men folks who have always respected and loved them. But in areas like inheritance, these days a lot of accommodation and acceptance have been made with social roles, responsibilities and changes.

The Aos also believed in certain taboos, for instance, persons who died of mysterious disease were isolated from the villages and their dead bodies were buried outside the village. They were not allowed to use the public burial as it might bring bad omen to the village.

Headhunting was not practiced as a social custom, though it was commonly practiced by many Naga tribes. The Aos practiced head-hunting for popularity and fame. The heads brought after a warfare signified 'bravery' and not victory. Victory is considered only when a village completely destroys the enemy's village or the other village surrenders. The head is boiled after which the skin and the flesh are removed. The skull is then smeared with rice. It is then hung on a tree.

The *Süngkong* (log drum) played an important role in the social function of the society. According to the Aos, whenever a village is established they would always make a *Süngkong*, to be kept in the village. Its use was to sound the warning in the event of an enemy's attack or to announce the bringing of an enemy's head to the village. It was believed among the Aos that whenever a *süngkong* or 'log-drum', is made, the village is blessed with honour and prosperity. Beating of the log drum differs for different situations and the beat varied according to the occasion like in the event of a war, fire in the village, or a head trophy being brought. For instance, when the chief of the village died, a three beat drumming style was played continuously till the burial of his body.

To the Aos, marriage is a sacred institution of the society. Marriage is not only necessary for biological necessity but also for social and economic reasons. The wife is the helpmate of her husband in all activities. According to Ao customs and traditions, only monogamous marriage is accepted and polygamy is prohibited.

Song also played an important role in the social life of the Nagas. Any public lecture, speech, storytelling or a casual discussion was followed by songs at intervals. Such an occasion without a song was incomplete; singing is an indispensable accompaniment of the Ao festivals and all Ao traditions of the past and notable events of the present are enshrined in their songs. The meanings in the songs are implied rather than expressed.

The Aos make use of proverbs, which reveal their rich culture and tradition. The elders use them not only in their everyday conversation but also in public gatherings and meetings. Proverbs not only teach the youngsters but they also bring out their cultural and traditional values. But today, factors like westernisation and Christianity have been a major contributory factor towards the loss of the old culture. The introduction of liberal education has been another major factor. The more 'educated' they became; the more alienated they began to feel from a way of life which seemed absolute and primitive (Ao, 1999: 176). The Ao - Naga literature is a reflection of the rich culture of the tribe. Though much of the traditional practices and beliefs which had been handed down through word of mouth or the oral tradition has lost its importance, yet the moral values that come along with the tradition is still relevant and continue to govern the people which finds its place in the written literature because we are living in an age where the written word reigns supreme (Ao, 1999: 178).

The present paper will make an analysis of the cultural values and practices of the Aos in Dr. Temsula Ao's collection of poems called *Songs From the Other Life* (2007). It is a collection of poems based on Ao folklore and myths, beliefs, cultural practices etc.

The old story-teller

I have lived my life believing
Story-telling was my proud legacy.
... Added to the lore.
... To wrench the thieving guts
Out of that Original Dog
And consign all my stories
To the script in his ancient entrails (SFTOL, 2007:11-13)

*SFTOL: *Songs From The Other Life.*

The art of storytelling among the Aos is as old as tradition. *Ariju* (bachelor's dormitory) and *Tsuki* (dormitory for unmarried girls) are the oldest social institutions for the boys and girls in the Ao society. A boy is initiated into the *Arijus* as early as twelve years of age. In the evening besides the defense training, the boys gathered together to narrate stories about warfare. Likewise at the *Tsuki*, the girls narrate love stories and folklores. In the poem, the narrator talks about the loss of culture in the modern Ao society. Much of political, social, historical and religious aspects of the tribe have been retained in the memory through the oral tradition. The storyteller in the poem nostalgically remembers how he once proudly carried on the legacy of storytelling from his grandfather. He referred to the stories he heard from his grandfather as his 'primary treasure'. He tells his stories with such passion as though they run in his blood, as each story 'revitalise' his life force. The stories remind him of his roots.

The stories he narrated were culturally important because they were about the origin of the Aos, how the forefathers founded the 'ancient villages' and 'worshipped the forces of nature' (SFTOL 12). The poem also focuses on the relationship between man and animals, which lived in harmony, as one according to the Ao myths of the story of creation. The storyteller talks of how his forefathers have warned the younger generations the danger of losing their identity, if they forget their past: "we would lose our history, territory and most certainly our intrinsic identity". The poet conveys the need and importance of storytelling by using the storyteller in the poem to emphasise his role as a narrator to let the younger generation develop a propensity for poetry and folklores, so that they grow up in wisdom possessing original ideas and a love for their own culture. But towards the end of the poem, the narrator sadly acknowledges the end of an era, replacing the old and past by a new era, 'insidiously displacing the old'. 'The mind once 'vibrant with stories,' is reduced to unimaginable stillness.

Soul-Bird

They are chanting prayers,
But I watch a lonely hawk
Soaring
Amidst the swirling
Blue of the vast sky.
... "See that keening bird in the sky?
  That's your mother's soul
    Saying her final good-bye,
It is over.
Come, let us go home now (pp. 14-15).

The Aos believed in life after death – to the Aos when a person dies his soul is taken to a village called *Asuyim* which means '*dead man's village*'. There is also an ancient Ao Naga belief that when a person dies, the soul takes the form of an insect, a bird or a caterpillar. The sighting of hawks soon after a person's death is considered to be a good omen signifying that the transition is complete and that it is the last appearance of the loved one on earth (SFTOL : 14). The poem begins with the 'chanting prayers', in the funeral gathering but 'amidst the swirling blue of the vast sky,' the narrator in the poem, notices a lonely 'hawk'. But grandmother refuses to accept the reality that her loved one is gone, guards the 'fresh mound', until she 'senses a presence hovering in the sky', the 'circling silhouette' of a hawk. The sight of the hawk brings comfort and an acceptance of 'the stark finality' to the grieving grandmother who tells the narrator,' that is your mother's soul saying her final goodbye, it's over. Come, let us go home now' (SFTOL: 15). The hawk signifies belief in a dead man's soul completing his journey on the earth, which bring comfort and consolation to the bereaved family.

The poem thus skillfully conveys the belief and cultural practices of the Aos concerning death.

A Tiger- woman's prayer

> you powers of the earth and sky,
> Who gave me this destiny
> Tell me what is happening
> ... Will dissolve my several selves
> Be they spirit, woman or tiger
>
> And raise a rainbow there
> Against our composite tears (pp. 19-21).

Lycanthropy is a common belief among the Naga tribes. Lycanthropy applies to metamorphosis into any life like the leopard, tiger, the wolf, the lion etc (Stirn and Ham, 2003: 76). Such persons exhibit some kind of supernatural powers in the form of physical and spiritual and are known as tiger-man and woman. The relationship between man and animals dates back to the myths, where human beings and animals lived together as one in a village called *merasha-yim* meaning (a place where animals and humans lived in an undivided society). Such men are known as medicine men, a witch doctor, a fortune teller etc. Besides foretelling the future, a tiger-man or a tiger-woman also heals different ailments through the indigenous medicines. The poem talks about the prayer offered by such a 'tiger-woman', who possesses the spirit of a tiger as the name suggests. She prayed and asked whether she is a spirit or a tiger. She seems to be confused and asking her role as a tiger-women. The tiger woman has more than one soul, one of which resides in an animal. According to this belief, the tiger, embodies the man or woman's spirit and is no different in appearance from other tigers in the forest except the particular animal has a strong sense of affinity and attachment to the person whose soul or spirit he is supposed to embody (Ao, 1999: 67). The tiger-woman talks of the 'the familiar steps that always stalk' (SFTOL: 19). This kind of powers are inherited from ancestors, or acquired through application to one who is reputed to be in possession of such power. The tiger-woman in the poem has inherited it from her grandfather, and entangled her 'in an –unseemly mesh of spirit, human and beast' (SFTOL: 20).

This poem highlights the belief of the Aos, like most Naga tribes, in lycanthropy that not only foretells the future but also heals illness. We see one, such in the tiger woman, who says "whether I be spirit, human or tiger."

Trophies

It is one of those crazy nights yet again;
The air is rent by blood-curdling yells
Of the warriors come home
With enemy heads which will hang
From the skull-tree in the village field
...
After vain glory
And vacuous reward... (pp. 54-56).

Headhunting is an ancient custom among the Nagas where the heads of one's enemies are brought home as 'trophies' and displayed at a public place. The human heads or 'trophies' were considered to be a gem or prized treasure to the villagers. The human heads are preserved by removing their flesh and hung to dry in the sun followed by rites and rituals of thanksgiving and celebration. A head-taker gained respect and admiration among his peers and villagers. A head-taker could be recognised by the decorative dress and ornaments he adorned himself with. These heads or 'trophies' were symbolic of powers, success and bravery, and was believed to be a source of good fortune for the villages.

This activity had several-cultural meanings. A human head was thought to bring good fortune to the villages. Enemy heads were brought home after the battle by the warriors. They would yell out loud cry as they entered the village gate, announcing their victory. We see such an incident in the poem, where: 'the air is rent by blood – curdling yells of the warriors come home' (SFTOL, 2007: 54). Among the Aos, the heads were taken to the log drum or to the village head tree. The Ao warriors' wives are known to have fed skulls, saying, 'I am feeding you. Bring your father and mother, and yours sons and daughter' (Stirn and Ham, 2003: 128). As seen in the line, "the warriors will hurl insults at the gory trophies." The fourth stanza of the poem onwards satirizes such meaningless acts of "these men, the father of my child among them, are an absurd lot, rejoicing over some ugly severed heads... Children." They don't seem to care for the women and children and their "home-fires often go unlit." The poet calls such acts as 'meaningless heroes'. And the wife in the poem warns her husband that if he doesn't pay heed to her cries and woes, she will return to her parents, "a widow and your son the orphan of an irresponsible father". The practice of headhunting was abolished by the British during their administration in the then Naga Hills. As in the oral histories of the different Naga tribes, the repeated emphasis laid on headhunting shows that it was a necessary strategy for the survival of each village community (Ao, 2001: 5). Prof. Temsula Ao in her paper entitled "Head-hunting: Some thoughts," cites that taking of heads began initially as a proof of success in warfare, gradually became the prime purpose for waging war. The phenomenon of head-hunting, being associated with so much of peace time activities like village organization, defense, travel, trade, language, art and culture has had a far deeper impact on the Naga psyche than meets the eye. To the British such a practice was nothing short of murder but to the Nagas it was an age old way of life (Ao, 2001: 5).

The poet is, through the poem, highlighting the gory practice of head-taking or headhunting and makes a mockery of the senseless customs of head-hunting practiced among the Nagas and the Aos in particular.

Man to woman

Woman, let me tell you the reasons
Why I have courted you these many seasons.

You may not be the prettiest
Nor the fairest of the village maidens

But when you smile
I see my world lit up in your face ...

But when I come, open the door wide

And let me walk to next year's Jhum by your side (pp. 57-59).

Marriage for the Aos is very important and it was considered not favourable to remain celibate, especially for a woman. Arrangements of marriages are not normally practised among the Aos. The boy and the girl meet each other on their own and marry with their parents' consent. Bride price and dowry is not practised among the Aos. Once the choice is made, a formal proposal is made by the boy's family. And after accepting the proposal, the marriage ceremony is organised, and the feast is given in both the houses. However setting up a new household entails a lot of responsibility which must be fulfilled before the marriage takes place. The burden falls on the groom as he is considered the head of the family and a patriarchal society demand of such social role of man. Custom demands that he must construct a new house before the marriage, where he will take the bride after the ceremony. The house is constructed with the help of his clansmen. The new house for the young couple symbolises the concept of total responsibility and independence of this new family unit in society. The courting scene of the man is seen in the line, "the rhododendron you wear in your ear close like the flame in my heart." He also compares the woman's curves with that of' "ripe banana." The man fondly remembers the gift – the *Sunak* given to him by his lover, which is (a traditional Ao Naga shawl for man is made of faded indigo and black yarn) (SFTOL: 59). The poem also mentions *Moatsu* festival, celebrated during the first week of May, invoking god's blessing for a plentiful harvest. *Moatsu* is a major Ao festival celebrated during the spring season, observed just after the completion of sowing the seeds in a new field. It is celebrated for six days with a lot of colourful traditional dresses, singing and drinking. He tells her that "After the harvest is over, I shall build a new house" (SFTOL: 58). This line brings out the Ao custom of marriage, where an Ao man has to build a house before he takes his wife to start a new life. The poem ends with man asking his lover to let him enter her door and begin a new life together. Not only is the poet bringing out the cultural significance of festivals as a means of social relationship but the poem also explains the old age concept of marriage.

Temsula Ao's writing is thus a reflection of the rich culture of the Aos. Though much of the traditional practices and beliefs which had been handed down through word of mouth or the oral tradition has lost its importance, yet the moral values that come along with tradition is still relevant and continues to govern the people which finds its place in the written literature. Culture is thus so integral to the Naga society and their quest for identity is rooted in itself.

REFERENCES

Ao,Temsula. (1999). *The Ao Naga Oral Tradition*. Baroda: Bhasha Publications.

Ao, Temsula. (2007). *Songs From The Other Life*. Pune: Grasswork Books.

Bakhtin, M. M. (1986). *Speech Genres and Other Late Essays*. Austin: University of Texas Press.

Jamir, N. Talitemjen. (1997). *Ao Naga Cultural Heritage*. Mokokchung: Private Edition.

Paniker, K. Ayyappa. (1997). *Studies in Commonwealth Literature*. Blackie and son Publishers.

Smith, Ronald W. and Frederick W. Preston. (1977). *Sociology-An Introduction*. New York: St. Martin Press.

Stirn, Aglaja and Peter Van Ham. (2003). *The Hidden World Of The Naga- Living Tradition in Northeast India and Burma*. Germany: Prestel Verlag.

11

Cultural Context in Literature: A Study of Easterine Kire's *A Naga Village Remembered*

Vizovono Elizabeth

Culture refers to a particular way of life. This can be reflected in various ways through the attitudes, beliefs, customs, values and activities of a group of people at a particular time. In literature, cultural context looks at the society the characters live in. It also includes how one's culture can affect one's behaviour and opportunities. Cultural theorists like Stuart Hall are of the view that the cross and interdisciplinary aspect is a focal point of cultural studies which has had important effects on the study of literature (Jordan and Weedon, 2006: 245). This perspective has highlighted the role of literature in society in new ways, enabling readers to look at literary texts in relation to cultural history, institutions, texts, forms and practices. The approach of cultural studies also considers that all works of imagination are cultural products. Since writers are inevitably influenced by their cultures, literature and culture are closely related. It brings forth the historical and emergent traditions and thoughts. Literature in this way, teaches to engage with the past and with others. Cultural knowledge can strongly affect a reader's interpretation of the text. Therefore, understanding and appreciating a literary text requires a proper consideration of its cultural context. Based on this framework, the present paper seeks to make a study of Easterine Kire's novel *A Naga Village Remembered* in relation to its cultural history. The study takes recourse to a cross and multidisciplinary approach based on literary, socio-historical, ethnographic and anthropological references.

A Naga Village Remembered, published in 2003, is the first novel written in English by a Naga. It is set in19th century Nagaland. The setting of the novel is the pre-colonial, pre-Christian world of the Naga, particularly the village of Khonoma, which resisted the British forces for almost fifty years until its fall in 1880. It was the last Naga village to withstand the might of the British, and the British administration was established in the area after the fall of Khonoma. This historical setting reflects the existing culture, beliefs and behaviour of the people. The novel serves as a good example to be examined from its cultural context because of the nature of its production. The story revolves around the battle of Khonoma and highlights the cultural life of the villagers before and during British colonialism. The author presents the narrative through a blend of fact and fiction. She has drawn heavily from historical events and incidents, and also from the memories of oral narrators. Some of the characters are historical figures from the time in which the story is set. The text and context of the story are therefore intrinsically linked together, demonstrating the role played by culture in challenging social power relations.

The narrative can be divided into two distinct parts – the first half which depicts the self sustaining, independent cultural way of life that sustained the village before the advent of the British, and the latter half which shows the impact of British colonial rule on the cultural way of life, disrupting it in such a way that the life of the Nagas would never be the same again. The conflict in the story is caused by the culture clash that takes place with the coming of the British. This paper focuses on this aspect by setting these two phases into contrast. It aims to highlight three main aspects i.e., the effects on the social, the historical and the religious aspects of Angami Naga culture as presented in the novel.

Culture performs a crucial educational role of passing down collective wisdom. This is aptly illustrated in the novel. The author delineates the culture of the village by making use of myth, incorporating cultural values, social institutions like the *thehou*, highlighting the observance of taboos and *genna*s, practice of spiritual beliefs etc. The morung was the traditional social institution of learning for the Nagas. For the men, it had two aspects – the *thehou* (men's hall/meeting place) and the *kichuki* (dormitory/sleeping place). It is noteworthy that the author portrays the *thehou* as central to the activities of the community in the novel. In *The Angami Nagas under Colonial Rule*, K. S. Zetsuvi (2014) notes that "it is in the *thehou* that the Angamis prepare their young men for life" (p. 24). This is where all the clan history, legends, songs and the traditional practices are taught. Charles Chasie (2017) corroborates that this was "where every member was thoroughly disciplined. From the *Thehou/Kichöki* would emerge the pride of the clan, fully prepared for life and to play their roles in society" (p. 25). The story opens with a messenger hissing a message conspiratorially to Kovi about a confidential meeting to be held that evening. The meeting is about an expedition of revenge on another village. The matter is a closed subject to the womenfolk of the village. It is strictly "man talk" (Kire, 2016: 21).

At the *thehou,* one of the elders instructs the young men that "a man is not a man if you let another man kill your kin and torch your houses and you do nothing about it" (Kire, 2016: 26). He explains that what "drives a man to battle, [is] the need to prove himself worthy of defending his village and his womenfolk, and to earn ornaments of war" (Kire, 2016: 26). This conversation informs the reader of the ingrained sense of honour in Khonoma men that made it culture bound for them to avenge the deaths of their kin. It also gives a glimpse of the pre-colonial feuds that frequently took place between the independent Naga villages and develops the context of warrior culture that was a part of the history and identity of the village.

Another important aspect is the author's incorporation of myth in the narrative. Through this, she demonstrates how knowledge is orally transmitted through storytelling and shapes the consciousness of the people. When Levi asks: "Do you know why we call the tiger 'elder brother'?" His brother replies: "Of course…every child of this village knows the answer to that question. It is because man and tiger and spirit were brothers once" (Kire, 2016: 34). The Tenyimia believe that man, tiger and spirit are the progeny of the union between Sky Father and Mother Earth. The author shows that this was common folk knowledge. In the novel, the myth serves as a conduit of the Naga worldview, illustrating how reality was perceived in the pre-colonial times. Levi had grown up hearing many stories such as that of *kirhupfümia*, whose existence was a mystery he could not understand. However he learnt of other truths that had no mystery surrounding them, such as the *genna* days that were never to be violated. His uncle Kovi had advised him: "Be humble, heed the taboos and there is no reason why you should not have a full and long life" (Kire, 2016: 73).

The social value of religious beliefs is also highlighted and it informs the reader of an alternative system of knowledge of indigenous people. The narrator describes cases of spiriting, during which the whole community goes in search of the missing person. A seer is consulted and the spirits are propitiated with a chicken sacrifice in exchange for the soul of the man. Zetsuvi (2014) notes that prolonged illness were also believed to be "due to the departure of the spirit from the body" (p. 29). Therefore sickness had to be averted by offering substitution in the form of chickens, old clothes, eggs etc. J. H. Hutton (1969) has also recorded witnessing such an incident in his book *The Angami Nagas*. The cultural life was governed by taboos and rituals, and it was believed that violating the taboos would incur repercussions. William W. Smith observes that "the religion of the Naga is intensely practical" (see Sharma and Sharma, 2006). For the Naga, "to be religious means to be true to the traditions of the tribe" and "everything in the routine of life is bound up with some belief, tradition or superstition, which is an integral part of the religion" (Sharma and sharma, 2006: 223).

This self-sustaining tradition of the village is disrupted with the coming of the British in the 19th century. The first direct contact between the Angamis and the British occurred when a British team passed through Angami territory in search of a direct route from Manipur to Assam. Before the advent of the British to Naga country, inter-village raids within the Naga villages as well as to the plain regions of neighbouring Assam took place frequently. The reputation of Khonoma had grown as a result of the triumphs in these raids. The

Government therefore decided to tame the Nagas through the intervention of a British officer. The British retaliated and punished the offending villages by burning them down. After the capture of Khonoma fort in 1850, since the British policy in India was shaped by their commercial interest, they tried to follow a policy of non-interference seeing that possession of the Naga Hills would be "costly" and "unproductive" and bring no profit to the Government (Mackenzie, 1981: 114). However, the Nagas continued to raid the British tea gardens. This finally forced the British to climb the hills. But as Charles Chasie asserts, "The Angami believed that if vengeance was not visited on the enemy, the soul/spirit of the deceased forbear would find no peace in the afterworld." For a Tenyimia "profiteering was not his normal motivation." He was "honour-bound" by his belief system to take revenge and redeem his honour. Therefore, from the Naga perspective, "they were getting back at the British Colonialists for first violating their territory" (Chasie, 2017: 35-36).

Against this historical background, the author shifts the narrative from the cultural life to the military activities of the British colonialists. Agitated over the audacity of Khonoma, they attempted to crush the village in order to stop uprisings from the others. Kire fictionally recreates history by introducing historical figures like the British officers G. J. Cawley, Colonel Johnstone and Brigadier General Nation along with the protagonists of the novel. The change in the way of life is seen in the natives being exploited and made to do coolie work under British imperialism. Feelings of bitterness and mistrust arose among the villages due to forced labour and imprisonment, and they finally decide "We are not going to be coolies anymore for the white man" (Kire, 2016: 106). On 14th October, 1879, when Mr.

Damant, Political Agent and the first Deputy Commissioner of the Naga Hills, marched to Khonoma with his troops, he was shot dead and his troops fled. This news inspired other neighbouring villages to join in the rise against the white man. Khonoma with her allies laid a siege of Kohima, the seat of British administration. Surrounded by Nagas, and cut off from essential supplies and communication, the British officers considered surrendering. However, the dramatic siege ended with the arrival of Colonel Johnstone, the Political Agent at Imphal, accompanied by 2000 troops provided by the Manipuri Maharajah. The Angami men dispersed to their own villages knowing that it was wiser to retreat.

The British made sure to punish Khonoma and reassert British supremacy. A strong punitive force was sent to Khonoma and the attack began on 22nd November, 1879. The British Government was determined to crush Khonoma once and for all: "So long as Khonoma is allowed to go unpunished over the murder of Damant, the other villages will make bold to rise against us. The spirit of Khonoma must be quenched" (Kire, 2016: 119). The little village was surrounded on all fronts. But they had strong mountain forts and caves afforded natural shelters. "The British had their cannons but the men of Khonoma were protected by the natural world they had always lived so close to" (Kire, 2016: 122). The land that had nurtured the village becomes a natural fortress to its people in their battle against the British. However, after a period of nearly four months of being cut off from supplies, scarcity of food finally made the villagers surrender on 27th March, 1880. Referring to this historical account, Julian Jacobs (1990) writes:

> The boundary of the 'administered area' was pushed further and further back into the hills .. The Nagas resisted this

> expansion, resulting in ten punitive expeditions between 1835-51. This culminated, albeit after an attempt at complete non-intervention, 1851-78, in an uprising in 1879 in which 6000 Angami Nagas laid siege to Kohima, the new British military base in the Hills. In retaliation, the village of Khonoma was subjected to very severe reprisals the following year. In some ways 1879- 80 marked the end of the military phase of colonial rule (p. 21).

The colonizer's power then became the dominant culture undermining and disrupting the native culture of the colonized. The treaty ended the battle but Khonoma had been totally razed to the ground and the villagers dispersed to neighbouring villages. All their granaries and crops too were destroyed. Kire's narrator comments that this was the "punishment for a people who had dared to control their own destinies" (Kire, 2016: 125-6). Finally, when the villagers were allowed to resettle their village, the women wept seeing their burnt homes, but "the men only felt a deep cold anger that would not go away" (Kire, 2016: 125-6). This anger would continue to have long lasting effects on the consciousness of warriors like Levi. When Levi returns to his village after the fourth burning, he sees it with new eyes:

> They returned but the village was no longer theirs for the white man had dispersed the clans of Khonoma. The dispossessed villagers found homes in other villages nearby. Deeply humiliated by the unaccustomed dependence on the charity of their hosts, many preferred to live in temporary shelters in the jungles" (Kire, 2016: 125-6).

This displacement destroyed the entire structure of the close-knit community. Kire highlights the deep bond that tied the men of Khonoma to their land. During the displacement, "they had longed for their village unbearably, dreaming of her by night, and able to look at her only from a distance by day" (Kire, 2016: 125-6). One of the biggest impacts of colonialism is the breaking of this great warrior spirit and sense of identity the land gave them. In her *Studies on Naga Oral Tradition*, Anungla Aier (2018) comments that "it is evident from the oral tradition of the Naga people that the security of the people of the village and the protection of the land were of paramount concern over all other aspect of life" (p. 21). Kire presents a human side to history by showing the emotional and psychological impact of colonialist activities on the natives.

The cultural values that sustained this proud village and its people are challenged further with the coming of the American missionaries. In the latter half of the novel, it is 1894, more than a decade after the peace treaty. The narrative shifts focus to the younger generation comprising Levi's children and their age-mates. A whole new era begins as a new culture and new way of life seeps into the society. Kire depicts the subtle way in which the white colonialists continued their civilizing mission in the Naga Hills. The introduction of Christianity and western education is presented through the white missionary Dr. Sidney Rivenburg, another historical figure. He was a Baptist missionary who had arrived in the Naga Hills as part of the civilizing mission of the British colonialists.

When he first came, he "had made very few converts." Seeing that there was "total absence of health care and awareness of the benefits of modern medical science," (Kire, 2016: 133) he returned to America for two years of medical study. In 1894, he returned feeling "more equipped" to serve the people under his mission. A new form of colonialism takes place as the preacher equips himself according to the needs of the people to make them accept his main mission i.e., to Christianize the natives. Instead of guns, he came with cure with his medical knowledge. There was a greater acceptance of him as he cured ailments with his medicines, and he could preach the gospel to his patients. Prior to his coming, the traditional "Bone-setters, Herbalists and Chicken sacrificers" (Kire, 2016: 133-134) had met the needs of the people's health problems. According to K. S. Zetsuvi (2014), "the impact of modern medicine was so great that it had shaken the foundations of tribal religion. In the tribal world-view, religion and illness were inseparable. The people believed that most sufferings and illness were the doings of gods to punish someone who had done something wrong. Curing illness was thus a religious function to be conducted by a priest" (p. 84). The core of their cultural belief was thus affected through this social transformation.

Rivenburg's medical practice was a means to an end – that of preaching the gospel of Christ. He soon learned to communicate in the local dialect and won the admiration of the Angamis. By affiliating himself with the natives, he won their favour without resistance. Moreover, he also ran an unconventional school at Kohima where he taught English and introduced formal western education. Notwithstanding the many positive changes brought about by the white man, the introduction of such new practices affected the material culture and way of subsistence of the community. Rivenburg's Mission School soon takes precedence over the traditional institutions like the *thehou* and the dormitories. With western education, English language and literacy are introduced for the first time to this people of oral tradition. It was Rivenburg who introduced a written script to the Angamis by writing primers in the local Angami dialect using the Roman script, and encouraged the students to converse in English. Thus, modern medicine, education and Christianity were introduced by the American missionary.

Rivenburg plays a pivotal role in ushering a new culture into the ways of the simple villagers. Though the Nagas had already experienced the superior military might of the white man, this missionary's conquest is quite different as he tries to win hearts favourably through the subtle means of education and medicine. The indigenous methods and way of life are superimposed by the wonders of western education and modern medical science coupled with the promise of salvation that he preached at every opportunity. The Nagas were introduced to the new ideologies as their ticket to a progressive modern world. However, the seed of the seeming benevolence was the 'white man's burden' and formed part of the colonial project of converting the Naga 'heathens.' As Paul Pimomo (2012) states in his review of Abraham Lotha's *History of Naga Anthropology (1832-1947)*, "colonialism and Christianity put an ideology and a mechanism in place for Nagas to abandon their structures of reality and society without being aware of what they were giving up in the process" (p. 196). In the novel, Kire demonstrates the repercussion of this sudden leap of cultural transition through Sato's encounter with Rivenburg's education and its effects on the former's family life.

Inato Yekheto Shikhu (2007) rightly notes that in traditional tribal societies such as the Nagas, there were no irreligious people because religion permeated all aspects of life. It existed "within the whole system of their being because to be truly human was to belong to the community," (pp.11-12) and to do so involved active participation in the beliefs, rituals and ceremonies of the community. Thus for the Naga, religion, culture and community were intrinsically bound together and could not be separated. Sato was caught between the guilt of being more attracted to the gentleness of Chaha's *Isu* and the happiness he found in learning at the Mission School. Meanwhile, his father was growing impatient and worried since Sato was old enough to be initiated, but "the time was never appropriate" as he was always "away at school" during major festivals (Kire, 2016: 136). Thus, with the introduction of education and Christianity, there are major changes that affect the social and cultural structures of the society and this is reflected in the conflict that arises in the family.

Levi roars "like a wounded tiger" (Kire, 2016: 141) when he learns of his son's conversion and aims for the spear, ready to kill his son who had betrayed him and brought shame to his warrior's name: "The shame of it or the pain of betrayal by a son – which hurt more he couldn't decide" (Kire, 2016: 141). Levi is a warrior's son, and a war hero who had fought the mighty British army. He had not forgotten the bitter experiences of his past encounters with the white man. Sato's experience of the white man is peaceful and educational because he has not experienced violence first hand from the white man like his father Levi.

For Levi, the white man is the enemy who plundered, destroyed and disrupted all that was dear to him. Therefore, he sees his son's conversion as a defeat at the hands of the enemy. The British themselves have recorded that their administration supported the American Baptist Mission with the motive of pacifying the Nagas and civilizing them. We see this illustrated very clearly in the conflict between Levi and his son. The white man could not destroy him with war and weapons but had conquered him through the subtle means of education. Paul Pimomo (2012) describes that the disruption of family ties demonstrates the way in which the Nagas were "socialized into the ideology of colonial subordination under the British" (p. 196). When his son Sato is lured away from his cultural roots, Levi takes it as a betrayal – a total negation of who he is. He disowns his son and the filial ties between them are severed forever. Sato walks the new path completely cut off from his family and village.

He is not the only one. The conflict between traditional culture and western influence caused discord in the community. There was great hostility towards the early Christian converts. The village elders declared: "You must not live with us. It will displease the spirits" (Kire, 2016: 143). The believers were excommunicated and had to live beyond the perimeter of the village. They were cut off from all links with their old village and subjected to sharp ridicule and persecution. Thus, the unity of the village was divided between the two groups following the old indigenous religion and white man's new religion.

Christianity was introduced as a tool for civilizing the natives. It began by condemning Naga cultural practices. The missionaries did not make things easy because of the way the Gospel was preached to the natives. In *The Naga Imbroglio*, Charles Chasie (2017) asserts that in the process of introducing Christianity, "condemning what was wrong took precedence over what was right... [*The Nagas were*] made to give up values because of the failure to interpret it in Naga cultural context" (pp. 121-122). Though it brought many positive things with it in the form of western education, literacy, personal hygiene, and a glimpse of the outside world, it cannot be denied that Christianity was introduced into

Naga society as a civilizing tool, and education was introduced under a colonial system which devalued indigenous culture. Since social values are the basis of an individual as well as folk-behaviour and form an integral part of their culture (Punia, 1993: 19-20), disruption of social values also disrupts the preservation of the heritage of the nation as a whole.

In the novel, Kire has very minutely and meticulously recaptured the essence of the cultural life that sustained this little warrior village. Festivals, gennas and taboos, rituals, kinship relationship, myths, beliefs, cultural practices and way of life - all these were manifested in the old religion. The chapters preceding the battle have a profusion of such descriptions but they are conspicuously fewer in the latter part of the novel where the traditional method of education in the *kichuki* is replaced by Rivenburg's Mission School. The focus is shifted to the new system of education in the more urban town of Kohima. The transition in the cultural way of life is apparent as the village takes a backseat and progress in the modern sense is sought away from home. This changed the mental outlook of the people.

By retelling and recreating the story of this village, Kire lays bare the price the Nagas had to pay in their leap from a near Neolithic era to the modern era in a lifetime. It is also a narrative of resistance, rewriting history from the native perspective. She resists depicting the white man in a negative light. However, in many ways, even the beneficent acts of the whites embody the ulterior motives of the colonialists. A lot of confusion and conflict in consciousness originated from the clash of two different cultures. The outcome is that of a new hybrid culture and identity which is neither wholly new nor old. The novel depicts how the clash of cultures had reshaped the social fabric of the society and its people. It illustrates the collective task of grappling with the challenges of the future. Therefore, viewing the cultural context of a literary work is an important tool for learning about a people's culture and history. This perspective helps interpret the text more accurately and enables a way for developing tools to adapt to the rapidly changing world.

REFERENCES

Aier, Anungla. (2018). *Studies on Naga Oral Tradition. Vol.1: Memories and Telling of Origin Myth and Migration.* Dimapur: Heritage Publishing House.

Chasie Charles and Harry Fecitt. (2017). *The Road to Kohima: The Naga Experience in the Second World War.* (2nd ed.). Barkweaver.

Chasie, Charles. (2000). *The Naga Imbroglio: A Personal Perspective.* (2nd ed.). Kohima: Standard Printers and Publishers.

Elizabeth, Vizovono. "Personal Interviews with Easterine Kire." 2008; 2009; 2011.

Pimomo Paul. (2012). A Review of Abraham Lotha's History of Naga Anthropology (1832 – 1947). In Eyingbeni Humtsoe–Nienu, Paul Pimomo, Venusa Tungi, *Nagas: Essays for Responsible Change.* pp. 193-197. Dimapur: Heritage Publishing House.

Hutton, J. H. (1969). *The Angami Nagas.* Bombay: Oxford University Press.

Jacobs, Julian. (1990). *The Nagas: Hill peoples of Northeast India.* London: Thames & Hudson Ltd.

Jordan, Glenn and Chris Weedon. (2006). Literature into Culture: Cultural Studies after Leavis. In Patricia Waugh (Ed.) *Literary Theory and Criticism*, pp. 245-255. New York: Oxford University Press.

Kire, Easterine. (2016). *A Naga Village Remembered.* (2nd ed.). Barkweaver Publications & Ura Academy.

Mackenzie, A. (1981). *The North-East Frontier of India*. New Delhi: Mittal Publications.

Nayar, Pramod K. (2019). *Contemporary Literary Theory and Cultural Theory: From Structuralism to Ecocriticism*. New Delhi: Pearson.

Punia, Deep. (1993). *Social Values in Folklore*. Jaipur: Rawat Publications.

Sharma, Suresh K., and Usha Sharma (Eds.) (2006). *Documents on North-East India: Nagaland*. New Delhi: Mittal Publications.

Shikhu, Inato Yekheto. (2007). *A Re-Discovery and Re-Building of Naga Cultural Values*. New Delhi: Regency Publications.

Thong, Tezenlo. (May, 2011). A Clash of Worldviews: The Impact of the Notion of Progress on Naga Culture, 1832 - 1947. *Journal of Race, Ethnicity, and Religion*, 2(5), 1-37.

Zetsuvi, K. S. (2014). *The Angami Nagas under Colonial Rule*. Dimapur: Heritage Publishing House.

12

Revisiting Culture and Tradition through the Lens of Mamang Dai's *Legends of Pensam*

K. S. Mariam

Ever since human civilization, there is a unique story behind every community and people to be told. Yet, living in a fast-paced world, people are overshadowed by globalization and in the process some stories from the past remain unrecorded and it is almost vanishing. However, literature is one source which people can rely on to understand one's own culture, traditions, myth and legends. Literature is a powerful source for preserving and transmitting people's unique identity through their distinct culture and tradition. It is born out of oral tradition which writers took pain to record and it gives aesthetic taste. Apart from the tradition of oral literature, writers also tend to reflect on their surrounding, events and life of people to come up with notable literary works. Having said that, it cannot be denied that literature is the reflection of society in which we live, and it is a treasure trove that preserves and reflects the rich culture heritage, traditional values and is a preserver of collective identity. In today's world, many writers from different regions regardless of their gender, race and ethnicity pen down various forms of writings that documented their culture, beliefs and traditional values, in their literary works as it permeates in society.

In this multi-dimensional world, it is through literature; people around the world are connected and are able to assimilate in spite of difference in culture, tradition, custom and ethnicity. Though living in a globalized world, there is a always a binary opposition and hierarchal structure in a society which often creates disparity, like rich and poor, civilized and uncivilized, elevated and marginalized group of people. In this light, the literature of tribal people usually the marginalized belonging to northeast India remained untouched and unnoticed from the mainland Indians for long. Yet, it cannot be ignored that the northeast literature has emerged in the realm of literary works through powerful writers like Mamang Dai, Easterine Kire and Temsula Ao to represent their unique culture and tradition. Among many other writers, Mamang Dai stands apart as she explores the unexplored, and her writings are perfect blend of documentation and creativity that transport reader to the aesthetic world and simultaneously, gives a clarion call to transform ourselves from being a mute spectator to preserve one's cultural identity through literature. The writing of Mamang Dai sheds light on different shades of predicament that tribal people have to endure in the midst of upheavals and turmoil and intricacies of tradition and modernity

Revitalizing Culture and Tradition: Mamang Dai's *Legends of Pensam*

Mamang Dai, of Arunachal Pradesh, is considered to be the first writer in English to contribute profusely towards the preservation of her native tribal culture and ethics. She is a poet, novelist and freelance reporter. Dai, who was conferred the Padmashree in 2011 for Literature and Education, has also been associated with the Arunachal Pradesh Literary Society, Sahitya and Sangeet Natak Akademi, Raja Ram Mohun Roy Library Foundation and the North East Writers' Forum in various capacities. However, Dai is principally known as a creative writer and a historian who writes about Arunachal Pradesh. She is the author of *Arunachal Pradesh: The Hidden Land*, a documentation of the culture and tradition of a state about which not much is known. Her creative writing includes three novels, *Legends of Pensam* (2006), *Stupid Cupid* (2009) and *The Black Hill* (2014). Mamang Dai talks of herself as an Itanagar-based writer.

The novel, *Legends of Pensam* is not just a product of Mamang Dai's power of imagination but a documentation of oral narratives of the Adi community in Arunachal Pradesh. The rich oral tradition, myths and folk-tales of the Adi community which have been passing on from generation to generation are made known to the world through this novel. Arunachal Pradesh one of the seven sister states, is vibrant in its traditions, mores and cultural beliefs system. Unlike, other novel which revolves around the protagonist and the events related to them, this novel is a series of interconnected stories which stresses on an entire community and simultaneously moves between individual and community. The epigraph of the novel states:

> In our language, the language of the Adis, the word 'pensam' means 'in-between'. It is the middle, or middle ground, but it may also be interpreted as the hidden spaces of the heart where a secret garden grows. It is the small world where anything can happen and everything can be lived; where the narrow boat that we call life sails along somehow in calm or

> stormy weather; where the life of a man can be measured in the span of a song (Dai, 2006: VI).

The novel consists of four sections titled "a diary of the world", "song of the rhapsodist", "daughters of the village" and "a matter of time". The first section, opens with the story of Hoxo, "the boy who fell from the sky" was taken home by Lutor, famous chief of the Ida clan of the Adis. When the villager asked about the child Rakut's father, who was with Lutor, replied, "There was a great noise and fire in the sky and then our son fell to earth" (Dai, 2006: 40). In the story Lutor was killed in a hunting accident, but people were not surprise or shocked as it is an event portended by his sighting of the water-serpent named Birbik:

> Anyone studying the signs could understand that something unnatural was bound to happen… now that Hoxo's father had seen the serpent… So no one was surprised when Hoxo's father was killed in a hunting accident shortly afterwards. A tragedy was expected (Dai, 2006: 10).

The tribal people have strange belief systems when it comes to unnatural death as they often associate it with the spirit of many kinds. They tend to be more irrational and illogical which modern people might find it hard to connect. Another accidental killing is observed in the novel with the strange case of Kalen, the hunter was shot death by Loma which he thought was monkey. When the hunters crossed the bridge to the village with the death body of Kalen, the lashings of the rope bridge came undone, and they toppled into the stream below. Bodak believed that it was a cursed afternoon, and that the men "had come back from the realm of malevolent spirits" (Dai, 2006: 15). Bodak's belief represents the entire community of Adis who observed that spirit has an important role to play when any misfortunate happens among their community. The Adi community also practices different customs as seen in the punishment meted out to a person who kills a fellow villager:

> The punishment for killing a man is death, unless a meeting can be called immediately and the aggrieved party is convinced that the matter is negotiable. In this case the poor friend was banished to live like an animal in the forest for a whole month. His closest kin could take him cooked food but there were so many taboos on the type of food he could eat that it was simpler to let him fend for himself. No one opposed the exile, least of all the man whose fate it had been to mistake a man for prey (Dai, 2006: 11).

The Adi community is governed by the law that Adis practise through their cultural standpoint without any other external interference. For some modern people, it might seem bizarre but for Adis it was their way of life.

Another incident in the first section, throws light on the narrator's friend Mona, who narrated about her daughter Adela, who had been diagnosed with autism, and how she and her husband had to leave Adela in a school for autistic children. Hoxo also narrated an incident that occurred in the neighboring village of Yagbo around the same time that Adela was diagnosed with autism. Kepi, the two-year old son of Togum, had fever, and after that he could cry, eat and sleep, but couldn't move. The parents went to the hospital, and consulted many famous Shamans. Someone from the village after almost a year remembered that Togum had shot a python and believes that it was the spirit of a snake that had coiled itself around the child. In the silence of Adela and Kepi, Hoxo narrates Mona and the narrator that it fell upon him to perform the snake ritual that would free the child, but it was too late, and "the spirits had moved away to a place beyond recall" (Dai, 2006: 24).The author Juxtapose the age-old cultural belief system of animistic faith practice by Adis and modern outlook between the treatments of children who suffered from same disease.

The story, titled "Pinyar, the widow", narrates the tragic tale of Pinyar who fall in love with Orka, a member of different clan, and bore him a child out of wedlock. Within a span a year, Orka abandon Pinyar and took the child with him. The villager does not sympathize with her as she has invited unhappiness on her own by going against their custom by loving someone outside their clan. After some year Pinyar was married to Lekon, but unfortunately tragedy struck when he was killed in a hunting accident. The Adis tribe is a staunch believer and upholder of their cultural belief and custom as reflected in the ostracism of Pinyar, living on the outskirts of village when her house is razed down by fire. However, the saga of tragedy continue in Pinyar's life when her son Kamur, chop off two of his children with dao in a fit of madness. The tribal people as usual choose to belief the force of spirit or the blood line behind this madness and were even ready to ignore the object dao which is stained with blood. As the matter of concern, "the community railed to restore sense and order" and things gradually returned to normal (Dai, 2006: 31). The animistic faith of the Adis, who believe in spirits and supernatural powers, was a faith of coexistence. They do not yield to any attempt at rational interpretation. But they are sustained by the community's unshakable belief in the stories and how they generate an understanding of the world. It is further reinforced through the words of Pinyar, "Faith is everything" (Dai, 2006: 35). However, change is something that is inevitable and this dimension is seen in the last story of this section. The narrator narrates how the incursion of the migluns brought them face to face with change. Hoxo puts it succinctly when he says:

> We saw a strange new glimmer in the distance. Our footsteps led us down unknown paths. We wanted more. Suddenly we knew more. There was more beyond our poor huts and cracked hearths where we once eased our dreams with murmured words and a good draft of home brew (Dai, 2006: 43).

The change which comes with the passage of time is swift and touches every aspects of life. The community of Adis who uphold animistic faith came across the new wind of modernity, the Christian religion and individualism as a way of existence. In this context, Harajit Goswami (2016) opines that:

> Mamang Dai's *Legends of Pensam* make a conscious effort not only to present the world view of marginalized tribe as it was in the past but also connects and relates the traditions and changes in cultural history of a people as they pass through a period of nativism, to being colonized by the British, and eventually stepping into the postcolonial era (p. 479).

The, "Songs of the rhapsodist", deals with four parts and the stories are narrated through myth and memory, stories of the lives of the ancestors in the form of the ritualistic song and dance performances of the ponung dancers. The rhapsodist is the miri, the great shaman. The narrator and Mona learns about how Noel Williamson, was killed when he was exploring the course of the Siang river in 1911 through the help of ponung dancer. Another aspect of Adis community is recounted by a rhapsodist, which showcases Adis' annual ritual of travelling to the snow-mountains to harvest the root of the deadly aconitum which is used to poison arrows. Another interesting tale which seems magical is recounted in "the case of the travelling vessel", by the headman of Komsing.

A vessel called a danki owned by the Lotang family of the Migu clan was treasured as an auspicious gift from the gods, responsible for the good fortune of the clan. Unfortunately, the vessel split into two as bad omen, followed by decline in the fortune of the clan. To restore the loss, an elaborate ritual was performed by miri from a neighboring but the miri decamped with a bag of stolen coins and heavy necklaces of precious stone. When the maternal uncle of the Migu clan chase, he finally manages to locate two women who were fighting for necklaces and he killed them both along with an onlooker in a fit of rage. After the fateful incident, he did not return to his village but got married and settled down in Sirum village. He returned back only after fourteen years, but a link had been established between the Migu and the people of Sirum as the headman concluded, history was a history of connections:

> There are many stories that link clans. Sometimes we forget how these connections were made, but everything is interconnected. Sometimes a connection is born in the middle of war. Sometimes it is through a woman, sometimes land, and sometimes it is through an object out of the past (Dai, 2006: 61).

Through the myth, the history of different clans from Adi tribe connection is linked. The remembered links of kinship are called up and word is sent to clan members to come to an aid of their brethren when needed.

The section called "daughters of the village" contains five parts of stories. The first two parts, "the words of women" and "a homecoming" focuses on narrator, who comes back and settles down in Gurdum town after living far away from her native place. It also throw light on their cultural belief where the narrator's mother was buried with her head pointing west, so that she face the east and walk into the house of sun. The life of village women in general is also depicted when Arsi complains about life and dreams of better life. She was admonished:

> In this one life it is enough work just trying to keep body and soul together. You must marry. A woman's marriage beads and the obligations she fulfils as wife and mother are the true measure of her worth (Dai, 2006: 76).

The lives of the village women are filled with hardship as their resilience against their plight remain unnoticed and ineffectual. It is the collective community wisdom which helps them come to terms with the inexorable laws of nature and society. Women are convinced to accept their fate and embrace a woman's lot as it is inevitable and natural.

The author talks about one's love for its root beyond other things in life through the story of Nenem a young girl of exceptional beauty, calm and unpredictable as the river. An enigmatic romance blossoms between Nenem and David a young British officer posted in the region, which was a rare occurrence during those time. However, when David is transferred and wants to take Nenem, she is unable to let go of her roots, her land and her people. She stays back, "No one dies of love. I loved him, and now I am enough on my own" (Dai, 2006: 109). Nenem console herself by getting married to Kao and had a daughter but when she has to leave her village and settle in some other place when flood destroyed her village she passed away. Nenem's life and death epitomize the pangs of transition from one way of life to another. Kao witness myriad forces were steeping slowly to encroach their old ways of life:

> He saw the children changing and learning new things, and he smiled when he heard them speak in a new tongue while writing words in new scripts that no one in the village could read (Dai, 2006: 130).

The last part is titled "a matter of time", and it focuses on how the change has affected the individual and the community. Development which comes at the expense of creating rift between tradition and modernity encroach into the pristine lands, "The village had moved to its own quiet rhythm for centuries, with old certainties and beliefs, but the road was changing all that" (Dai, 2006: 148). The people were torn between tradition and modernity and helpless observed that the old way of living was lost:

> The old days of war and valour had vanished. They had surrendered their lands to the government and now the road and the things that came with it seemed to be strangling them and threatening to steal their identity like a thief creeping into their villages and fields (Dai, 2006: 157).

When changes engulfed the traditional tribal societies, the author is apprehensive about the future. Rakut puts it succinctly when he says:

> We are peripheral people. We are not politicians, scientists or builders of empires. Not even the well-known citizens or the outrageous one. Just peripheral people, thinking out our thoughts' (Dai, 2006: 190)

As change is inevitable, Rakut further argues that change is something that one should not be afraid of, "Change is a wonderful thing! It is simply a matter of rearrangement, a moment of great possibilities! Why should we be afraid? ... We have nothing to fear" (Dai, 2006: 190-91).

Reviewing *Legends of Pensam*, Bhattacherjee (2006) observes that many 'worlds' have been "silenced at the altar of progress" by the more powerful lot and he believes that literature can undo this damage by bringing back these lost worlds. He says that, "Mamang Dai's *Legends of Pensam* is a valiant attempt to discover the secrets of one such lost place" (Dai, 2006: 35).

Mamang Dai is not just a writer who focuses on aesthetic sense but she act as a conservator and guardian of culture and tradition by preserving it through literature. Dai as an insider did a commendable work as she is not just an observer but she breathes life to her vanishing culture and tradition through her novel *Legends of Pensam*.

Literature is a treasure trove where distinct cultural identity is preserved and allows the past glory to remain intact through myths, folklore and oral tradition. Mamang Dai through *Legends of Pensam* documented the rich tribal culture and traditions and how it has evolved with the passage of time. The cultures of Northeast India are facing tremendous challenges from education and modernization bring about the loss of distinctive identities of the tribal which can be restored through literature, enabling the younger generation to understand and appreciate their culture and custom. Globalization which shakes the very foundation of tradition through modernity should be balance through the help of literature in order not to erase identity to anonymity.

REFERENCE

Bhattacherjee, Kallol. (2006). Flight of the Hornbill. Rev. of Legends of Pensam. *A Review of Books*, 11(11), 35.

Dai, Mamang. (2006). *Legends of Pensam*. New Delhi: Penguin.

Goswami, Harajit. (2016). Post colonialism and the Retrieval of the Past: A Critical Study of Mamang Dai's Legends of Pensam. *International Journal of English Language, Literature and Humanities*, 4(11), 467-481.

13

Festivals as Cultural Heritage: Sekrenyi Festival of the Angamis

KEDIVONU KHARUTSO

Introduction

A festival is a special event celebrated by a community with ceremony and ritual to fulfil specific purposes. It is the outward manifestation of the identity of the community and provides a distinctive identifier of place and people. Festivals perform the vital role of connecting the present with the past while inculcating the spirit of communal solidarity and cooperation to work towards common goals.

Since time immemorial, festivals played an important role in the life of the Angamis. Festivals constitute an integral part of the Angami social life and relate to strong beliefs in the power of supernatural elements and community bonding. Agriculture being the main occupation of the Angamis, all their festivals is intimately connected with the various agricultural activities. For the celebration of the various festivals, the Angamis follow the lunar calendar known as the *Khrü-phrü*. The months in the *Khrü-phrü* are related to the various stages of agricultural cycle. The Angami annual agricultural cycle begins with the sowing season. Each village follow its own calendar. Therefore, the Angami village do not celebrate the festivals at the same time. The agricultural cycle of the Southern Angami is ahead of that of the Western, Northern and the Chakhro villages. Subsequently, the festival dates in the Southern villages fall earlier than the rest of the other Angami villages. Though there exist a variation of duration and date, ritual performances and the sequences of events from one village to another, and more so from one region to another, the meaning and purpose of the festival remains the same.

Sekrenyi festival

Sekrenyi also known as *Phousanyi* (festival of purification) is the biggest and the most important festival of the Angamis. It is celebrated in the month of *Kezei* (February) by the northern and western Angamis and in *Rüde* (December) by the southern Angamis. It is celebrated for seven to thirteen days. *Sekrenyi* is celebrated to ensure good health of the village community throughout the coming year. For the northern and the western Angamis, *Sekrenyi* marks the beginning of the New Year, when the people purify themselves to start everything afresh.

The village elder/priest makes the announcement of the advent of the festival and to make necessary preparation for the celebration. Women engage themselves in weaving new shawls for the male members of the family, for every male wear the new shawl during the purification ritual. Moreover, *Sekrenyi* is the most colourful festival for the Angamis. It is during this festival that both male and female, old and young adorn in their best attire. It is a time to showcase ones rich cultural attires. Besides, the Angamis male makes new hearth, new fire, new cups/mugs and spoons etc. during this festival. For them 'new' indicates newness of life and purification.

Four-five days ahead, before the actual celebration or *genna* period starts, every household would be involved in brewing rice-beer for the festival (*thenyi thou zhuo*). On this day *genna* is observed. The next three-four days are working days for the people to complete their unfinished works before the festival starts.

The festival begins with *kizhie/kide* ritual (sanctification of the house). This ritual is performed by the lady of the house. On the first day of the festival, she will take a few drops of *zumhou* which is specially prepared for this ritual in miniature plantain leaf cups and tied to the central post of the house and all the paddy barns (*chü)*, praying to the Supreme Being to bless her home with good health and prosperity. *Zumho* is prepared from the soaked rice which is kept ready on the eve of *Kizhie*. The next day, early morning, the lady of the house roughly pound the soaked rice, mix with water and add yeast as it's done in preparing *zutho* (rice beer). After this, she takes a few drops of the *zumhou* and performs the *kizhie* ritual.

The second day of the festival is called *Sekre. Sekre* generally is the occasion on which male children leaves the "women's side" (Hutton, 1969: 204). Prior to the day, the menfolk clean the village well and watch it so as to prevent it from defilement. No one is allowed to fetch water from the village well till the ritual is over, hence, the women fetched and store water before the well is cleaned. On *sekre* day, all the male folk go to the village well early in the morning where they wash themselves, their weapons and tools, then they sprinkles water on their new shawls, the white *mhoshü* and black *lohe* in a ritualistic manner by pronouncing that all their misfortunes and illness have been washed away. This ritual is known as *Dzüseva* (touching the sleeping water). This ritual symbolized the purification of soul. The men then fetch some water and walk back home. On returning home, every man will make a new hearth in the central room and light the fire by traditional method (*Meyoshü/Seguomesu*). After this an unblemished cock will be killed by strangling it with bare hands. It is considered a good omen if the right leg falls over the left leg. The cock killed is then cocked in a separate pot being prepared for the purpose. With the cooked meat the head of the house (father) will then perform the *chii pe/chiisepe* rite to ward off all sicknesses and misfortunes from the family. The head of the family will take a few pieces of cooked meat or liver, put it on plantain leaf, break the meat/liver into pieces and then take some *zutho* (rice beer). He will then go behind the door and throw the meat ritualistically as he chant to the spirits to let his enemies eat the meat and be lured/make weak so that he may kill/overpower them and also to let his food and drinks always be bountiful (field work). The male will dine together separately till the *genna* is over. The women and men can share food or dine together only after the end of the *Sekre* (purification ritual). The end of *Sekre* is called '*pruo*'. This is usually done on the second day of *sekre* before the sun sets. The male will don their shawls; take their weapons viz. spear, dao, gun and go down behind the village gate (*kharu*). They will then shook their shawls in the air, pierce the ground with their spear, give some blind shot in the air calling for the spirit of Sekrenyi (*Sekreseno*) to return to him soon. If the *genna* meat could not be finished, the remains should be distributed to the widows and orphans or to young girls who have not reached puberty.

In some villages, the eve of *kizhie* is a day for slaughtering animals (cows, pigs etc.), while other; on *kizie* morning all the animals meant for the festival will be killed. The *kizhie* day is a day for collecting/carrying firewood, wood for the new hearth and also for making new hearth, spoons and mugs etc. On *Sekre* day all the meat are prepared/cooked for the whole festival period. On the second day of the festival, *Sekre* meat and brew is given to their maternal uncles and goes to seek their blessings. The maternal uncles receive the Sekre meat and brew in return give back meat share from their own house. It is believed that next to the spirits, the maternal uncles are the most important in a man's life and as such this honour is given to them.

From the fourth day, three days session of singing and feasting begins. In one of these days, there is community gathering where the young men are taught the art of war fare, traditional male dance etc. On this day, the Sekrenyi song *Sokese* is sung by some of the male groups. It is a song wishing a person good health, to enjoy the festival and also to celebrate together the following year. Young people sit together and sing songs throughout the day feasting with rice beer and meat. Young boys and girls from other *khels* are invited and feasted together with meat and rice-beer. Great amount of pork, beef, and dog meat are consumed.

On the seventh day young men go hunting and on the eight day the bridge-pulling/gate-pulling ceremony are performed and also inter-village friendship visits are exchanged. Gate pulling is an important ceremony of the Angamis. Since ancient time, *Kharu* (village gate) served as a means of defence for the whole village. Before the old *Kharu* decays the villagers will make a new *Kharu* to replace it. *Kharu* is hewn out of a piece of solid wood. It is usually the largest and the best tree in the forest, so to fell it, an unblemished cock is offered as sacrifice to please the *Terhomia* (the spirit of the forest). Few months ahead, the *kharu* will be prepared with all the carvings and kept ready for the gate- pulling ceremony. On the eight day of Sekrenyi, all the men folks in their ceremonial dresses will take part in the gate pulling ceremony. Until the *kharu* is erected, the whole village will observe *genna*. Inter-village visit begins on the eight day of the festival. All the men folk of the invited clan/ *khel* will wear their best traditional dresses specially the warriors who earned special decoration for their bravery and proceed to the host village. On their arrival, they are welcome with great hospitality by the host village. It is said that everyone from the host village will come and choose their guest. If the guests are fewer in number, there will be a lot of tussle over the guest because everyone wants at least a guest in their house. The visiting guests are given the best food and drink to feast on. On the third day the guest will be given a large amount of meat and rice beer as return gift. These inter village visits served as good-will mission to ensure peace and understanding between two villages or clan groups. "Many clans have long standing ties of friendship with particular clans in other villages and the memory of such ties is preserved and kept green by these visits" (Hutton, 1969: 211). *Thenyi Mi/Meivi genna* is observed on the eleventh and twelfth day respectively which mark the close or end of the festival. Until the close of the festival is announced no one goes to the field.

Conserving and Sustaining Cultural Heritage

Sekrenyi festival is not only an occasion of ritual sacrifices and feasting of meat and rice-beer but have social and cultural contexts. It provides the platform to display the rich and unique cultural traditions of the Angamis. This festival is accompanied by folk songs and dances, display of ceremonial dresses and ornaments, indigenous games and sports through which cultural heritage is transmitted to the young generations. Sekrenyi festival conserve and sustain the Angami culture and tradition by keeping cultural elements, such as food, art and craft, clothing, language, value and belief system etc. alive.

Sekrenyi festival disseminates the rich cultural values cherished by their ancestors. Through this festival, the values and beliefs of the people are rejuvenated, giving meaning to the social, political and religious life of the people celebrating them. In the olden days the Angamis were known for reverence to his community, sense of justice, equality, integrity, work ethic, honesty, generosity, hospitality and religiosity. The Sekrenyi festival exhibits and reinforces this value system. Nekha (2015) points out that festival is one of the oldest institutions for imparting social and cultural values to the people (p.24).

Sekrenyi festival is generally accompanied by a number of religious ceremonies and *gennas* (anything forbidden). Basically rituals are performed and sacrifices are offered to appease the harmful spirits so as to avert troubles and destructions. The Angami traditional religion was based on oral doctrine propitiating deities and spirits. For the Angamis festivals and religion are two faces of a coin. Agriculture being the prime occupation of the Angamis all the major festivals is connected with the agricultural operation and their traditional beliefs and practices are mainly characterized by this occupation, while the entire activity of the agricultural operation is controlled by their religion. Mathur (1992) states that "religion, much like other cultural information is inter-generationally transmitted through the process of enculturation with emphasis on oral tradition" (p.135).

According to Maitra (1991), the participation of young ones is very significant. They learn the rituals and customs so that they can take over in future (p. 85).

The Sekrenyi festival is an occasion for universal celebration where every person of the village participates. It is an event for establishing new relationships and renewing old ones. It also helps to spread message of brotherhood, friendship and peace within and outside the village community. The observance of *genna* days, participation in gate pulling, singing and dancing, games and sports etc. indicates the sense of responsibility every individual feels towards the welfare of the village. "The *gennas* are public rather than private affairs. They are performed keeping the community rather than individual at the central position. They provide ample opportunity to work in collectivity as going out to hunt or fish, cooking on the single hearth and feasting thereby strengthening the adhesivity between individuals and reinforcing solidarity and common identity" (Mathur, 1992: 133). Sekrenyi brings equality and unity among all the villagers.

Besides feasting and merry-making, in the festival, competition and exhibition of indigenous games were done. *Phyieda* an indigenous game is played by menfolk from Southern Angami. The '*ophyie*' stem (dwarf bamboo like stick) used for playing the game. The game is played by hitting the '*ophyie*' on a clearing called '*tetsii*' so that it takes off as far as it possibly can. The player whose *ophyie* goes the farthest score one point and the team which get the maximum points is declared as winner. This game is played between peer groups, competing with each other. The women group also play an indigenous game called *Thulo-va*, played with a seed of creeper plant peer group wise. Wrestling, the most popular sport item of the Angamis is held during the Sekrenyi festival. Wrestling is done by applying one's hands around the back of the opponent and applying clever tricks so as to fall him flat on the ground. It is a great test of stamina needing great skills and energy (Zetsuvi, 2014, p.30).Young wrestlers are trained and prepared during the festival to participate in the inter-khel wrestling competition. *Khouthuo* (top spinning), *Mesi Kedzieguo* (muzzle loading gun competition), *Phita Meshü* (spear kicking) etc. are some of the other sports played during the Sekrenyi festival.

In all the festivals food constitute an important element. Like the other Naga tribes, rice beer and meat has been in use among the Angami people for centuries.The unique food system and culinary knowledge that have been inherited from one generation to another makes them culturally distinct. Sekrenyi is an occasion for unlimited consumption of *zutho* (rice beer) and meat. During the festival the best breed of pigs and cows are slaughtered for the feast. The festival manifests their ethnic food habits, surplus and the accumulation of wealth of the individual and the community. In short, the traditional food of the Angamis reflects their cultural identity. The Sekrenyi festival helps in the preservation of the traditional knowledge of food habits and transmission of the associated heritage.

During the festival, Angami men and women dress themselves in their best traditional attire. Sekrenyi festival not only serves as means to unite the community but also provides the occasion to display the rich material cultural traditions of the Angamis. The dresses and ornaments display the skill and artistic quality of the Angamis. Dress language has being seen to be a mirror of their culture and positively affects their culture in that it is used as a tool to transmit their cultural values and norms to the next generation. Shimray (1986) states that, dress is one of the most effective mediums of expression of preserving one's cultural identity (p. 220). In the olden days, during the festive season the art of craving new household articles and making traditional dresses has been taught to the sons and daughters by the parents or elders. While menfolk skilfully carve spoons, plates etc., for the festival, womenfolk weave shawls with different colours, patterns and designs which are worn during the festival. Through the festival, knowledge and skills related to crafting and weaving are transmitted orally from generation to generation both within and outside of the family circle.

Sekrenyi festival provides a rich set of practices and performances including forms of folk songs and dance. It offers an important way of socialising, providing a sense of rootedness and connection to the past. During the festival various forms of dance are performed. '*Phita*' (folk dance) are performed by young and the old comprising of both male and female. *Phita* is a folk dance in which dancers move their hands and legs in harmony with the rhythm of the songs on the different tunes and beats. The knowledge and skills of *Alo-khwe* (traditional male dance), *Mepfü* (shrill quivering yell) and *Ruüshükhwe* (demonstration art of warfare) are transmitted through demonstration. Warrior dance with furious movements depicting the act of contest/challenge against the enemy is performed by elder to the young generation. Young boys start to learn during the festive occasion by taking part in folkdance along with the older group of performers. This save these arts form from getting into oblivion.

Music is an indispensable part of Angami Sekrenyi festival. Feasting is always accompanied by singing of folk songs. During the festival the various peer groups spend hours feasting and singing. In the process the younger generations learn the folk songs from them. While singing the Angamis play a single string musical instrument called '*Tati*'. The folk songs composed on traditional themes are derived from oral discourse which is passed on from generation to generation. The folk song reflects the richness of thought and artistic talent of the Angamis. It also acts as the medium for the expression of ideas and emotions held in common by the community. Jadave (2013) points out that the cultural traits of their rich folk heritage can be discerned mostly in their folksongs and rhymes (p.65). It is vital mainspring in their traditional education and remit of the people's culture.

Conclusion

The Angami Sekrenyi festival is thus, not only an event of feasting but throw light on the various aspects of the Angami society, culture and tradition. It reflects the dynamic value systems of individuals united by the same customs, images, collective memory, habits and experiences. It is an occasion when they learn the basic principles of community living, folk songs, dance and folk-lore which were passed down from one generation to another through their memory in spoken language. Similarly, attire they adorn during celebration display, express and shape cultural identity, imbuing it with a directly material reality. Through the celebration of the festival the community feelings have been retained and are being revived to renew and reaffirm the Angami ethnic solidarity. The very acknowledgement and celebration of Sekrenyi festival continued to preserve and maintain the rich cultural heritage and also perpetuate the collective identity of the Angamis. Today, Sekrenyi festival has become the cultural identity of the Angami people fostering unity among them.

REFERENCES

Biswas, S. (2002). Preservation of Tribal Culture in Northeast India. In Sengupta (ed). *Tribal Studies in Northeast India.* New Delhi: Mittal Publication.

Haksar, Nandita. (2011). *ABC of Naga Culture and Civilisation.* Bibliophile South Asia.

Hutton, J. H. (1969). *The Angami Nagas.* London: Oxford University Press.

Jadave, Kishore. (2013). *Folklore and its Motifs in modern Literature.* New Delhi: Manas Publications.

Kikhi, K., D'Souza, A., Hibo, H. (2009). *Angami Society at the beginning of the 21st Century.* New Delhi: Akansha Publishing House.

Maitra, K. (1991). *Nagaland Darling of the North-East.* New Delhi: Mittal Publication.

Mathur, Nita. (1992). Religious Ethos of the Angami Nagas. In Subhadra Mitra Channa (Ed.) *Nagaland: A Contemporary Ethnography.* New Delhi: Cosmo Publication.

Nekha, K. N. (2015). *The Nagas: Culture and Education.* Dimapur: Heritage Publishing House.

Nshoga, A. (2009). *Traditional Naga Village System and its Transformation.* Delhi: Anshah Publishing House.

Shimray, R. R. (1986). *Origin and Culture of Nagas.* New Delhi: Somsok Publications.

Venuh, N. (2004). *Naga Society: Continuity and Change.* Delhi: Shipra Publication.

Verrier, Elwin. (1969). *The Nagas in the Nineteenth Century.* Oxford University Press.

Zetsuvi, K. S. (2014). *Traditional Culture of the Angami Nagas.* Dimapur: Heritage Publishing House.

14

Colonial and Postcolonial Imagery of the Early Nagas: Text, Context and the Discourse of Difference

TEMJENWABANG

I

> *Now a few words about these savages of the hills (the Aos and Angamis). They are run of blood and war. Their fighting is all hand to hand, with big knives and spears...But as our Indians prized a scalp, so these men glory in the head of a warrior; and as, among some of the tribes, a man is hardly considered a man till he has taken human life, so they are not always very particular whether the man they kill is an enemy or not, provided, if not an enemy, it is done in secrecy.* (E.W. Clark quoted in Barpujari1986, 267)

Throughout known human history, the march of society has revolved around the vices as well as better aspects of civilization. Parallel to these developments, somewhere back in time, in a 'secluded' corner of the Northeastern part of India, Nagas are believed to have actively indulged in a practice called 'head-hunting'. When the first 'histories' of the Nagas was put to writing by westerners; a significant body of descriptive writing by surveyors, soldiers and administrators, anthropologists and missionaries began to build up. Ever since then, Europeans have struggled to make sense of the apparent 'ethnographic chaos' they perceived around them (Imsong, 2004: 2). There came the multitude of descriptions of the Nagas. They represented the Naga inhibited areas as the abode of savages, barbarians and blood-thirsty head hunters: "We found the Assamese Valley surrounded north, east, and south by numerous savage and warlike tribes whom the decaying authority of the Assam dynasty had failed of late years to control..." (Mackenzie, 1884: 7). These were the first assumptions made to the unknown Naga land (apart from the people in the plains of Assam).

With regard to this, contemporary perception on the early Nagas still fall within the boundaries of misconceptions and reality from inside as well as from outside. An interesting aspect to this is the portrayal of the early Nagas as 'savages' in most colonial writings as such this continues to be referred sporadically by the media, professionals, intellectuals and laymen alike. This is either in support of or against the term itself. To consider some contemporary opinions: *"Missionaries came from the West with western bias who called the tribal 'heathen', 'savage', 'wild', 'native' and 'uncivilized'... (Christianity) in the long run opened the minds of 'savage' and 'wild' people and began to change their social and cultural life"* (Bendangyabang, 1998: 272); *"Nagaland was once as dark as Sheol, the reason being the influence of demons was very great. The whole atmosphere was of fear which affected the daily life of big and small alike in addition to lawlessness in society"* (Epao, 1998: 20); Suriya (2004) also admittedly wrote that he entered "Nagaland burdened with preconceptions and prejudices" while Bonita Baruah (2004) echoed, "The North-East; unknown, remote, exotic and barbaric...and at best, a region to be regarded as a museum piece, a subject of anthropological study". Suriya further says that the Nagas themselves have lamented on the fact that most of the non-Nagas consider them as "those naked, dog-eating, headhunting savages". Welman (2005) observed that even before he made entry into Nagaland, he was informed that Nagaland as "a land full of headhunters and warmongers" (p. 9); and Jamir (2000) viewed that his fore-fathers' mode of contacts was mediated only through the "savage practice of headhunting" (p.7). There is, therefore, a vital link between the constructed image of the early Nagas and the received understanding of the same in the postcolonial context based on these diverse opinions and portrayals in literature. At best we can assume they were pre-mediated and pre-informed postcolonial opinions, assertions and statements. And to understand these postcolonial opinions, the dynamics and the diffusion of the idea from the colonial period should also be understood.

II

Across the continents, wherever colonialism happened, the colonial subjects were often placed under a Eurocentric prism to an extent the rich legacies of the societies were denied. When the colonial masters encountered the Nagas, this 'colonial rhetoric' came in the form of objectifying the Nagas as savages: "...the paths are panjeed and our 'savage' allies (Nagas) were of use in clearing away the obstructions" (McCabe, 1882); S.A. Perrine applauded M.M. Clark as "...the first woman messenger of the Cross to a savage tribe of head-takers in the Assam range of the Himalayas" (Purakal, 1984: 153); "The Nagas were warned not to take the law into their hands, and the planters advised to cultivate a good understanding with their savage neighbours and to avoid engaging hillsmen…" (Mackenzie, 98); "I would soon be among real 'savages'…" (Haimendorf, 1939: 2). These portrayals and depictions were linked to the perception of the writers and the contexts that inescapably dictated them. Indicative to understanding this context are works done by Patrick Moloney (2001) *Savagery and Civilization* who traces the Victorian discourse of savagery on the natives of New Zealand as well as the historical development of the usage of the term 'savage'; Simon Ryan's (1996) C*artographic Eye* discusses a similar situation of the aboriginals of Australia who were perceived and labeled as degenerate society by the European explorers and travelers in their writings; Dorinda Outram (1995) *The Enlightenment* locates the Tahitians within the European discourses on the 'civilized', the 'exotic' and the 'savages'; Toby Freund (2001) *Occidental Tourist* posits a discourse on the 'Iberians' by the Europeans in a similar context. All these writers observed there was a systematic project of subjecting societies under the Occidental paradigm and Eurocentric cosmos. Inspired by the Lanmarckian and Darwinian Theories (Murray, 1979: 95) they labeled the various societies to the perceived or observed hierarchy in their normative scale of Civilization.

Although the discourse on savagery has begun since the sixteenth century (Breisach, 1983: 178), it was only by the end of the eighteenth century that a standardized description of savagery gained currency in Britain which was popularly considered as a condition of 'vagrant liberty'; savage nations were nomadic, lacking any permanent abode, and had no laws. According to Moloney (2001), Adam Smith used this theoretical construct where savage nations were understood to lack property rights in the territory they occupied, and were therefore valuable to acquisitions of territory by European states as an ideological justification for the Europeans to dominate over other societies (p. 154). By the turn of the 19th Century, savagery was considered as a stage in human development. But the Europeans used this scale to affirm and re-create their own identity. While the savage state was the antithesis of their commercial and civilized society, it was also a picture of their infancy. It would excite nostalgia and romanticism, but also embarrassment and rejection (Marnie, 2004: 340-341). It is also through this virtue that Marx defined a capitalist society emerging from a feudal society; Weber was to write about the rationalization and the disenchantment of the old world; Durkheim about the change from mechanical to organic forms of solidarity. Each conceived of the new world in contrast to 'traditional society'; and behind this 'traditional society' they discerned a primitive or primeval society (Kuper, 1988: 4). The influence of this trend is evident on later scholarships, especially when Hodson (1922) gave a powerful introductory in his study; *The Primitive Culture of India* (1922): "...existing savage races are not merely peoples who have been left behind in the stream of progress... we can safely accept the primitive character of their mentality and take them as guides to the history of mental development, though they are very questionable value as guides to the order of social development" (p.1). There was a standardized model of savagery created by the Western discourse that underpinned European policy and practice on the other societies in the first half of the nineteenth century (Freund, 2001: 1). By then, it has become a powerful ideology used by different groups to meet their justifying ends. And in doing so, the meaning underwent changes in order to accommodate the justifications and as Said (1978) puts it in his seminal work Orientalism, 'classificatory practices in knowledge construction' (p. 202).

The generous and non-critical usage of the label like savagery and its persistence, even sporadically, suggest that mapping mentalities in the texts and contexts were overlooked, if not ignored by most postcolonial studies. The treatment of the Nagas as savage had varying degrees according to the background of the colonial observers. For the administrators it was a civilizational distinction between the superior and the inferior: F.E.Younghusband is said to have opined that "no European can mix with non-Christian races without feeling his moral superiority over them…our superiority over them is not due to mere sharpness of intellect, but to the higher moral nature to which we have attained in the development of the human race" (cited Bell, 1994: 177). For anthropologists they considered this treatment to be devoid of societal prejudices and anomalies. Like their most reflective societies, they looked back in order to understand the nature of the present, on the assumption that modern society had evolved from its antithesis. Finally missionaries, the term stood synonymous with 'heathen', 'wild', 'nimrods', 'barbaric', 'headhunters' and 'savages'. The dominance of the Christian worldview is apparent in Clark's writing when she observes, "… in this rude population-largely demon-worshippers- is found a virgin soil, the richest in all this valley for gospel seed-sowing"…"The Nagas, once civilized and Christianized, will make a manly, worthy people" (p.3). This justified the triumph of Christianity as a great leap towards 'civilization'. In all these treatments, the term 'savage' stood in as a key label of the Nagas. Thapar's statement echoes in this context: "*In the writing of Indian history, we have become accustomed to packaging our past and identifying it with labels.*

Such labels, even where they may include a variety of activity and experience, tend to force interpretation into a single category so that the infinite shades of difference within them disappear. When this happens, the historical perspective comes to be governed by the tyranny of labels: a condition which requires the historical unpacking of the categories and redefining of the contents" (Thapar, 1996: 3).

III

Beyond the conditioned perception and portrayal, there lies a 'paradigm' which influenced 'repeated portrayal' of the Nagas as savages. Most of the Europeans who wrote on the Nagas lived and interacted with them, have appreciated their ways of life, hospitality, the generosity and their bravery, but have often portrayed the Nagas as savages. J.P. Mills contended that the "Naga customs and practices is incomparably better than that of a Western city dweller" (Mills, Fifth Pacific Science congress, 1933) though he still considered the Nagas as savages. An underlying factor to this dichotomy is the determination to be always different from the Nagas, a strong sentiment many European observers shared in their interaction with many other societies. This 'discourse of difference' was a justification, not to the Nagas but to their European counterparts. The need to justify that in spite of living and working among the Nagas, they were still Europeans, different from the Nagas becomes evident through such persistence in their writings: "...We like to be in correspondence with the outside - the civilized and the Christian world! Ours is a dark, dark corner. O, so dark would it be to us, were it not for the light of the countenance of the blessed Redeemer, shining in our pathway! (Clark's letter of 1871 cited in Bendangyabang, 1998: 42). In most cases, the colonial authors came forth as 'heroes' in their narratives. And at stages, even if the authors were not threatened, it is nevertheless still possible for the authors to present the indigenous as inherently dangerous situation so as to reflect a meaner and larger-than-life image of the subjects under discussion to the readers and listeners drawing in awe and admiration to the 'heroes' of the narratives. The distancing of the 'observer' from the 'observed', and disassociation from the subject society maintained an exotic, romanticized difference that the West had always maintained: "*...This is a fine book for vacation reading. It smells of the forests, kindles the imagination, warms the heart, is better than a novel, for it is not only full of romance, but is true*". W.E.Witter's introductory on M.M.Clark's, *A corner in India*; Haimendorf: *The Naked Nagas* and *Return to the Naked Nagas* (Chapter VII, *Fishing with the Tactful Savages*). Peter Robb (1997) says that in the course of thenineteenth century, as evangelical, romantic and utilitarian influences grew, and as the British rule became more established, "the difference was emphasized" (p. 29).

All these discourses seem to have emerged from an 'anthropological treatment of other cultures' that was already taking place in the West (Kuper, 1988: 8). According to Cohn (1997) anthropology became a "cultural project of colonialism" (pp. 11-12). Colonial anthropology envisaged and encouraged colonial officers *as well as anthropologists* (italics mine) to make more systematic studies of the language and culture of the peoples they administered, which were subsequently embodied into administrative strategy (Bush, 1999: 36). British anthropology 'constructed a distinct identity' dependent on its relationship with imperialism. From administrators and anthropologists to the missionaries and lay Europeans, the anthropological treatment of other cultures took place within the colonial discourse. Earl Winterton's remark on the Nagas, "that is the most interesting ethnological race of people divided by 500 or 1000 years from the rest of India", stands witness to the then ongoing discourse going on in the West (as cited by Elwin, 1961: 58).

The savagery-civility context also reflected in the first generations of the Westernised Nagas who unwittingly underwent a process of alienation and negation within as observed by many: *"Ao pastors encouraged the Ao Christians to go out of the village to show contempt for heathen customs"* (Hutton, 1919-1920); "To be a new believer, one has to shed or to do away with all the customs and practices of the traditional way of life. Thus Christianity had a profound impact that led to unforeseen results" (Yhome, 2001: 70-71); "the Naga saw his own customs condemned by the missionaries; he learns to despise his own tribe and cultural inheritance. Christianity and Naga culture seem to him (the Naga) opposite poles" (Haimendorf, 1939: 54-55).

Conclusion

According to Sen (2004), defining the 'other' was an exercise to accommodate and appeal to defining the 'self' (pp.109-129). The discourse on the 'savage societies' was a binary construction of 'self' and 'other'. The Westerners who extensively observed and wrote on the Nagas were products of a larger discourse that was taking place in Europe. Each group had a context - the administrators' depiction reflected superiority, the anthropologists' depiction identified a stage in the societal progress towards civilization, and the missionaries' portrayal as based on their Christian worldview that many 'societies living in the darkness' or ignorant about the 'Gospel' were indeed 'savages' whose conditions needed to be brought out from darkness to light towards, modernism and civilization through the 'Gospel' and 'education'.

That the continuum in most of the postcolonial writings on the Nagas highlights attempts to disassociate the postcolonial Naga society from their ancestral past; there was 'othering' within the Nagas - the 'other' being the Naga ancestors. As of what initiated the discourse, we can premise that the colonial imagery on the early Nagas is ethnographic in nature and hence devoid of enabling historical narratives. This then brings in other implications, firstly, colonial imagery of the early Nagas as 'savage' was an offshoot of Western ethnographic discourse of self and the other; secondly, this imagery was internalized in the postcolonial context; thirdly, this operated within a discourse of difference. From an enlightened modern perspective, the postcolonial writers and readers picked up the label 'savage' and interpreted it in the light of the contemporary context which has very negative connotations. In other words, the meaning of the term 'savage' of the contemporary context underwent changes over the long historical development; as such contemporary parlances equated it. Since portrayals become a historical symbolism, the residual elements of the western discourse on savagery will continue to remain relevant so as long as there is no effort to re-map mentalities in resolving the conflicting worldviews.

REFERENCES

Ao, A. Bendangyabang. (1998). *History of Christianity in Nagaland: A Source Material.* Bangalore: Shalom Ministry Publications.

Barpujari, H. K. (1986). *The American Missionaries and North East India: 1896-1900 A.D.* Guwahati and Delhi: Spectrum Publications.

Baruah, B. (2004, October 10). The North-East: The India we don't Know. *Special Report; Sunday Times of India*. Hyderabad.

Breisach, E. (1983). *Historiography: Ancient, Medieval, and Modern*. Chicago and London: The University of Chicago Press.

Bush, B. (1999). *Imperialism, Race and Resistance*. London and New York: Routledge.

Clark, M. M. (1907). *A Corner in India*. Philadelphia: American Baptist Publication Society. Reprint Gauhati: Christian Literature center (1978).

Cohn, Bernard S. (1997). *Colonialism and its Forms of Knowledge: The British in India*. New Delhi: Oxford University Press.

Elwin, V. (1961). *Nagaland.*Shillong: Research Department, Adviser's Secretariat.

Epao, V. (1998). *From Naga Animism to Christianity*. (2nd edition). Dimapur: Hindustan Print-o-Print.

Freund, T. (2001). The Occidental Tourist: Discover, Discourse, and Degeneracy in S. Africa. *Michigan Journal of History*. Retrieved October 6, 2018 https://michiganjournalhistory.files.wordpress.com/2014/02/freund_toby_the_occidental_tourist-1.pdf

Furer-Haimendorf, Christoph Von. (1939).*The Naked Nagas: Head Hunters of Assam in Peace and War. London:*Meuthen & co. Ltd.(Reprint 2004). Guwahati, Delhi: Spectrum Publications.

Gregory, D., Ron Martin and Graham Smith. (1994). *Human Geography: Society, Space and Social Science*. New York: Palgrave Macmillan.

Hodson, T. C. (June 30, 1909). Head-Hunting among the Hill Tribes of Assam. *Folklore*, 20(2).

Hughes-Warrington, M. (2004).*Fifty Great Thinkers in History.* London and New York: Routledge.

Hutton, J. H. (n.d.). *Memoir of time in the Naga Hills as a Deputy Commissioner 1919-1920.* Digital Himalaya Project. Retrieved August 1, 2018, from http://himalaya.socanth.cam.ac.uk/collections/naga/coll/23/records/list/coll/index.html

Imsong, A. (2004). *Myth and Ancient History: Case-study of Ao-Naga Myths.* (unpublished M.phil. dissertation) Department of History: University of Hyderabad.

Jamir, S. C. (2000, July).*Bedrock of Naga Society.*(2nd edition). Nagaland Pradesh Congress Committee.

Kuper, A. (1988).*The Invention of Primitive Society: Transformation of an Illusion.* London and New York: Routledge.

Mackenzie, A. (1884).*The North East Frontier of India.* (Photo reproduction). Mittal Publications: New Delhi, 1999.

McCabe. R. B. (n.d.).Tour Diaries of Deputy Commissioner, Naga Hills, 1880-1882. *Assam Secretariat, APPTT and Political Department, Political Branch, 1882*: File No-13, Record Cell, Kohima.

Mills, J. P. (1933). The Effect of the Naga Tribe of Assam of their contact with Western Civilization. Fifth Pacific Science congress, Victoria, Vancouver.

Moloney, P. (2001, October).Savagery and Civilization: Early Victorian Notions.*New Zealand Journal of History,* 35(2).

Murray J. L. (1979).*Man, Mind and Science.* New York: Columbia University Press.

Parasher-Sen, A. (2004). *Subordinate and Marginal Groups in Early India*(Ed.). Delhi: Oxford University Press.

Purakal, J. P. (1984).*Baptist Missions in Nagaland.* Calcutta: Firma KLM Pvt. Ltd.

Said, E. (1978). *Orientalism.* London: Routledge.

Suryia, J. (2004, October 9). No dogs, please, we're Indians. *Times of India*: Hyderabad.

Yhome, K. (2001). *Origins of Naga Political Consciousness in the Early Twentieth Century.* (unpublished M.Phil Dissertation). Department of History: University of Hyderabad.

15

The Study of Customs and Traditions in Khezhakeno Village: Some Reflections on Changes and Continuity

VELHOU KOZA & TSUTSHOWE-Ü SEKHAMO

Introduction

Custom is a universal practice and each society has their own specific way of doing something. They are means to preserve a culture and transmit it to the succeeding generations. Custom is a common way of doing things; it acts as an effective means of social control. In simple words, Customs are the long established habits and usages of the people, while tradition contributes a sense of comfort and belonging. Custom is a social phenomenon and are the often repeated practices of the people. According to Kingsley Davis, *Customs refers primary to practices that have often been repeated by a multitude of generations, practices that tend to be followed simply because that they have been followed in the past* (Rao, 2015). It is the socially accepted ways in which people do things together in personal contacts. Tradition, on the other hand, refers to the beliefs and practices handed down from the past. Traditionalists see tradition as static. They urge that the traditional values and practices have to be adopted and preserved because they were found useful in the past. They are thus hostile to innovations that violate previous practices. According to Edward Shils, tradition or traditionalistically – oriented action is a "self-conscious deliberate affirmation of traditional norms, in full awareness of their traditional nature" (Ahuja, 2005).

Culture and society are essentially related as no human society can exist without culture and no culture can exist except in a society. Therefore, all changes in culture bring about social change. Changes in any aspect of culture, material or non-material are cultural change. Such changes take place because of diffusion and acculturation. Culture change also takes place through internal development-inventions and discoveries (Kikhi, 2012).

Africa is the origin place for myriad tribes. Presently there are about 3,000 diverse African tribes, each generating their own fascinating tribal traditions and customs. Some display love for the opposite sex through C*ourtship Dance* (Wodaabe tribe of Niger), while others showcase their rich attires in the W*edding Ceremony* (Ndebele, South Africa). *The Bull Jumping* of the Hamar is performed to bring dignity to both the initiate and his family. *Spitting of the Maasai* of Kenya and Northern Tanzania is performed to wish someone good luck and blessings while the *Ritualistic Healing Dance* of the San of South Africa, Namibia, Botswana and Angola is performed to cure diseases. The *Lip Plates* of the Mursi and the *Red Ochre* of the Himba is a traditional way practiced by these women for adornment (Lesley Marchant, 2018). From these multiple examples one can detect that each practice is unique and has its own reason for functioning in the society.

In the same manner, Naga society has its own rich cultural practices that have been passed down from generation to generation. Nagas have found a way to preserve their culture through customs and traditional practices. Folklores and myths help in remembering certain important events or to immortalize warriors of their village. The ornaments and particularly the clothes of the Nagas reflect a concern for minute identification of social organisations and status. The designs and colour of clothes symbolize ascribed status such as village, clan, and morung membership and achieved status arising from head taking and feasting exploits (Jacobs, 1990).

This paper is an attempt to appreciate some of the customs and traditions of Khezhakeno village. It will analyze the changes undergone and the impact it has on the village. Some of the essential customs and traditions of the village such as food, festivals, dress, marriage system, oath taking, traditional games, and honorary ritual *Xhachi* and so on are reflected in this paper. The study on customs and traditional practices of Khezhakeno village are based on the primary data collected from the research fieldwork. The list of the participants (respondents) in this study is indicated at the reference list. The secondary data were gathered from different sources such as books, website and souvenir. The study thus aims to project the changes and continuity in relation to customs and traditional practices of Khezhakeno village.

Brief Background of the Village

Khezhakeno is a village located in Phek district of Nagaland. The village is well known as a historical site and one of the oldest migratory trajectories undertaken by some Nagas. This ancestral site derived its name from 'Khezha' language '*Kozabomi*' which means, *the native people of Kozu*. The village is divided into three khels i.e. Upper khel (*Chisomi*), Middle khel (*Zhipfhemi*) and Lower khel (*Komuno*). *Chisomi* khel comprises of two sub-khels called *Tepfuno* and *Abvümi* while *Zhipfhemi* khel has *Thasomi* and *Tshemiladumi* as the sub-khels. Some of the historical sites or monuments of Khezhakeno village are *Zhinhaka* (Nose of the lake), *Chinisabe*, *Tso Tawo* (Spirited Stone) and *Tsopoupe Chitude* (a stone believed to touch the sky). At present the village is declared as a Christian village. Language constitutes an essential element of culture. The Kozabomi (people of Khezhakeno) speak the dialect called as *Kozale*.

Custom and Traditions of Khezhakeno

The people of Khezhakeno preserve their customs and traditions in the form of folklores, folksongs, dress and games etc. Some old practices are still evident in day to day social habits and activities. The performance of traditional songs and dance is an essential custom of this village. In various occasions or feast, *Lü* (song) and *Salü* (traditional song in Khezha dialect) are performed to entertain the crowd. A funeral rite called *Pra-Tshü* is performed on the events of death of a villager. Domestic animals are slaughtered and their meats are distributed to the villagers, either to the whole village or some selected few. Before the colonial period, the people of Khezhakeno have various customs and traditional practices and from which some significant practices are discussed below.

Rünyie

Rünyie is a festival and celebrated during December month after all the harvest is done. In Khezha language, *Rü* means Paddy and *Nyie* means Festival. This festival is celebrated to prevent any bad omens and seek blessings for the newly harvested paddies. *Bulie* rite and fasting are performed during this time. It is interesting to note that the Kozami or Kozabomi perform fasting only during this festival time (Fasting in Khezha dialect is also known by *Tekukhu, Lua* or *Movoa).* This is followed by feast and celebration where young boys will blow *Kobolichie* instrument and buffalo horns (horns can be blown only during this specific period). Girls will play an indigenous game called *Tholotsü. Rünyie* festival lasts for about 3 months and irrespective of rich and poor, everyone will gather together and drink rice beer. This festival is also known by another name called *Kenyikhrü.* Other important festivals of Khezhakeno village *are Lekhenyie, Selunyie, Rünyie,* and *Neikoe* (*Lawonyie*).

Xhachi

Xhachi (offering meat and rice beer) is a traditional practice of the people in Khezhakeno. It is practiced to honour their parents and elders. Through this the youngsters demonstrate their love and respect for them. In this, rice beer filled in a clean dried gourd and a plate filled with cooked meat is distributed to the elders in the month of December. This old custom of *Xhachi* is practised even today with some alteration i.e. rice beer is not used.

Pumi-xhachi is another similar practice or an extension of *Xhachi.* It is the custom of offering cooked meat to the elders of family and clan members. *Pumi-xhachi* is performed mainly to get the blessings of the elderly people. A noteworthy point observed in this practice is that, on the death of the elderly person, three basket of paddy will be distribute to all those person who have given him meat when he/she was alive.

Bulie

Practiced in the month of November, *Buliekhrü* derived its name from *Bulie* ritual. In this ritual, the villagers pray to the Supreme Being to bless the newly harvested paddy (*Rube* in Khezha). The ritual is for bountiful harvest so that the family can survive with it until next harvest. As per the ritual, the recently harvested paddy would be taken out from the *Bu* (*Granary basket*) and dried (*Pho*) in the sun. After this, rice chaff (*Be Mimhi)* is removed and the paddy would be brought and stored back in the *Bu.* While pouring the paddy into the *Bu,* they would utter/say *Toh Mupu Molo* (May it never fall short/finishes). They would also take out a small portion of grains for *Rü-Michi* (Paddy Seedling). In case of spouses *Kaminhi* rituals were performed for three days, whereas, for the widows *Tomemi*, it was a day affair (Zehol and Zehol, 2015: 18).

During *Bulie* ritual, common people also called as *Kozabomi* fast for one day i.e. from morning till evening. On the other hand, *Chimi* or *Rich People* who have performed the *Feast of Merit* will fasts for three days. During fasting period they drink only the water that has been soaked in handful of ritual performed rice. In this ritual called *Bulie,* few pieces of grains of paddy are collected from each granary which is soaked in water. On the third day, around evening, the owners of the house cuts a branch from the oak tree and stick the fresh branch at the entrance of their houses. After this the fast is considered complete and he can have his meal. Once the fasting ritual is completed, on the 4th day, cows are set free from the village and let loose to the jungle, that same night trumpets were blown to signify the coming days for feast and festival.

Dress and Indigenous Method for Producing Textiles Materials

Primitive technological methods were used for manufacturing clothes. The locals produce clothes mainly for personal consumption. Materials required for weaving were collected from the tree barks locally called *Khro* and *Medimelü* (*Medimelü* produces light reddish colour). The collected bark is dried, soaked and later peeled into thin threads. The peeled one is cooked with ash and water and later taken to the river, beatenand washed thoroughly. Once cleaned, the threads are dried in the sun and the process of weaving starts. The materials woven from these plants usually last for ten years and up till 1950s this method was largely practiced in the village.

Since the method for manufacturing was not easy and quantity of clothes produced were less, young boys start covering themselves only when they reach the age of 10 and girls at age 7 or 8. *Chichümüna* and *Zho Mene is* short-length wrap around worn by men. Women cover the lower part of the body with a cloth wrap around. The upper part of the body is covered with a small cloth that will be tied on one side of the shoulder, locally called *Lashe Menyi*. Rich women, on the other hand use two clothes i.e. *Lashe Menyi* and *Rhasorha*. Some elder womenfolk in the village still knows the process of producing the materials made from natural fibres but they don't practice that anymore due to modern influence. It thus becomes essential to preserve such traditional methods of manufacturing clothes. Traditional shawls like *Kozara*, *Kozara'*, *Medimelüra*, *Tophara*, *Thovora* and *Khrora* are worn by men and *Kapomene* (Wrap Around) are worn by women in olden days.

Rice Beer

Rice has been the staple food for the Nagas from ancient times. It is also the reality that some Nagas being fond of local drinks, half of the rice cultivated goes in the manufacture of local drink called rice beer. Consumption of traditional rice beer was considered as a part of staple food by the *Kozami* ancestors. Rice beer is brewed from local sticky rice (*Mvükrürü Be*). Before Christianity, Khezhakeno people in general preferred drinking rice beer instead of water and so huge quantity of rice was used for manufacturing the local beer. This in turn can lead to economic loss. It was also a custom to serve rice beer and meat during the festivals or feast to the family members, neighbours or guests. However, with the change of time, practice of drinking traditional rice beer declined. Other daily commodities for consumption are green leaves attained from garden or forest. Except for rice beer,the consumption habits of the locals remain similar to this day.

Thozo

Thozo (thozozo) in Khezha dialect means test of luck. The significance of *Thozo* is to test their luck on whether they could hunt animals or not when they go for hunting. It will show signs on whether they will be successful in their search for animals. A plant known as *Lenu* in Khezha dialect is used to perform this ritual. Hunting was very common in the traditional time in Khezhakeno and they took keen interest in huntingwild animals and birds. The Kozabomi people would preserve the various animal skulls that they had hunted during their time.

Traditional Games

Since early times, *Mono* (Wrestling) remained a very popular sport. This sport is played especially after the harvesting season. On the event of the game, two elders from opposite side select a player each for the match and scoring is based on best of three.The winner can also challenge anyone or vice versa. Wrestlers of different villages challenging the champion were common. The challenger can challenge the opponent anywhere and anytime. If the challenger is defeated, as a custom they will quietly go back to their own village. It is also considered a great shame for the defeated village. Some other indigenous and traditional games are *Thucho* (High Jump), *Phekete* (Traditional Bamboo Race) and *Tsoliphe* (Go Carting) and *Tholotsü* is (Traditional game played by the girls in the village).

Tashü (Oath)

When any conflict or disputes arises between individuals or groups an act of *Tashü* (Oath Taking) is performed to claim one's right. Oath taking is known to all the Nagas, some takes the soil in the hand and take oath to prove their innocence while others look for signs in cutting of a bamboo, eating a segment of soil from the disputed land. Stumbling while walking is also considered as a sign of guilt and this is another method for oath taking. The method of oath taking is also prevalent among the *Kozabomis.* During the *Rünye* time, right before the feasting part, the khels will gather in their respective meeting place (an raised platform). *Mowo* (Chief/Priest) will state all the misfortunes that will befall upon those people who are guilty of any crime. After his every sentence, all the men folk will repeat after him, accepting the consequences if they take this oath wrongly. The oath, in short stated that those who use black magic, poison, steal, seduce other's women will lose everything and vanish.

In the past, for Khezhakeno people, oath taking was considered something very sacred and no one dared to take oath to support a guilty man. Apart from an individual oath taking, there are two more types of oath taking. First is *Chu Phu*, where clan members will take oath in support the victim/accused. If oath is falsely taken, it is believed that curse will befall upon the whole clan. Second type is *Lekha Tophu*, where family members will take oath in support of the victim/accused. In this case curse will befall on the family and his generations if the oath is faulty.

Zatsü

Zatsü is a status given to an individual when he completes a series of feasting ritual. A ritual performed under this is systematic and takes years to complete. This ritual is concerned with feasting the whole village and for this not everyone can perform it. The person who plans to feast the whole village first will butcher three or four buffaloes. The meat is distributed to the whole village so that they can cook and bring it on the feasting day and the owner will provide them local rice beer. In the first year, after harvest, the concerned person performs *Meyie* where he hosts feast for the whole village with local rice beer. After a year or two, if he can afford another feast, than he can perform *Yiepa* for the whole village. The succeeding year, he can perform, *Zatsu* which will continue for two days (also called *Lhepho* and *Tasiso)*. After this the villagers will erect a monolith in his name. After this he is eligible to wear two shawls i.e. *Liketsura* (buffalo head shawl) and *Terüde* (shawl with big white stitch). Only those who have performed a ritual called

Zatho can also use a cup known as *Whutha*. In Khezha dialect, *Whu* means Banana and *Tha* means Long. The name *Whutha* is derived from the way the cup is made, banana leaf stitched with bamboo fibre.

Gathering of the Youths

Youth gathering is an old traditional practice of the Kozabomi community and has been practiced up to this day with some modification. In the past, a group of boys will select one particular *Lüzü* (Girl's dormitory) of their choice and offer *Se* (basket of meat) to them who shares the meat amongst themselves. In return they invite the boys and provide brewed rice beer for them. On that day the boys will sit in one corner and the girls will sit in another corner. They will drink beer and tease or praise each other. The girls were so bashful that they will show only their face and cover everything with a shawl. Boys will tease them stating that they can see their toe and the girls will quickly cover it. This practice continued for a long time however in due course of time modification came with the influence of Christianity. At present with the inclusion of some old ideas, such youth gatherings are done outside the church premises or in respective *khels*, usually after the harvest season.

Marriage system

Khezhakeno village permits the monogamous form of marriage. The marriage system in the traditional and modern day in Khezhakeno village is different. The study indicated that their traditional marriage system was quite ritualistic. When the son attain the age of marriage his parents sends proposal through the elders who act as middleman. Once consented, two elderly men will go to pick up the bride. On their way back one older man will walk in the front and the other behind the bride. The bride will carry local rice beer which will be consumed after they reach the groom's house. The man walking behind will not enter the groom's house but the man in front will take the bride inside the house. Before entering the old man will place an iron item usually a spade (*Kapfü*) on the doorway and let the girl step on it before entering. This custom is practiced so that the bride maintains her cool temperament. Later two young boys will be invited and sweet rice beers were offered. These boys will be asked to sing a song and once they do the marriage ceremonial will be considered complete. For the male child, the older brother has to leave the parents' house and live in a separate house however they will get better field. When the youngest son gets married, parents usually leave the house and give the house to the youngest son.

Trial marriage in olden times was practiced in Khezhakeno village. It signifies the traditional way of selecting life partners for a boy and a girl by undergoing the procedures of marriage system. Bride and the groom perform a ritual known as *Bo De* wherein they will remain locked inside the house on the first day after marriage. The *Kozabomis* (people of Khezhakeno) practice trial marriage which lasts for three days. In the olden days it was customary for girls to have short hairs before marriage, so the desire to keep long hairs made them agree to marry anyone who proposes her. After the trail marriage is completed, the girl gets the liberty to stay or leave her husband. If she decides to leave and go back to her parents, then she will be called as *Nheyi/Lheyi* (Once Married). With the change of time, various changes were brought in the marriage system. Parents do not take active role in selection of life partners anymore.

The influence of western education brought by the Christian missionaries also changed the matrimonial system and hence the village don't practice the old system anymore.

Conclusion

With the advent of Christianity, modernization, westernization and advancement of technology, some old customs and traditions have been altered in the Naga society. The advent of Christianity in Nagaland especially has brought tremendous transformation. With the transition of time along with the other societies, Khezhakeno village also have undergone changes. The people of Khezhakeno have effectively adapted to the changes which is observable through various aspects such as religion, house construction, dress, food habits and professions. At the same time, attempts were made to uphold some of their traditional customs and practices and are still in use. With the coming of Christianity in the village, festivals of Christianity such as Christmas, Easter Sunday have great significance and celebrated enthusiastically. Even to this day, the custom of *Xhachi* is prevalent and is performed during Christmas time with certain modifications.Nowadays, with relatives and families scattered in different places, instead of cooked meat, raw meats are usually sent to the elders as a practice of *Xhachi* (an act of honour to relatives). In the past, *Bulie* rites were performed where people fast for three days. At present, fasting for three days is also common.The only difference is that, now fasting is performed to please Jesus and not the Supreme Being.To this day, gatherings of youths in the form of campfires are still practiced where they have a time of excitement or merry making. In trial marriage, as the girls want to keep long hairs they ended up marrying anyone who proposes her first irrespective of choices. With the advent of Christianity, trial marriage practice is not prevalent in the village. The influence of western education brought by the Christian missionaries has changed the matrimonial system.

The system of passing knowledge in the form of folktales and folk song is still practiced. Stone erection is still practiced on important days like memorials or agreements. Old customs and traditions continued to strive despite the changes and thus help in retaining their ethnicity. It is evident from the study that though the *Kozabomi* people have accepted the changes yet these new customs and practices have not let them to completely abandon their traditional culture. Though the description of all the customs could not be elaborated in detail, this study portrays the rich culture, customs and traditions which define ones identity and uniqueness in Khezhakeno village.

REFERENCES

Ahuja, Ram. (2005). *Indian Social System*. New Delhi: Rawat Publications.

Jacob, Julian. (1990). *Hill People of Northeast India: The Naga Society, Culture and the Colonial Encounter*. London: Thames and Hudson Ltd.

Rao, C. N Shankar. (2015). *Sociology- Principles of Sociology with an Introduction to Social Thought*. New Delhi: S. Chand and Company Pvt. Ltd.

Zehol, Lucy and Zehol, Kevekha Kevin. (December, 2015). Festivals: A Celebration of Life - The Naga Case-A Reflection. In Chisomi Youth Organisation, Khezhakeno Village. *Golden Jubilee Souvenir*, p.18.

Lesley, Marchant. (August 13, 2018).7 *Amazing African Tribal Traditions*.

https://blog.rhinoafrica.com/2018/08/13/7-amizing-africa.com. 30-10-2019. 10 pm.

Personal Interview with

Thochü Koza, Male. Personal Interview. 22-10-2019.Khezhakeno Village.

Tirilhou-o Koza, Female. Personal Interview.23-10-2019. Khezhakeno Village.

Athou Koza, Female. Personal Interview. 25-10-2019.Khezhakeno Village.

Avi Koza, Male. Personal Interview. 24-8-2019.Khezhakeno Village.

16

From Traditional to Modern: A Discourse on Education and Subsequent Cultural Change in Mizo Society

LALLIANZUALI CHHANGTE

Every society has a culture that exerts a strong influence on the actions and beliefs of its members. Just as culture is universal, education is also part of any given culture. The concept of 'Culture' was first explicitly defined in 1871 by the British Anthropologist Edward Burnett Tylor. He used the term to refer to "that complex whole which includes knowledge, belief, art, morals, law, custom, and any other capabilities and habits acquired by man as a member of society" (Tyler, 1871: 1). Since then, anthropologists and other social scientist have offered numerous refinements and variations on this definition, but all have agreed that culture is learned behaviour in contrast to genetically endowed behaviour. Education in its broadest sense may be understood as a wholesome process of human learning by which knowledge is generated and passed on from one generation to another. Some people regard education as the process by which individuals are helped to become the best they can become based on their ability, whereas others see education as the development of the intellect through which the learners acquire essential cognitive and social skills and perennial knowledge (Pai, 1990: 3). Whatever perspectives one may have, there is no denying that education is a crucial socio-cultural process. Education and culture are intimately connected. Culture influences and shapes education, while education in turn influences and shapes culture. No part of the educative process, neither its contents nor products, is free from cultural influences (Pai, 1990: 4). On the other hand, education affects culture by influencing how people think, believe, judge and act. According to George F. Kneller (1971), "Education is the means by which society provides for the transmission of its culture, for without a viable culture, there is no common life by which men are associated. Education may be defined as the inculcation of knowledge, values, skills and attitudes by means of institutions that have been created for this end" (p. 50).

Both education and culture have remained an integral subject matter among scholars of different disciplines in Mizoram. Several works are available concerning Western education in Mizoram. As formal education began with the arrival of the British, some British administrators and missionaries have given information on the growth of formal education and British policy towards education in the Lushai Hills in their reports. In the post-Independence period, scholars have worked on various aspects of education such as the growth of education, educational administration, educational systems ranging from elementary to university, from training to technical institutions etc. Notable among the history of education in Mizoram are those by Lalbiakliana (1979) and J. V. Hluna (1992). An interesting work on the topic is that of Laksmi Bhatia, in which she tries to explore and analyze the critical aspects of education and society. She has attempted to understand the Mara community of Mizoram through the lens of education. Likewise, many scholars such as Lal Dena (1988), Sangkima (1992), Chittaranjan Nag (1993), Nunthara (1996), Mangkhosat Kipgen (1997), have worked on the changes in Mizo society. However, emphasis have been mainly on Christianity and the impact of colonialism on Mizo society. In view of all the works related to education and culture, there was hardly any study that critically examined the inter-relationship between culture and education. To fill up the gap in the cultural history of Mizoram, I have worked on the various factors, patterns and spheres of change and continuity in Mizo society and culture. The relationship between education and culture occupies an integral part of my ICCSR Sponsored Post-Doctoral Research (Chhangte, 2021). This paper is primarily based on the project report.

This paper examines the concept, methods and practice of traditional Mizo education. Also, it highlights the process of how Western education replaced the conventional system of education which in turn brought about numerous changes in Mizo culture. In this study, traditional education has been used to refer to the method of education practised in the pre-colonial period and the formal or Western education introduced during the colonial period by the British.

I

The traditional Mizo society was a close-knit and homogenous society based on shifting cultivation where each family strived to produce enough for a year. Extensive cooperation within the family and in the community was vital to survive amidst rugged hilly terrain and occasional threats from their enemies. Hence, the education of the youth was part and parcel of the traditional culture. The main aim of traditional Mizo education was to produce an honest, respectable, skilled, and cooperative individual who conformed to the social order of the day. However, education was in no way structured or formalized; instead, the young ones learnt the necessary skills and knowledge through the situational observation of and participation in daily routine. After weaning in traditional society, children were cared for not only by the mother but increasingly by a wide range of other kin such as older siblings, aunts, uncles, and grandparents. Consequently, each child formed close ties with several kinsmen. They played freely during the day, which enabled them to explore their natural surroundings either alone or with siblings or playmates. Children engaged themselves in various games and activities, for instance, wrestling, jumping, climbing, racing, balancing and swimming, which enabled them to develop their physical well-being. Much of the children's play imitated the activities of their parents and thus rehearsed adult roles. The home was an important place where a child was moulded to become a responsible individual. Children were taught by parents the moral requirements of the community, and they were severely reprimanded if they behaved in improper manners. They were also taught the family history and knowledge necessary for survival in an agrarian society. Mealtime was usually the time when the family discussed important matters. Storytelling and proverbs were important pedagogical tools employed by parents and other extended family members to teach children about moral and ethical behaviours.

Traditional Mizo education was pragmatic as it emphasized total involvement and active participation of the learner. When boys reached five to six years, they usually accompanied the father at his workplaces or the jungle trapping wild animals and birds. They were also made to look after domestic animals like *mithun*s and goats. Boys were expected to bear hardships without complaints. Girls from a very early age helped their mothers in household chores, collecting water and firewood. Girls usually between the age group of six to twelve who could carry *em* (traditional basket) were called '*thingtang kai rual*'. After reaching the age of twelve, they were called '*tu ha hem rual*', and they began to accompany their parents in the fields. They were also made to learn spinning and weaving. Thus, girls were drilled in their future roles as home-makers. By early adolescence, Mizo children were already conversant with the topography of their community and could distinguish between fishing and hunting seasons and knew when to plant crops and when to harvest them.

An important feature of traditional education was its emphasis on promoting harmony and cooperation in the community. Traditional education sought to produce men and women who were not self-centred, putting the group's interest above their interest and dutifully fulfilling social obligations. It aimed to inculcate among the youths the spirit of *tlawmngaihna*, the traditional code of conduct that puts others above self. *Zawlbuk*, the bachelor's dormitory, played an important role in imparting these values to the youth. Boys were admitted to *Zawlbuk* when they reached the age of six or seven years. They became *Thingnawifawm* (those who collect firewood) boys. They were duty-bound to works related to laundry, running errands, collecting and carrying firewood for the *Zawlbuk* and also collecting bamboos and stones when graves were dug by the *tlangval* (bachelor). Names would be called out every morning and evening to ensure the attendance and performance of the works assigned. If any boy was found to evade his duty, he was disciplined by the young men in *Zawlbuk* in the presence of all the other boys. N. E. Parry remarked (1976), "The younger boys are obliged to work for the older, are taught to wrestle, are punished when disobedient, and are generally imbued with a sense of public school spirit, with excellent effect on their character in afterlife" (p. 28). A boy was promoted from the status of a *thingnawifawm* boy to being an inmate of the *Zawlbuk* when he reached the age of fifteen. The bachelor members had to do all those heavy works and social services beyond the capacity of *thingnawifawm* boys. After dinner, young men would go to assemble at *Zawlbuk* for a light gossip to relieve their day's tedium. Apart from the young men, the older men and married men also paid a visit to tell the success story of some powerful chiefs, brave warriors, and the history of the people to those who gathered in the *Zawlbuk*. Therefore, besides acting as a place for training a person to be disciplined, obedient, industrious, and a fine hunter, *Zawlbuk* served as an important centre for transmitting and keeping alive the culture. It functioned as a powerful instrument to embed into the minds of its inmates a lifestyle best suited to their society.

Thus, in traditional Mizo society, education was multidimensional shaped out of its culture. It, therefore, served two main purposes-firstly recruitment to membership in the cultural system in general so that one became a responsible member of the society and secondly, maintenance of the cultural system by organizing the educational system to inculcate cultural values, attitudes and beliefs.

II

Formal education among the Mizo began to take root with the British annexation of the Lushai Hills. The pioneer missionaries, J. H. Lorrain and F. W. Savidge reduced *the Duhlian* language into the written form using the Roman script. They opened a school at Aizawl on 1st April 1894 with only two pupils at Thangphunga Veng (Chaltlang). But the school was soon closed as they wanted to concentrate on translation work. Pu Buanga compiled a *Grammar and Dictionary of the Lushai Language (Lushai into English)* containing 7000 words, published in the later part of 1899. D. E. Jones (Zosaphluia), who succeeded the first two missionaries, reopened the school on 28th February 1898. The first Government school for the Mizo was established on 21 August 1897, using Bengali a medium of instruction. However, the natives found it challenging to learn the Bengali script with which they were taught and did not fare well.

The new schools had little attendance in the beginning. As already discussed, Mizo children from an early age had indispensable roles in meeting the family needs. Parents preferred to send their children to *jhum* rather than to the school. The early students appeared to be loafers who attended school simply to escape their chores to many Mizo parents. According to them, *Zawlbuk* was there to educate them by storytelling, impart practical knowledge in the art of survival, while the new school did not seem to have any special value and prospect to offer. Very few Mizo families were inclined to send their girls to school. "Who would work if the girls were sent to school?" was always their questions (Chapman & Clark, 1968: 13-14). Girls in the school were thought to be socially spoiled because they could not effectively perform the ordinary household chores and morally degraded because they adopted Western dress. The mission, with the help of the Government, adopted certain methods to encourage schooling, such as granting a '*kuli awl*' (exemption from forced labour) to those who passed Upper Primary Examinations and to parents who sent their girls to school, and grant of scholarships to brilliant students. The Government also allowed the entry of female missionaries to promote female education in Mizoram.

Enrolment in mission schools increased remarkably in the subsequent years, and the number of literates also grew. The 1901 census records show that there were 736 male literates and 25 female literates in Mizoram. The Mission continued to open more schools in villages as well, and by 1903, there were fifteen schools in North Mizoram, including two night schools. Of these schools, six were in Aizawl town, and the remaining schools were in villages (Rohmingmawii, 2013: 204). When Assam Chief Commissioner Sir Bamfylde Fuller visited Mizoram in 1903 and found that the mission schools were doing better than the government school, he instructed the Superintendent to submit proposals for handing over the education of the district to the missionaries. Thus, the proposal was approved by the Government, and accordingly, on 1 March 1903, all the Government schools in Mizoram were put under the supervision of the mission in the person of Rev. E. Rowlands, who was an Honorary Inspector of Schools. Financial aids were provided to the schools by the Assam Government in addition to the salaries given to the teachers. However, the cost incurred by the Government on the education of the Mizo had never exceeded 16 paise per head of the population per year during the forty years of British administration (McCall, 2003: 232). In 1904, the Upper Primary School was introduced, and the course of studies, prepared by the Director of Public Instruction in consultation with the Superintendant of the Lushai Hills, was also introduced (Sangkima, 1992: 89). The Lunglei Sub-Division was put under different inspector of school in September 1904, and Savidge was appointed Honorary Inspector of schools in this area.

In the post-Independence period, there was a growth of higher education in the region. Since 1944, Middle schools known as Middle Anglo Vernacular Schools were opened in various villages. The first High School, called the Mizo High School, was opened at Aizawl in 1944 with 56 students. In 1948, another High School was opened at Lunglei and also at Champhai in 1950. In 1952, the direct responsibility of supervision of primary and middle schools in Mizo District was undertaken by the Government of Assam. On 15th August 1958, 'Aijal College' was established by a group of Mizo elders to become the first institution of higher education in Mizoram. After the political status of Mizoram was raised to a UT in 1972, there occurred tremendous progress in the education sector. The Directorate of Education was set up with senior officers to man it. A centre for training school teachers, the District Institute of Education and Training (DIET), was first established in September 1973. An academic wing of the Directorate of Education, Mizoram State Council of Educational Research & Training (SCERT), was started in January 1980. Two years after Mizoram attained the status of a full-fledged State on February 20, 1987, the Directorate of Education was bifurcated into Directorate of School Education and Directorate of Higher and Technical Education. A new Directorate called the Directorate of SCERT was created in 2008 by taking out SCERT and DIETs from the Directorate of School Education. Mizoram University, a central university under the University Grants Commission, Government of India, was established on 2 July 2001 by the Mizoram University Act (2000) of the Parliament of India.

The literacy rate of Mizoram has seen an upward trend. In 1901, no less than 2.5 percent of the male Lushai population knew how to read and write; some had acquired the knowledge to enable them to assist the government officials in carrying out the census (Zorema, 2007: 70). By the turn of the century in 2001, the literacy rate in Mizoram stood at 88.80 percent, of which male and female were 90.72 percent and 86.75 percent literate, respectively. According to the 2011 Census, the literacy rate was 91.33 percent. Male literacy stands at 93.35 percent, while female literacy is 89.27 percent (Mizoram Population 2011 Census, n.d.). At present, there are numerous educational institutions, right from pre-school to university levels, run by the Government of Mizoram, Society or individuals.

III

British colonialism led to the introduction of a regimented and schematized Western education system commonly known as schooling. Western education was consistent with the goals of imperialism: the economic and political control of the people in one country by the dominant class in another (Carnoy, 1974: 3). The imperial powers attempted through formal education to train the colonized for roles that suited the colonizer. Macaulay's Minute clearly stated the purpose of Western education in colonial India: " We must do our best to form a class who may be interpreters between us and the millions whom we govern...a class of persons, Indian in blood and colour, but English in tastes, in opinions, in morals and in intellect" (Nurullah and Naik, 1951: 136). The colonial administrators were interested in formal education in the Lushai Hills to produce literate natives to fill minor administrative positions and also create a group of natives who would be faithful to the colonial Government. The Government was, however, indifferent to the plea for the establishment of high schools because they preferred to have more village schools where elementary education was imparted. The first high school was opened only in 1944. The colonial Government also grasped the opportunity of propagating its imperialist agenda to the new literate group by launching the first official monthly journal *Mizo leh Vai Chanchinbu*, in November 1902.

For the Christian missionaries, education was an important tool to propagate Christianity among the Mizo and civilize the so-called 'savage tribes'. Since the missionaries had the full authority to make the curriculum, write textbooks, train and recruit the teachers, Biblical teaching occupied an important place in the school. Missionaries, through the kind of education they offered, also helped in promoting the stability of the colonial regimes. They carefully tried to infuse or introduce the interest of the 'motherland' in the teaching materials and in shaping the whole educational structure (Dena, 1988: 7). By asserting the superiority of the White culture, they became a conduit to imperialism and the indoctrination of the Western culture. *Duhlian Zir Tir Bu* (Primer textbook), which was printed in 1915 and 1929, included these lines:

> "There are five kinds of people in the world: the black, the brown, the yellow, the red and the white people. All are but one. The vast majorities are the yellow people; the white people are the wisest, they are also the most powerful." (Lalthangliana, 2001: 563).

This textbook also contained lessons such as *Bawiah awm tha rawh* (Be a good servant), *Puakphurh haw suh* (Do not resent impressed labour), underlining an urge to be submissive to the colonial authority.

The curricular content of the school introduced the Mizo to a culture that was completely alien to them. The natives had no part in the development of the scope and contents of schooling. The school curricula were formulated, fashioned, and relished with Western cultural ideals and values. Schools were detached from the social fabric of society. Most of what was taught in colonial schools had little to do with traditional values and practices. Those who attended the schools were obligated to adapt to the European standards of dressing, culture, and values. The sense of identity, connectedness, and understanding of their own culture eluded the pupils. They were sandwiched between the new, enforced ideas of the colonizers and the formerly accepted traditional ideals. Within a short time, they began to change significantly towards acting in ways inappropriate with traditional culture. Without question, the new educational system created conflicts between generations and disrupted the transmission of traditional culture. The new educated elite saw themselves as having the 'mind' of Europeans and presented themselves as more civilized and enlightened to their fellow men. They were staunch supporters of the colonial rule in Mizoram. A number of articles were written by this group in *Mizo leh Vai Chanchinbu* explaining the benefits of colonial rule and how progress was possible only with the help of the British. They wore Western dresses, cut their long hair short, and consequently repudiated many aspects of traditional culture that they believed were inconsistent with Western culture and values. They became prime movers in the movement for the abolition of chieftainship, an important institution that had upheld traditional customs and values in traditional Mizo society. McCall remarks that education "has beckoned young Lushai towards distant lands and ideas, rather than towards the land of their birth, the land of their future" (McCall, 2003: 205). All these conditions combined to precipitate a new kind of value system and lifestyle, which was in discrepancy with the community's traditional ethos and social order.

Western education, in many ways, was responsible for the disappearance of one of the most interesting characteristics as well as an important guardian of the traditional culture, the *Zawlbuk*. As formal education provided an opportunity for advancement in political and social stature and material wealth, parents now preferred to send their children to schools instead of *jhum* or *Zawlbuk*. The attendance of *Zawlbuk* fell rapidly, and its relevance came to be debated. The new elite class were also in favour of abolishing the *Zawlbuk*. The *Zawlbuk* was condemned quite wrongly as an evil place where people drank while the practice of *tlawmngaihna* was neglected (Parry, 1976: 22). *Zawlbuk* fell into complete disuse in the course of time, and by the late 1930s, there were hardly any *Zawlbuk* in most of the Mizo villages. An institution that reinforced discipline and cooperation in the community gave way to a new institution that fostered competition rather than the cooperation that characterized the traditional Mizo society. The purpose of education became more individual-oriented instead of community-oriented. Competition, the keynote of school life, is in many ways responsible for the degradation of moral and ethical values among the youth in Mizo society.

By providing a means to salaried jobs, Western education led to the creation of an educated elite class that was distinctive and propertied. And it was the children and relatives of this salaried class for whom access to higher education became possible. In this way, this new elite class enjoyed advantages not readily open to the ordinary and typical villager whose resources for education, after the free primary course, could only be derived from the toilsome labour of producing surplus crops (Mc Call, 2003: 206). In present Mizo society, material wealth has become an important social marker resulting in the emergence of social differentiation on the basis of wealth. This materialistic worldview has resulted in the deterioration of moral values in Mizo society. With the spread of education and the modern value system, there has been a growing individual economic interest. The spirit of individualism in the form of personal preference is becoming the basis of kinship relations. The obligatory kinship duties, intimacy and a sense of belonging to oneness as a kin group have undergone deterioration in the changing economic situation.

Within the family, formal education has changed family relations and roles. Education of children both in academics and vocational, which was once one of the most important functions of the family, has passed on to the hands of the professionals. Providing the best education for their children becomes the utmost priority of the parents. The father, unlike traditional society where he taught his children, especially the sons, the art of survival in the jhum economy, now assumes the role of financial provider. Children are not expected to contribute to the maintenance of the households. Parents prefer much that their children devote themselves wholeheartedly to their schoolwork rather than doing anything else at this point in time. The childhood and adolescent years of young people are spent in preparation for their future career. In the traditional family, children were an economic benefit and having many children was an asset. Today in the Mizo family, a child puts a large financial burden on the parents. The frequently heard phrase in the family has become, "we are doing everything for our children", which shows how much the family revolves around the children.

Education and employment enable women to acquire greater independence from traditional patriarchal constraints. In many families, women are the primary or secondary contributor to the family's income which allows them to have more influence in the decision-making within the family. The husband-wife relationship seems to be more cordial and open among the educated couple, usually belonging to the age group of 20 to 40. Young married couples are now more assertive in showing their affections towards their partners, while older couples tend to feel more constrained by customs. Division of labour based on sexes has been disappearing fast among the educated, westernized families. Men are now more involved in what was traditionally women's domain. Household works are increasingly shared by both the wife and the husband. In selecting a marriage partner, the traditional values like expertise in war and hunting or physical beauty and skill in domestic works have lost their significance. Education, apart from other factors, has become important criteria of mate selection. The most eligible bachelors are those with white-collared jobs or one who can give financial security to his wife.

IV

Education is an essential component of human development. Mizo traditional education was intrinsically intertwined with their culture. It utilized a variety of learning techniques

to mould an individual to become a responsible member of society. It was relevant to the needs of society. Colonialism disrupted traditional education and introduced a new form of learning that fostered materialism and individualism. Education came to be viewed as an exciting opportunity to climb the social ladder and enjoy a life free from manual works. Even in the post-Independence period, very little has changed in the philosophy, curriculum, context and contents of education in Mizoram. Education is still designed after Western models and paradigms. Therefore, there is a need to re-conceptualize formal education to shake off its colonial groove. This does not mean that formal education is without any benefits and that a Mizo must be solely educated in traditional knowledge and methods. Cumulative events such as British colonialism, the Western-style education that colonization brought, and the current forces of economic and cultural globalization have all led to a present that differs from the past. In today's global world, education should attempt to integrate desirable traditional culture with current and appropriate formal educational content and process to produce individuals who understand their cultural roots and are sensitive to the realities and needs of the present.

REFERENCES

Carnoy, Martin. (1974). *Education as Cultural Imperialism*. New York: Longman.

Chapman, E. & Clark, M. (1968). *Mizo Miracle*. Madras: The Christian Literature Society.

Chhangte, Lallianzuali. (2021). Mizo Society and Culture: Change and Continuity. *The Post-Doctoral Fellowship Report, submitted to The Indian Council of Social Science Research, New Delhi.*

Dena, Lal. (1988). *Christian Missions and Colonialism*. Shillong: Vendrame Institute.

Hluna, J.V. (1992). *Education and Missionaries in Mizoram*, Gauhati: United Publishers.

Kipgen, Mangkhosat. (1997). *Christianity and Mizo Culture*, Aizawl: The Mizo Theological Conference.

Kneller, George F. (1971). *Foundations of Education* (3rd ed.). New York: John Wiley & Sons Inc. (Original work published in 1963).

Lalbiakliana. (1979). *Mizoram Zirna Chanchin*. Aizawl: Social Education Wing.

Lalthangliana, B. (2001). *Mizo Chanchin*. Aizawl: Remkungi.

McCall, A. G. (2003). *Lushai Chrysalis*. Aizawl: Tribal Research Institute. (Original work published 1949).

Mizoram Population 2011 Census. https://www.census2011.co.in/census/state/mizoram.html.

Nag, Chitta Ranjan. (1993). *The Mizo Society in Transition*. New Delhi: Vikas Publishing House Pvt. Ltd.

Nunthara, C. (1996). *Mizoram: Society and Polity*. New Delhi: Indus Publishing Company.

Nurullah, Syed and Naik, J. P. (1951). *A History of Education in India*. London: Macmillan.

Pai, Young. (1990). *Cultural Foundations of Education*. New York: Macmillan Publishing Company.

Parry, N. E. (1976). *The Lakhers*. Calcutta: Firma KLM Pvt. Ltd. (Original work published in 1932).

Rohmingmawii. (2013). Christianity and Society in Mizoram. In Malsawmdawngliana & Rohmingmawii (Eds.), *Mizo Narratives: Accounts from Mizoram*, pp.193-240. Guwahati: Scientific Book Centre.

Sangkima. (1992). *Mizos: Society and Social Change*. Guwahati: Spectrum Publications.

Tyler, E. B. (1871). *Primitive Culture*. London: John Murray.

Zorema, J. (2007). *Indirect Rule in Mizoram 1890-1954*. New Delhi: Mittal Publications.

17

Hydropower Development in Northeast India and its Impact

Roja Ahmed

Climate Change

Climate Change is one of the biggest environmental threats in today's world. The United Nations Framework Convention on Climate Change (UNFCCC) defines climate change as "a change of climate which is attributed directly or indirectly to human activity that alters the composition of the global atmosphere and which is in addition to natural climate variability observed over comparable time periods" (UNFCCC, 1994: 7). It also defines adverse effects of climate change as "changes in the physical environment or biota resulting from climate changes which have significant deleterious effects on the composition, resilience or productivity of natural and managed ecosystems or on the operation of socio-economic systems or on human health and welfare" (UNFCCC, 1994: 7). According to UNFCCC, "climate change will have wide-ranging effects on the environment, and on socio-economic and related sectors, including water resources, agriculture and food security, human health, terrestrial ecosystems and biodiversity and coastal zones. Changes in rainfall pattern

are likely to lead to severe water shortages and/or flooding" (UNFCCC, 1994: 8).

There are eight states in the Northeast Indian viz. Assam, Arunachal Pradesh, Manipur, Meghalaya, Mizoram, Nagaland, Sikkim and Tripura. The northeastern region of India which is a biodiversity hotspot is exceptionally rich in varied flora and fauna. The growing concern on climate change and its effects on biodiversity has become a major issue globally. Loss of biodiversity can be a great threat to the existing ecosystem of the region. According to the Indian Network for Climate Change Assessment (INCCA), the Northeastern region of India has been considered among the four major eco-sensitive regions and biodiversity hotspots ("Climate Summit", 2011). According to a report of the Indian Network for Climate Change Assessment (INCCA), "Northeast India is vulnerable to water-induced disasters because of its location in the eastern Himalayan periphery, fragile geo-environmental settings and economic-underdevelopment. The powerful hydrological and monsoon regime of the region, especially the Brahmaputra and the Barak (Meghna) river systems are both a resource and a source of vulnerability. Moreover, the average state of economic development and growth in the Northeast Indian region is lower than other parts of the country. The average per-capita income of the region is 30% less than the national average. Assam and Manipur have the lowest per-capita income in the region. The region has higher incidence of poverty, even when compared with states having similar average per-capita income. Increasing population and declining land fertility, comparatively greater reliance on natural resources (e.g. forests) are both restrictions on the protection of the ecosystem in the region ("Climate Summit", 2011: 34).

Dams

Dams have been defined as, "massive barriers built across rivers and streams to confine and utilize the flow of water for human purposes such as irrigation and generation of hydroelectricity. This confinement of water creates lakes or reservoirs" ("arch. mcgill", [2021).] With the boom of industrialization the idea of hydro-electric dam building received a tempo and therefore dam-building efforts expanded in the nineteenth century (Werner, 2015: 2). According to International Rivers Network, over 800,000 dams have been built worldwide for various purposes. Dams are constructed mainly for drinking water, electricity generation, flood mitigation, irrigation, water supply for domestic and industrial use etc. India too has constructed around 4300 large dams and is on the verge of building many more. Plans to etch around 200 dams in the hydrologically rich but geologically fragile Eastern Himalayan region of the northeastern India have raised a matter of grave concern among the environmentalists and the social activists. A dam which is higher than 15 metres is considered to be a large dam ("Greenhouse Gas Emissions", May 2007). China tops the list of building dams followed by US and India ("Greenhouse Gas Emissions", May 2007). Already eight ("walkthroughindia," 2010-2021) mega dam are operational in the northeastern region, excluding several other small dams.

i) Ranganadi Dam having a height of 68m and 405MW is situated in Yazali of Arunachal Pradesh.

ii) Lower Subansiri Dam, with a height of 116m and 2000MW is situated in the border between Assam and Arunachal Pradesh.

iii) Doyang Dam is situated in Nagaland having a height of 92m and 75MW.

iv) Khuga Dam situated in Manipur has a height of 162m with an installed capacity of 7.5MW.

v) The Tuirial Dam is situated in Mizoram with a height of 74m and an installed capacity of

vi) Gumti Dam, situated in Tripura has a height of 30m with an installed capacity of 8.6MW.

vii) Umiam Dam, situated in Meghalaya with a height of 27.5m

viii) Rangit Dam which is situated in Sikkim has a height of 45m and has an installed capacity of 29MW.

Although dams are well-planned structures but they are viable to failures as well. There have been many instances of dam failures worldwide. The recent example of dam failure is from Brazil, where people faced grave disaster after a dam crumbled at an iron ore mine killing at least 84 people and leaving hundreds of people missing ("Brazil's Brumadinho Dam", January 2019). The disastrous incident occurred in the Brumadinha town of South-Eastern Brazil in the state of Minas Gerais. This is the second dam failure in 3 years in Brazil.

Environmental Impact of Dams

Around 104 million metric tonnes of methane is emitted from reservoir surfaces, turbines, spillways and rivers downstream annually from the large dams worldwide. Dams are the largest single anthropogenic source of methane and therefore, methane emissions from dams are responsible for at least 4% of the total global warming impact of human activities. According to the Inter governmental Panel on Climate Change, methane has a warming impact 72 times higher than carbon dioxide if measured over 20 years and

25 times higher measured over 100 years ("Greenhouse Gas Emissions", May 2007).

"The fuel for the methane, carbon dioxide, and nitrous oxide released by dams is the rotting of reservoir-flooded vegetation and soils and the organic matter (plants, plankton, algae, etc.) that flows through, and is formed in, reservoirs during their existence. The gases are released at the reservoir surface, at turbines and spillways, and downstream of the dam. Greenhouse gases are often generated by numerous other dam-related effects, including fossil fuels and building materials used during dam construction; land clearance for relocation areas, power lines and access roads; and the extension of irrigated farmland, which is a significant source of methane pollution. The trapping of sediments in reservoirs may act as a carbon sink; it may also indirectly increase the concentration of carbon dioxide in the atmosphere by reducing the amount of river-borne sediments available to fertilize oceanic plankton, which are important consumers of carbon dioxide. Much of the dams' effect on global change is attributed to releases of methane at spillways, reservoirs and downstream. Methane is created at the bottom of the reservoir. When it falls to the surface more of the methane is oxidized to carbon dioxide in the atmosphere, a much less powerful greenhouse gas. But when methane-rich deep water is released at the dam the pressure acting upon it suddenly drops and most of its dissolved methane is emitted straight into the atmosphere" ("Greenhouse Gas Emissions", May 2007). The blocked water in hydroelectric dams also causes methane to discharge into the atmosphere ("Brief introduction to Hydroelectric Dams", 2009). The north-eastern region of India consists of 60% of forest cover and therefore the government of India has taken up

Climate Change Adaptation Project in some of the states of the region. It will help facilitate resilience among the people against the impact of climate change (MDONER, 2012-13). According to the World Bank (June, 2005) says that "the Himalayan hydropower sites are, from a social and environmental perspective, among the most benign in the world"

Ranganadi Dam: The Ranganadi Hydro Electric Project is a 405 MW concrete gravity dam having a height of 68m and a length of 340m. The project is located in Yazali of the Lower Subansiri District of the state of Arunachal Pradesh in the Ranganadi Basin (NEEPCO, 2021). The building of the dam has led to the drying of the river downstream which has severely affected both human and aquatic lives. It has also made extinct certain variety of fishes like noka, tangar, ngurap and ngoh which were available before the construction of the dam ("Ranganadi Dam in Arunachal", May 2017). The Ranganadi dam has severe downstream impacts both in the Ranganadi valley and the Dikrong Valley. The water from the Ranganadi dam is diverted by releasing into the Dikrong or Pare River through an 8.5KM long diversion tunnel ("Comments on Scoping Clearance Application of Panyor HEP", November 2013). By doing this, they are altering the flood regime of both the Ranganadi and the Dikrong Rivers and thereby the Ranganadi Dam is reducing the capability of the various methods which the downstream dwellers used to adopt otherwise. This has ultimately resulted in severe dam-induced floods in the downstream areas. The recent example is from July 2017 and 2018 when NEEPCO's unwarned release of water created a deluge in Lakhimpur, Dhemaji and Bishwanath districts affecting almost 24,000 people ("Assam Flood Situation Grim", July

2018). The Ranganadi Dam was constructed with the aim of mitigating flood along with generating electricity. But according to some household interviewees the completion of the Ranganadi Dam has instead aggravated the flood flow in the downstream areas. According to them the water released from the dam is causing more destruction to them because of uninformed and frequent floods than before. According to them earlier they were aware of the occurrence of natural floods and would thereby prepare beforehand to survive the floods. But after the building of the dam, water is released from the spillway without any proper prior information causing havoc to the downstream dwellers. Furthermore according to the interviewees the dam-induced flood carries much more sand than the natural floods and has therefore caused problem for agriculture. Hydropower development along the Brahmaputra basin completely depends on river flows and that is being affected by climate change in the region. In summers, the increase in glacial melt of the Himalayas further aggravates the problem of flooding in the Brahmaputra basin. In winters, climate change impact will decrease the river flow in the long run and thereby threaten the livelihood of the riparian communities.

Climate Change will have further impact due to a number of dams being planned in the region since dams modify river flows that are already being hampered as a result of climate change. At least 168 large hydroelectric projects have been planned in the northeastern region of India, identified as 'India's future powerhouse' that is going to have disastrous impact on the region's rivers and landscape (Vagholikar and Das, 2010). A large network of dams are bring encouraged in the region in spite of the fact that the region is ecologically and geologically fragile, seismically active and culturally sensitive region. Rivers are an integral part of the lives of people of northeast India especially Assam and Arunachal Pradesh. They use the river system in various ways such as fishing, water for drinking and for livestock rearing, and for various religious and recreational activities.

Cultural Impact

Although dams are built for various purposes that include harnessing electricity, water supply, irrigation, flood mitigation, construction of dams can lead to loss of cultural assets which can be in the form of underground remains of significant historical or religious importance. One of the most important cultural impacts of construction of dams is that they disrupt the relationship of the indigenous population with the river. Northeast India is known for its varied cultural diversity and most of its population follows traditional resource-based livelihood. The government has aimed to intervene in the hydrology of the region by planning to construct 168 large hydropower projects in the Brahmaputra basin and 22 in the Subansiri basin (Dutta, 2012). In order to build the Gumti dam in Tripura, a large area of lands inhabited by tribal population was inundated, thus affecting their livelihood patterns and cultural ties. In Manipur, after the creation of the Loktak reservoir, livelihood of local communities was disturbed after many varieties of fishes and aquatic vegetation became extinct. The Ranganadi Hydroelectric project has had severe downstream impacts since it was commissioned. The Project diverts water from the Ranganadi River to the Dikrong River thereby reducing its flow in the Ranganadi River. This has impacted the livelihood patterns of the downstream dwellers to a great extent.

The Misings are among the indigenous communities of Northeast India who live along the banks of the Brahmaputra and Subansiri Rivers. Construction of dams has led to their displacement, thereby disturbing their livelihood patterns. Local economies and livelihoods depend largely on the Brahmaputra River and its riparian ecosystems. Fishing community has been affected, agricultural lands have been lost and the locals have been deprived from the available natural resources. The ongoing Lower Subansiri Hydroelectric Project will impact Majuli, the largest river island which is an important center of Assamese culture. The reservoir will also submerge a number of forests and wildlife habitats like parts of Tale Valley Sanctuary, Tale Reserved Forest and Panir Reserved Forest in Arunachal Pradesh and Subansiri Reserved Forest in Assam (Menon and Kohli, 2005: 44).

Conclusion

According to "Climate Vulnerability Assessment for the Indian Himalayan Region Using Common Framework," Assam is the most vulnerable state towards climate change among twelve Himalayan states of India. Efforts to construct hydroelectric projects along the Brahmaputra basin are worsening flood conditions instead of mitigating it. It is also having severe impact on the river's flows and thereby reducing winter season flows. All these factors are contributing to the impact of climate change on the flow of rivers. Riverine communities living in downstream areas have their own strategies and methods to survive summer floods. But it seems these strategies and adaptive methods will no longer work anymore as a result of climate change impounding the flood problems. The hydropower building efforts along the Brahmaputra will further aggravate the existing environmental concerns and adding to climate change impact upon the region.

REFERENCES

Assam Flood Situation Grim: CM asks NEEPCO Not to Release Water From the Ranganadi Dam. (July, 2018). *The Times of India.*

Brazil's Brumadinho Dam Was Certified 'stable' weeks before it collapsed. (January 2019). *CNN.* https://edition.cnn.com/2019/01/30/americas/brazil-dam-collapse-vale-mining-regulations-intl/index.html

Brief Introduction To Hydroelectric Dams: How They Work, Advantages and Disadvantages. *Bright Hub Engineering.* https://www.brighthubengineering.com/building-construction-design/42794-how-does-a-hydroelectric-dam-work/

Climate Change: Impacts, Vulnerabilities and Adaptation in Developing Countries, Chapter II, p.8. *UNFCC.*

Climate Summit for a Living Himalayas. (Bhutan, 2011). *Thematic Area - Biodiversity; Contribution for Indian Part of East Himalaya*, p.34.

http://environmentportal.in/files/file/Biodiversity%20Paper%20-%20INDIA.pdf

Comments on Scoping Clearance Application of Panyor HEP on Ranganadi River in Arunachal Pradesh. (November, 2013). *SANDRP.*

Dutta, R. (2012). Lower Subansiri Hydroelectric Power Project and future of the Subansiri River Ecosystem. *Annals of Biological Research*, 3(6), 2953-2957.

Greenhouse Gas Emissions From Dams. (May 1, 2007). *International Rivers, People, Water, Life.*

http://www.arch.mcgill.ca/prof/sijpkes/arch374/winter2001/dbiggs/what.html

http://www.walkthroughindia.com/walkthroughs/the-8-mega-dams-of-north-east-states-of-india/

https://www.indiawaterportal.org/sites/indiawaterportal.org/files/Damming%20Northeast%20India_%20Kalpavriksh_%20Aaranyak_ActionAid%20India_2010.pdf

India's Water Economy: Bracing for a Turbulent Future. (June, 2005 Draft). *World Bank.*

Menon, Manju and Kanchi Kohli (Eds.) (June, 2005). *Large Dams For Hydropower in Northeast India: A* Dossier. New Delhi: Kalpavrtiksh.

North Eastern Electric Power Corporation Limited. *Ranganadi Hydro Eectric Project.* https://neepco.co.in/projects/hydro-projects/ranganadi-hydro-electric-project

Ranganadi Dam in Arunachal Hits Ecology and Human Life. (May, 2017). *The Citizen.*

https://www.thecitizen.in/index.php/en/NewsDetail/index/3/10691/Ranganadi-Dam-in-Arunachal-Hits-Ecology-and-Human-Life

United Nations Framework Convention on Climate Change: Convention. *UNFCC,* 1994 Article 1, p.7https://unfccc.int/files/essential_background/background_publications_htmlpdf/application/pdf/conveng.pdf

Vagholikar, N. & P. J. Das. (2010). *Damming Northeast India: Juggernaut of hydropower projects threatens social and environmental security of the region.* Kalpavriksh, Aaranyak and Action Aid India.

Werner, Hanna. (2015). *The Politics of Dams: Developmental Perspectives and Social Critique in Modern India.* New Delhi: Oxford University Press.